D0759505

Developing Reflective Judgment

Patricia M. King
Karen Strohm Kitchener

*The authors contributed equally
to the writing of this book;
their names are listed here
in alphabetical order.*

Developing Reflective Judgment

*Understanding and Promoting
Intellectual Growth
and Critical Thinking
in Adolescents and Adults*

PROPERTY OF
CLACKAMAS COMMUNITY COLLEGE
LIBRARY

Jossey-Bass Publishers · San Francisco

BF
447
.K56
1994

Copyright © 1994 by Jossey-Bass Inc., Publishers, 350 Sansome Street,
San Francisco, California 94104. Copyright under International, Pan
American, and Universal Copyright Conventions. All rights reserved.
No part of this book may be reproduced in any form — except for brief
quotation (not to exceed 1,000 words) in a review or professional
work — without permission in writing from the publishers.

Substantial discounts on bulk quantities of Jossey-Bass books
are available to corporations, professional associations, and other
organizations. For details and discount information, contact the
special sales department at Jossey-Bass Inc., Publishers.
(415) 433-1740; Fax (415) 433-0499.

For sales outside the United States, contact Maxwell Macmillan
International Publishing Group, 866 Third Avenue, New York,
New York 10022.

Manufactured in the United States of America. Nearly all Jossey-Bass
books and jackets are printed on recycled paper containing at least
10 percent postconsumer waste, and many are printed with either soy-
or vegetable-based ink, which emits fewer volatile organic compounds
during the printing process than petroleum-based ink.

Library of Congress Cataloging-in-Publication Data

King, Patricia M., date.
    Developing reflective judgment : understanding and promoting
intellectual growth and critical thinking in adolescents and adults
/ Patricia M. King, Karen S. Kitchener. — 1st ed.
        p.   cm. — (The Jossey-Bass higher and adult education series)
(The Jossey-Bass social and behavioral science series)
    Includes bibliographical references and index.
    ISBN 1-55542-629-8
    1. Judgment. 2. Critical thinking. 3. Reasoning. I. Title.
II. Series. III. Series: The Jossey-Bass social and behavioral
science series.
BF447.K56 1994
153.4'6 — dc20   93-43164
                                                                  CIP

FIRST EDITION
HB Printing   10 9 8 7 6 5 4 3 2 1   *Code 9426*

A joint publication in
**The Jossey-Bass
Higher and Adult Education Series**
and
**The Jossey-Bass
Social and Behavioral Science Series**

Consulting Editor
Student Services
**Ursula Delworth
University of Iowa**

Contents

ix

Tables, Figures, and Exhibits

Text Tables

xi

Exhibits

Preface

This book summarizes more than fifteen years of theory building and research on the Reflective Judgment Model. Our work on the model began in a graduate seminar on college student development organized by Clyde A. Parker at the University of Minnesota. These Friday afternoon seminars ran for several consecutive quarters in the mid 1970s and provided one of the most intellectually stimulating experiences of our careers. It was during those seminars that we became acquainted with each other and decided to pursue jointly our interests in understanding late adolescent and adult development.

The first seminar focused on William Perry's (1970) model of college students' intellectual and ethical development and its implications for teaching, counseling, and advising college students. We were also aware that many psychologists, including Piaget, Binet, and Wechsler, had described and studied other aspects of the intellect. We then began to ask questions about the nature of the intellectual development that Perry described, what differentiated it from other models of intellectual development, and what questions needed to be addressed to establish its validity as a description of college student development.

While we were examining psychological theories of intellectual development, we also examined educational philosophers' descriptions of "good thinking." John Dewey's (1933) work on reflective thinking was especially influential in our own work in this area. He described a type of thinking that focuses on problems for which no clear-cut solution can be identified by using only inductive or deductive logic; solutions to these problems involve other characteristics of reasoning. As we studied these ideas and people's responses to such problems, we began to see that the "other characteristics" involved epistemic assumptions. We found that people's assumptions about what and how something can be known provide a lens that shapes how individuals frame a problem and how they justify their beliefs about it in the face of uncertainty. Influenced by Dewey's observations, we now think of reflective judgments as beginning with an awareness of uncertainty. Such judgments involve integrating and evaluating data, relating those data to theory and well-formed opinions, and ultimately creating a solution to the problem that can be defended as reasonable or plausible.

The model itself evolved over many years as a result of a variety of influences. Foremost among these were the people we interviewed about their epistemic assumptions and the way they justified their beliefs in the face of uncertainty. We and other colleagues have now interviewed more than seventeen hundred people, ranging from fourteen-year-old high school students to retirees over the age of sixty-five. On the basis of our interviews and our understanding of the assumptions behind people's reasoning in the interviews, we abstracted seven distinct sets of epistemic assumptions and concepts of justification, which form the basic description of the Reflective Judgment Model.

A second influence resulted from our interest in understanding how and why different forms of reasoning evolve. For this we turned to other theorists. Jean Piaget and Lawrence Kohlberg were the most influential theorists on cognitive and moral development we looked at. We also examined the work of others who were studying and formulating new models of adolescent and adult cognitive development (Basseches, 1980;

Broughton, 1975; Kramer, 1983; LaBouvie-Vief, 1982; Sinnott, 1984) for insights into the developmental differences that we and others observed in the responses to the Reflective Judgment Interview.

Third, we were aware that what we were calling reflective judgment was related to what other researchers were studying as critical thinking and intelligence and that while certain aspects of the definitions overlapped, other aspects were quite distinct. Work in these related areas stimulated us to clarify the distinctions between the constructs. The three influences— listening to the words of the people we interviewed, reading other theorists' descriptions of the content and mechanisms of post-adolescent intellectual development, and attempting to delineate the distinctions between our own and other approaches—helped us refine our characterizations of the stages of the Reflective Judgment Model described in this book.

Throughout the process, we were also informed and challenged by the observations of those whose lives are directly touched by students. We had frequent discussions with many groups of people who were concerned about students' intellectual development: with educators who were intentionally stimulating reflective thinking in the high school, college, and graduate students they taught; with student affairs staff on college campuses who were privy to students' informal observations about their classes, their learning, and their own development; and with our own graduate faculty colleagues who were teaching courses or conducting research on college students and their developmental characteristics. Our discussions with these groups of people helped us ground our questions, claims, and recommendations in the context of the "real lives" of developing people. We hope we have been true to their insights and experiences.

Purpose

The first purpose of *Developing Reflective Judgment* is to describe the Reflective Judgment Model in detail and to provide examples from our interviews of each of the stages. Further, although many journal articles and book chapters have been written on the model and on its supporting data, no single source has assembled the data so that they could be summarized and critically evaluated. This leads us to the second purpose of the book: to provide a comprehensive review of the research on the Reflective Judgment Model and the Reflective Judgment Interview.

Since we teach in university settings (in the fields of higher education and student affairs and counseling psychology) and are committed to improving the lives and educational experiences of students, our third purpose is to address the implications of the model for students' education. We define education broadly to include many interactions a student may have that serve an educational purpose. In doing so, we are acknowledging that development occurs in a variety of settings and that individuals in many roles may serve as teachers in fostering reflective thinking. In this book, we suggest ways in which the Reflective Judgment Model may help educators think about their interactions with students and more effectively teach them to make reflective judgments, both in classrooms and in the educational community at large.

Audience

Although we began studying development in college students, the Reflective Judgment Model has broader applicability, since it describes the development of epistemic assumptions and concepts of justification from late childhood through adulthood. It even has implications for characteristics that are generally associated with old age, such as wisdom. As a result, we hope that the book will appeal to educators, practitioners, and researchers who work with or study learners across the life span.

The book was written for four audiences. First, it is our hope that *Developing Reflective Judgment* will be of immediate interest to educators who work with college students in various settings; to these educators, we offer a description of the stageby-stage development of the ability to make reflective judgments, a skill that many individuals and institutions of higher education purport to teach. The book is also written for those who are attempting to promote critical thinking among high school and noncollege students, as well as adult learners. People who teach graduate students will also find our description of the development of reflective thinking relevant in determining what reasoning skills are consistent with graduate-level preparation. Our concluding chapter on fostering reflective thinking in college contexts should be of particular interest to educators who work with college students. As noted earlier, the definition of reflective judgment is consistent with but distinct from other definitions of critical thinking. Early in the book, we discuss the similarities and differences and suggest that the Reflective Judgment Model provides a unique contribution to the literature on critical thinking because the model focuses on thinking about ill-structured problems, a neglected aspect of critical thinking. Our model has implications for the teaching of that type of problem solving because it describes reflective thinking about ill-structured problems as the outgrowth of a developmental process.

While other books focus on general principles for enhancing college teaching or suggest specific strategies for improving students' reasoning skills, this work is distinctive in two respects: (1) it describes the series of stages that lay the foundation for and lead to reflective thinking, and (2) it, and the developmental model on which it is based, are explicitly grounded in an extensive research base. The research presented here is organized by respondents' age and education level, to make it easier for teachers to locate the findings for a given age or class level.

Second, we believe that the book will be useful to those who teach about college students in higher education programs, counseling programs, and student affairs preparation programs. In addition, we hope the book will be valuable to practitioners in other helping professions, such as counselors, clinical psychologists, and social workers who seek to understand normal development so that they can better understand divergent developmental paths.

Third, college faculty and administrators with responsibility for the assessment of college outcomes should find this book of interest because it documents a progression in reflective thinking across the college years. Researchers and evaluators may be particularly interested in the measurement of the Reflective Judgment Model, outlined in Chapter Four (which includes a list of characteristics desirable in a measure of reflective thinking, and a description of the psychometric properties of the Reflective Judgment Interview), as well as in the chapters that summarize the research findings. These findings include both cross-sectional and longitudinal research on the Reflective Judgment Model — including the results of our ten-year longitudinal study, some of which have not been reported elsewhere — and research on the relationship between Reflective Judgment Interview scores and a variety of other measures of intellectual development and the development of character.

Fourth, this book should be of interest to developmental psychologists who seek to understand the nature and mechanisms of cognitive development in adolescents and adults. The detailed presentation of the Reflective Judgment Model, the explanation of the measurement properties of the Reflective Judgment Interview, and the description of the longitudinal and cross-sectional data base should provide psychologists with sufficient information to make an independent judgment about the validity of the model, the need for future refinements, and new directions for research.

Overview of the Contents

The book is divided into nine chapters that define and describe the development of reflective thinking as articulated in the Reflective Judgment Model, provide evidence for the model, and discuss its educational implications. Chapter One sets the stage for the remainder of the book by defining reflective judgment as one aspect of critical thinking that has often been neglected in the study of intellectual development. In Chapter Two, we discuss stage-related assumptions that underlie the Reflective Judgment Model, including our use of the word *stage*. We then relate our model to current work in developmental psychology, using Fischer's skill theory (1980) to refine the meaning of stages in our model, and we describe the implications of an epigenetic model for the development of thinking skills.

In the second half of the chapter, we relate the Reflective Judgment Model to prior models of epistemological development, including those of Perry (1970), Broughton (1975), and others. We conclude this chapter by relating our model to contemporary models of epistemological development, noting points of similarity and points of departure.

In Chapter Three, we describe the seven stages of the Reflective Judgment Model in detail, illustrating the internal coherence of each stage and showing how later stages build on earlier ones. Verbatim statements from people we have interviewed illustrate how individuals' assumptions about knowledge and justification are reflected in their responses to ill-structured problems.

Chapter Four focuses on the assessment of reasoning skills. It contrasts the components necessary for assessing reasoning about ill-structured problems with those found in other common measures of thinking, including formal operations, postformal reasoning, and critical thinking. This chapter sets the stage for Chapter Five, which describes the assessment procedures used in measuring reflective judgment and reviews the data pertaining to the reliability and internal consistency of the Reflective Judgment Interview. The chapter concludes with a summary of alternative approaches to and new developments in the assessment of reflective judgment.

Chapter Six, prepared with the collaboration of Phillip K. Wood, is in many ways the centerpiece of the book. It focuses on the research that has been conducted on the model and addresses the following questions: (1) Does reflective judgment develop between late adolescence and middle adulthood? (2) How do high school, college, and graduate students reason about ill-structured problems? (3) Does students' reasoning improve with additional exposure to and involvement in higher education? (4) Do adult learners differ from traditional-age students in their reflective thinking? (5) How does the reasoning of adults with no formal background in higher education compare to the reasoning of those who have earned a college degree? (6) Are there gender or cross-cultural differences in the development of reflective thinking? We open the discussion by describing our ten-year longitudinal study of three cohorts of students and summarize the findings from other longitudinal studies. Next, we present the general patterns of development in reflective judgment based on the seventeen hundred individuals who have been assessed in cross-sectional studies using the Reflective Judgment Interview. The results are summarized for each of the following groups: high school students, traditional-age college students, adult learners in college, graduate students, and nonstudent adults. While the focus of the discussion is on college students, it also has implications for younger adolescents and for adults who have not attended college. Because of the length of Chapter Six, we offer a detailed summary of the findings at the end of the chapter. This may suffice for those whose work or interests do not require the level of detail provided in the chapter and its accompanying statistical tables. Others may prefer to start with the summary before exploring the individual sections on which the summary is based.

In Chapter Seven, we examine the relationship between the Reflective Judgment Model and other measures of intellectual development. The chapter draws on theoretical arguments and data from individual studies to evaluate the relationship between reflective judgment and other intellectual processes. The companion chapter, Chapter Eight, describes the relationship between the development of reflective judgment and the development of character—specifically, moral and identity development. We discuss how each of these relationships affects education.

The last chapter, Chapter Nine, focuses on the implications of the Reflective Judgment Model for college teaching and for student development on the college campus. We make specific suggestions based on the typical patterns of development for different age and educational groups (see data in Chapters Six, Seven, and Eight), for encouraging students and supporting their progress in making reflective judgments.

Two major resources are included at the end of the book. Resource A includes a variety of materials on the Reflective Judgment Interview (RJI), including both standard and discipline-based interview problems, as well as procedures for conducting and scoring the RJI. Resource B contains eleven statistical tables. These tables are intended for researchers who desire a more in-depth look at data from individual studies that are presented in general terms in Chapters Five, Six, and Seven. Specifically, the tables include reliability data on the RJI, a complete listing of individual scores on the RJI from the ten-year study discussed in Chapter Six, a compilation of RJI scores from all available studies by each of the five age/educational levels discussed in Chapter Six, and correlations between the RJI and other measures of intellectual development.

Acknowledgments

The Friday afternoon seminars where we began the thinking that resulted in this book were led by Clyde A. Parker, who was then a professor at the University of Minnesota. His gift for stimulating thinking, for making students reach beyond their own expectations, and for caring deeply about those he mentored provided much of the inspiration for our work. Others who attended those seminars, both faculty members and students, also contributed their time, talents, and encouragement. In particular, James R. Rest and Mark L. Davison (University of Minnesota), Mary M. Brabeck (Boston College), and Elizabeth Reynolds Welfel (Cleveland State University) have provided us with many insights and much support throughout this project. Over the last ten years, our colleagues Phillip K. Wood (University of Missouri, Columbia) and Cindy L. Lynch (University of Denver) have contributed substantially to our conceptualization of reflective judgment and especially to its measurement. We offer our heartfelt thanks to each of these friends and colleagues.

We also wish to acknowledge the financial support of the following organizations: the National Institute of Education, the Spencer Foundation, the Ohio Board of Regents, the Fund for the Improvement of Postsecondary Education, the American College Personnel Association Theory and Research Board, the University of Denver, and Bowling Green State University. Without their assistance, the Reflective Judgment Model might have remained at the level of interesting speculation, without the research base that has so richly enhanced our understanding of reflective thinking.

We would also like to express our appreciation to our colleagues in the College of Education at the University of Denver and in the Department of Higher Education and Student Affairs at Bowling Green State University for their sustained support of our work. We extend a special note of thanks to other colleagues who reviewed earlier versions of these chapters for sharing their time and talents with us. In particular, we wish to thank David Finster, Thomas Klein, Barry M. Kroll, Katherine Nevins, and Phillip K. Wood for their many insightful comments.

Throughout the years and the many professional activities that culminated in the writing of this book, we have each enjoyed and thrived on the long-term, unwavering support of our husbands, Timothy King and Richard Kitchener. Each of these men made substantive contributions not only to our well-being but to elements of the book as well. Each has served by personal example as a model of a reflective thinker. Our children, David, Brian, and Ellen King and Greg and Brian Kitchener, have served as tangible, visible examples of the miracle of intellectual development we have tried to describe here. They have stimulated us to come up with better answers to their difficult questions and in the process, have contributed greatly to our own intellectual development as well. To these individuals, we offer our love as well as our gratitude.

December 1993

Patricia M. King
Bowling Green, Ohio

Karen Strohm Kitchener
Denver, Colorado

The Authors

Patricia M. King is associate professor and acting chair of the Department of Higher Education and Student Affairs at Bowling Green State University. Previously, she was assistant vice president for student services at Ohio State University and senior research psychologist at the University of Iowa. She earned her B.A. degree (1972) in English from Macalester College and her Ph.D. degree (1977) in educational psychology (psychological foundations of education) from the University of Minnesota.

For the past fifteen years, King's research and writing have focused on the intellectual and moral development of college students, in both classroom and cocurricular contexts. She has twice received the College of Education and Allied Professions Research Award (1984 and 1989) at Bowling Green State University. She currently serves as president of the Association for Moral Education and is a member of the American College Personnel Association and the Association for the Study of Higher Education.

Karen Strohm Kitchener is professor in the College of Education and director of the counseling psychology program at the University of Denver. She received her B.A. degree (1965) in history from the University of California, Santa Barbara, and her M.A. degrees (1968 and 1971) in education from Claremont Graduate School and in counseling psychology from the University of Minnesota, respectively. She received her Ph.D. degree (1978) in counseling psychology from the University of Minnesota.

Kitchener's main research activities and writing have focused on the areas of adolescent and adult cognitive development and ethical issues in psychology. She received the Ralph Berdie Award for Research on College Student Development (1983) from the American Association for Counseling and Development and the Contribution to Knowledge Award (1992) from the American College Personnel Association, which also elected her Senior Scholar in 1993. In 1992, she was chosen University Lecturer at the University of Denver, presenting as her lecture "The Development of Critical Reasoning: Does a College Education Make a Difference?" Kitchener is coeditor of *Adult Cognitive Development* (1986, with R. A. Mines) and has written numerous journal articles and book chapters. She is currently a member and fellow of the American Psychological Association and a member of the American Association of Counseling and the American College Personnel Association.

Developing Reflective Judgment

Chapter One

Reflective Judgment: A Neglected Facet of Critical Thinking

One of the most important responsibilities educators have is helping students learn to make defensible judgments about vexing problems. This idea has emerged as an underlying theme in several national proposals for educational reform. These proposals have emphasized the need to teach students to make interpretive judgments about the world's complex issues (Association of American Colleges, 1985; National Commission on Excellence in Education, 1983; Study Group on the Conditions of Excellence in American Higher Education, 1984). One of the most compelling statements from these reports is offered in a volume entitled *The Challenge of Connecting Learning* (Association of American Colleges, 1991, pp. 16–17): "In the final analysis, the real challenge of college, for students and faculty members alike, is empowering individuals to know that the world is far more complex than it first appears, and that they must make interpretive arguments and decision-judgments that entail real consequences for which they must take responsibility and from which they may not flee by disclaiming expertise."

The focus of this book is on the process by which people become increasingly able to make such arguments and judgments. While much attention is given to college students, the

1

ideas presented here have implications for the development of
these abilities for a broad cross-section of adolescents and adults.

How do people decide what they believe about vexing
problems? We began to explore this question more than fifteen
years ago by asking people to discuss with us how they arrived
at their judgments about complex and controversial problems.
In doing so, we found that many people struggle with questions
such as the following: How can I say I know anything about
an issue if even the experts disagree about it? How can I justify
my answer to a question if there is uncertainty about the correct answer? Are the opinions of experts any better than my
own? Excerpts from three of these discussions follow, showing
some of the different approaches we observed. The topic of conversation in these excerpts is the safety of chemical additives
in food. The following comments were made by a high school
student.*

I: Can you ever know for sure that your position that Nutra-
sweet is safe is correct?

R: No. I don't know for sure because I don't manufacture it.

I: OK. Do you think we'll ever know for sure?

R: If somebody more or less had the guts to stand up and go
and do all the research on it and find out.

I: So you think someday we'll know?

R: Yes.

I: When people disagree about the safety of chemical additives [in foods], is it the case that one opinion is right and the
other is wrong?

R: Some people's opinion is right, and they can more or less
prove that they are right, and the other people that are wrong
maybe can't prove it.

I: And "right" in what way? What do you mean by "right"?

*In the dialogues, *I* represents the interviewer, *R* the respondent.

R: They can back up their opinion. They have the facts to show they are right.

From this respondent's perspective, the problem itself is not a perplexing one; it is one for which a correct answer exists or will exist. Finding the right facts will lead to certain knowledge. Interpreting the facts is not mentioned as a part of the process of arriving at a decision.

Other people used a different approach when discussing this issue, as illustrated by this undergraduate student:

I: Can you say you will ever know for sure that chemicals [in foods] are safe?

R: No, I don't think so.

I: Can you tell me why you'll never know for sure?

R: Because they test them in little animals, and they haven't really tested them in humans, as far as I know. And I don't think anything is for sure.

I: When people disagree about matters such as this, is it the case that one opinion is right and one is wrong?

R: No. I think it just depends on how you feel personally because people make their decisions based upon how they feel and what research they've seen. So what one person thinks is right, another person might think is wrong. But that doesn't make it wrong. It has to be a personal decision. If I feel that chemicals cause cancer and you feel that food is unsafe without them, your opinion might be right to you and my opinion is right to me.

I: Could we ever say that one opinion is in any way better and one is worse?

R: I don't think so.

I: Can you tell me why not?

R: Just because the opinion that a person has is based upon what he believes, and so you wouldn't be able to say that one person's opinion is better than another's because it's just an opinion.

For this respondent, knowledge about problems like the safety of chemical additives in foods is never available with certainty. As a result, the person argues that it is not possible to make a judgment about whether or not a chemical additive is harmful. Rather, one simply has an opinion, and one cannot evaluate the strengths or weaknesses of an opinion.

By contrast, when asked the same questions, another group of individuals argued that, although we can never be certain that our judgments about complex problems like this one are true or correct, we can nevertheless come to defensible conclusions about such problems. The following excerpt from an interview with a graduate student illustrates this reasoning style.

I: Can you ever say you know for sure that your point of view on chemical additives is correct?

R: No, I don't think so. I think given that any theorem has to start with assumptions that are not necessarily true, then even if the internal argument in your system is completely consistent, it might be that the assumptions are wrong. So, just from this standpoint, we can't always be sure. I think we can usually be reasonably certain, given the information we have now and considering our methodologies.

I: Is there anything else that contributes to not being able to be sure?

R: Yes. Aside from assumptions, it might be that the research wasn't conducted rigorously enough. In other words, we might have flaws in our data or sample, things like that.

I: How then would you identify the "better" opinion?

R: One that takes as many factors as possible into consideration. I mean one that uses the higher percentage of the data that we have and perhaps that uses the methodology that has been most reliable.

I: And how do you come to a conclusion about what the evidence suggests?

R: I think you have to take a look at the different opinions and studies that are offered by different groups. Maybe some studies offered by the chemical industry, some studies by the government, some private studies, a variety of studies from a variety of different areas. You wouldn't trust, for instance, a study funded by the tobacco industry that proved that cigarette smoking is not harmful. You wouldn't base your point of view entirely upon that study. Things like that have to be taken into account also . . . you have to try to interpret people's motives and that makes it a more complex soup to try to strain out.

People who use this reasoning style acknowledge the uncertainty of knowing, but even though they accept the uncertainty, they also argue that a judgment that is "reasonably certain" can be constructed on the basis of available data and existing methodologies. We believe this third style exemplifies the kind of reasoning that the Association of American Colleges (1991) had in mind when it suggested that the challenge for college students and faculty is to understand the complexity in the world but still take the responsibility to make judgments and draw conclusions.

In examining hundreds of responses such as the foregoing, we observed several consistent patterns in the way people approached complex issues. We found that the way people justify their beliefs is related to their assumptions about knowledge. This led to the development of a model of cognitive development that describes how people justify their beliefs when they are faced with complex or vexing problems; we call this the Reflective Judgment Model. In this book, we describe our model, present its extensive research base, and explore the implications of our findings for educational practice.

Before describing the model that resulted from the interviews, we think it is important to clarify first what it means to engage in reflective thinking (as we use the term), to show how this type of thinking is different from other types of reasoning commonly referred to as critical thinking, and to identify the types of problems to which reflective thinking skills are applied. Having laid this foundation, we provide a brief overview of the Reflective Judgment Model. (A detailed description of the model is given in Chapter Three.)

What Is Reflective Thinking?

John Dewey (1933, 1938) provided one of the earliest exposi-tions of reflective thinking. He observed that true reflective think-ing is initiated only after there is recognition that a real prob-lem exists. Such real problems, he argued, cannot be answered by formal logic alone. Rather, they are resolved when a think-ing person identifies a solution to the problem that temporarily closes the situation. True reflective thinking, he noted, is un-called for in situations in which there is no controversy or doubt, no concern about the current understanding of an issue, or in which absolute, preconceived assumptions dominate. For ex-ample, the high school student in the first interview excerpt given above did not engage in reflective thinking since he did not ac-knowledge that a real problem exists.

According to Dewey, a person makes a judgment, what he called a reflective judgment, to bring closure to situations that are uncertain. In such uncertain or problematic situations, there is no way to apply a formula to derive a correct solution and no way to prove definitively that a proposed solution is cor-rect. He suggested that situations may be problematic for a va-riety of reasons, such as the unavailability of or the impossibil-ity of attaining data necessary for solving the problem. Examples of other problematic situations include deciding whether a given product is safe to ingest, deciding which candidate to vote for in an election, and determining what really happened in a histor-ical event. Individuals who do not recognize that such situa-tions are truly problematic cannot make reflective judgments.

However, individuals who do not recognize uncertainty may be able to solve other kinds of problems, such as figuring out the circumference of a circle, translating a set of instruc-tions into a computer language, or playing a game of chess, quite adequately. These activities do not require reflective thinking in the way Dewey used the term. Mathematical formulas, logic, or rules of play may be adequate to derive successful solutions to these problems. While such activities require intelligence and astute thinking skills, and even one type of critical thinking, they are not truly problematic and (as discussed below) are characteristic of a different type of problem.

Simple logic or formulas are not adequate for solving the kinds of problematic situations that are truly controversial; nor are they adequate for making judgments when there is an inadequate data base. Instead, part of the process of forming a reflective judgment involves identifying which facts, formulas, and theories are relevant to the problem and then generating potential solutions. These strategies must then be evaluated for their relevance and validity.

In addition, according to Dewey (1933, 1938), the problem solver engaged in reflective thinking must evaluate the potential solutions to the problem in light of existing information, information that may be incomplete and unverifiable. Formal logic is insufficient for such purposes. Instead, other criteria, such as coherence of the argument, fit with other data and arguments, explanatory power of the solution, plausibility, and so on, must be used. The process is guided by the need for a solution to the problem and is characterized by an interaction between the basis of the proposed solution and the reasoning of the problem solver. The process is imperfect not only because of limitations of the available information but also because of the limitations of the knower. Reflective thinking requires the continual evaluation of beliefs, assumptions, and hypotheses against existing data and against other plausible interpretations of the data. The resulting judgments are offered as reasonable integrations or syntheses of opposing points of view. Because they involve ongoing verification and evaluation, judgments based on reflective thinking are more likely to be valid and insightful than are beliefs derived from authority, emotional commitment, or narrow reasoning (Dewey, 1933, 1938). Further, unlike authority-based beliefs or emotional commitments, judgments derived from the reflective thinking process remain open to further scrutiny, evaluation, and reformulation; as such, reflective judgments are open to self-correction.

In summary, reflective thinking is called for when there is awareness of a real problem or when there is uncertainty about a solution. Reflective judgments are based on the evaluation and integration of existing data and theory into a solution about the problem at hand, a solution that can be rationally defended as most plausible or reasonable, taking into account the sets of conditions under which the problem is being solved.

Reflective Thinking and Critical Thinking

The terms *reflective thinking* and *critical thinking* are sometimes used interchangeably, even by Dewey (1933, 1938). For example, the definition of reflective thinking just discussed contains elements that are similar to other current definitions of critical thinking, such as that of Lipman (1988, p. 39), who argues that "critical thinking is skillful, responsible thinking that facilitates good judgment because it (1) relies upon criteria, (2) is self-correcting, and (3) is sensitive to context." However, there are two major differences between typical descriptions of critical thinking and our conception of reflective judgment: the epistemological assumptions on which the thinking person operates and the structure of the problem being addressed. Both are tied to Dewey's observation that awareness of uncertainty must exist prior to the initiation of reflective thinking.

The Neglect of Epistemic Assumptions in Models of Critical Thinking

Traditional attempts to define critical thinking typically reflect two perspectives. From one perspective, critical thinking is viewed as synonymous with logic or the hypothetico-deductive method. For example, textbooks such as *Logic and Critical Thinking* (Salmon, 1989) focus on inductive and deductive logic skills. From another perspective, critical thinking is seen as a process of inquiry or problem solving (Ennis, 1985a; Glaser, 1985; Lipman, 1988). While the second perspective is closer to our understanding of reflective judgment, both approaches are limited by the assumption that critical thinking consists primarily of a set of skills or general principles that one can apply in order to solve problems. The educational assumption associated with this view is that learning those skills or principles and how to use them will lead to critical thinking.

By contrast, rather than logic, basic differences in assumptions about what can be known and how knowing occurs differentiate authority-based thinkers from those who use reflective thinking (Kitchener and Kitchener, 1981). Deductive and inductive logic cannot totally account for naturally occurring, rational problem solving because a person may argue validly using formal logic but still use authority as the basic criterion for truth. People who assume that knowledge is authority based also assume (consistently so) that an authority can provide a solution for the problem. Within this worldview, uncertainty does not really exist. Although there may be temporary uncertainty while the individual seeks an authority who knows the answer, there is no perceived need to evaluate the evidence or generate a solution for a problem because it is assumed that the authority ultimately knows the answer.

Those who see critical thinking as only problem solving fail to acknowledge that epistemic assumptions (assumptions about knowledge) play a central role in recognizing a problematic situation. They often see a close relationship between such thinking and the scientific method. Typically, they specify a set of steps for approaching a problem, such as formulating and then testing hypotheses. What is missing from this approach is the understanding that such steps cannot be applied if the individual fails to recognize that a problem exists and that this recognition itself is predicated on other assumptions about knowledge (for example, that it is gained through inquiry). By contrast, we argue that epistemic assumptions constitute a fundamental difference between children's and adult's problem solving and that it is only in adulthood that individuals hold the epistemic assumptions that allow for true reflective thinking. (Evidence in support of this assertion is presented in Chapter Six.)

Problem Structure

The second issue that distinguishes our work on reflective think-ing from traditional work on critical thinking relates to the struc-ture of problems on which the thinking is focused. Problem struc-ture is defined as the degree to which a problem can be described completely and the certainty with which a solution can be iden-tified as true or correct (Wood, 1983). For example, problems that can be solved using deductive logic (All men are mortal; Plato was a man; therefore, Plato was mortal.) may be consid-ered puzzles. Puzzles can be described with a high degree of completeness, certainty, and correctness; Churchman (1971) has named these well-structured problems. Since well-structured problems have single correct answers that are ultimately avail-able, the task for the problem solver is to find and apply a decision-making procedure to find, compute, or remember the solutions. In Churchman's words (1971, p. 143), puzzles are "mental exercises concocted so that one model or way of think-ing is the appropriate pathway to a solution." As noted elsewhere, such problems "do not require considering alternative argu-ments, seeking out new evidence, or evaluating the reliability of data and sources of information" (Kitchener, 1983, p. 224). Paul (1990) has called these problems monological, noting that they can be answered within a single frame of reference with a specific set of logical moves.

However, no problem ever presented is perfectly struc-tured, as noted by Commons, Stein, and Richards (1987) and Churchman (1971). For example, even the equation $5 + 5 = x$ is ambiguous since it does not specify the base in which the prob-lem should be solved. However, some problems are much far-ther along the continuum from low to high structure than are others (Wood, 1990). Given base 10, the equation $5 + 5 = x$ is very high in structure and will accordingly be considered a well-structured problem in this discussion.

Problems such as overpopulation, hunger, pollution, and inflation are a different kind of problem. They cannot be de-scribed with a high degree of completeness or solved with a high degree of certainty; in fact, it is sometimes difficult to determine when a solution has been reached. Churchman (1971) calls such problems ill structured and suggests that they are of greater interest in understanding the real-world problem solving of adults. (We recognize that the terms *well* and *ill* carry connotations in other contexts that differ from those presented here in the context of problem structure. We use these terms here to be consistent with their meaning and use in related literature.) In Paul's (1990) terms, these would be multilogical problems since whole frames of reference compete for their solution. Wood (1983) has observed that ill-structured problems result when either the acts open to the decision maker, states of nature, possible outcomes, or the utility of the outcome is unknown or not known with a high degree of certainty. For a comparison of well- and ill-structured problems, see Table 1.1.

The solution to ill-structured problems depends on a much

Table 1.1. A Comparison of Well- and Ill-Structured Problems.

	Well-Structured Problems	*Ill-Structured Problems*
Definition	Can be described with a high degree of completeness	Cannot be described with a high degree of completeness
	Can be solved with a high degree of certainty	Cannot be resolved with a high degree of certainty
	Experts usually agree on the correct solution	Experts often disagree about the best solution, even when the problem can be considered solved
Examples	Converting a unit of measure between its English and metric equivalents	Determining what really happened at the Hue massacre in Vietnam
	Solving for *x* in an algebraic equation	Judging the adequacy of a theoretical proposition
	Calculating the trajectory of a rocket's flight	Predicting how to dispose of nuclear waste safely
Educational Goal	Learn to reason to correct solutions	Learn to construct and defend reasonable solutions

more complex process than the application of an algorithm. For example, Paul (1990) notes that we must evaluate the logical strength of one frame of reference against another by using criteria that are not necessarily peculiar to either. We contend, however, that in order to make such a comparison a person must hold the epistemic assumption that each solution may have some validity and may contain some error and that there may be no absolutely correct choice between them. Even developing a strategy to pick a solution, integrate several solutions, or develop a more general synthesis involves assessing the relative validity, fruitfulness, or truth value of each possible solution. Such an enterprise moves beyond simple knowledge of alternatives or skill in applying critical thinking principles. Rather, it involves an understanding of knowledge itself, or what we have called epistemic cognition, defined as "the process an individual invokes to monitor the epistemic nature of problems and the truth value of alternative solutions" (Kitchener, 1983, p. 225). It includes a person's knowledge about the limits of knowing, the certainty of knowing, and the criteria for knowing. It can be distinguished from cognition, the premonitored cognitive processes on which knowledge of the world is built (such as reading, memorizing, and computing), and from metacognition, the cognitive processes invoked to monitor progress on cognitive tasks (Kitchener, 1983).

Most tests of critical thinking address either well-structured problems or a mixture of well- and ill-structured problems. For example, two popular measures of critical thinking, the Cornell Critical Thinking Test (CCTT) and the Watson-Glaser Critical Thinking Appraisal (WGCTA), reflect different degrees of problem structure. Examination of these two measures suggests that the CCTT (Ennis and Millman, 1971) measures one's ability to solve well-structured problems, while the WGCTA (Watson and Glaser, 1964) reflects a combination of well- and ill-structured problems (Brabeck, 1983b; King, Wood, and Mines, 1990; Mines, King, Hood, and Wood, 1990). Thus, they invoke cognitive or metacognitive processes rather than the epistemic assumptions of the respondents.

In summary, our model of reflective thinking differs from current models of critical thinking in two respects. First, it acknowledges the importance of epistemic assumptions to the reasoning process. Throughout this book, we argue that educators cannot ignore individuals' epistemic assumptions if they want to help their students be reflective thinkers.

Second, our model focuses explicitly on how people reason about ill-structured problems. We endorse Dewey's (1933, 1938) contention that true reflective thinking is uncalled for unless real uncertainty exists about the possible solution(s) to a problem. If educators neglect to engage students meaningfully in addressing ill-structured problems and if researchers fail to include ill-structured problems in their assessment of critical thinking, the teaching and evaluation of these important skills will also be neglected.

The Reflective Judgment Model

As noted earlier, the Reflective Judgment Model (Kitchener and King, 1981, 1990a, 1990b) describes a developmental progression that occurs between childhood and adulthood in the ways that people understand the process of knowing and in the corresponding ways that they justify their beliefs about ill-structured problems. In other words, the model describes the development of epistemic cognition. As individuals develop, they become better able to evaluate knowledge claims and to explain and defend their points of view on controversial issues. The ability to make reflective judgments is the ultimate outcome of this progression.

This developmental progression in reasoning is described by seven distinct sets of assumptions about knowledge and how knowledge is acquired. Each set of assumptions has its own logical coherency and is called a stage. Each successive stage is posited to represent a more complex and effective form of justification, providing more inclusive and better integrated assumptions for evaluating and defending a point of view. Further, each set of assumptions is associated with a different strategy for solving ill-structured problems. Specifically, the more advanced sets allow greater differentiation between ill-structured and well-structured problems and allow more complex and complete data to be integrated into a solution. These stages are summarized in Exhibit 1.1.

Exhibit 1.1. Summary of Reflective Judgment Stages.

Pre-Reflective Thinking (Stages 1, 2, and 3)

Stage 1

View of knowledge: Knowledge is assumed to exist absolutely and concretely; it is not understood as an abstraction. It can be obtained with certainty by direct observation.
Concept of justification: Beliefs need no justification since there is assumed to be an absolute correspondence between what is believed to be true and what is true. Alternate beliefs are not perceived.

"I know what I have seen."

Stage 2

View of knowledge: Knowledge is assumed to be absolutely certain or certain but not immediately available. Knowledge can be obtained directly through the senses (as in direct observation) or via authority figures.
Concept of justification: Beliefs are unexamined and unjustified or justified by their correspondence with the beliefs of an authority figure (such as a teacher or parent). Most issues are assumed to have a right answer, so there is little or no conflict in making decisions about disputed issues.

"If it is on the news, it has to be true."

Stage 3

View of knowledge: Knowledge is assumed to be absolutely certain or temporarily uncertain. In areas of temporary uncertainty, only personal beliefs can be known until absolute knowledge is obtained. In areas of absolute certainty, knowledge is obtained from authorities.
Concept of justification: In areas in which certain answers exist, beliefs are justified by reference to authorities' views. In areas in which answers do not exist, beliefs are defended as personal opinion since the link between evidence and beliefs is unclear.

*"When there is evidence that people can give to convince everybody
one way or another, then it will be knowledge; until then, it's just a guess."*

Quasi-Reflective Thinking (Stages 4 and 5)

Stage 4

View of knowledge: Knowledge is uncertain and knowledge claims are idiosyncratic to the individual since situational variables (such as incorrect reporting of data,

Exhibit 1.1. Summary of Reflective Judgment Stages, Cont'd.

---

data lost over time, or disparities in access to information) dictate that knowing always involves an element of ambiguity.
Concept of justification: Beliefs are justified by giving reasons and using evidence, but the arguments and choice of evidence are idiosyncratic (for example, choosing evidence that fits an established belief).

> *"I'd be more inclined to believe evolution if they had proof. It's just like the pyramids: I don't think we'll ever know. Who are you going to ask? No one was there."*

Stage 5

View of knowledge: Knowledge is contextual and subjective since it is filtered through a person's perceptions and criteria for judgment. Only interpretations of evidence, events, or issues may be known.
Concept of justification: Beliefs are justified within a particular context by means of the rules of inquiry for that context and by context-specific interpretations of evidence. Specific beliefs are assumed to be context specific or are balanced against other interpretations, which complicates (and sometimes delays) conclusions.

> *"People think differently and so they attack the problem differently. Other theories could be as true as my own, but based on different evidence."*

Reflective Thinking (Stages 6 and 7)

Stage 6

View of knowledge: Knowledge is constructed into individual conclusions about ill-structured problems on the basis of information from a variety of sources. Interpretations that are based on evaluations of evidence across contexts and on the evaluated opinions of reputable others can be known.
Concept of justification: Beliefs are justified by comparing evidence and opinion from different perspectives on an issue or across different contexts and by constructing solutions that are evaluated by criteria such as the weight of the evidence, the utility of the solution, or the pragmatic need for action.

> *"It's very difficult in this life to be sure. There are degrees of sureness. You come to a point at which you are sure enough for a personal stance on the issue."*

Stage 7

View of knowledge: Knowledge is the outcome of a process of reasonable inquiry in which solutions to ill-structured problems are constructed. The adequacy of those solutions is evaluated in terms of what is most reasonable or probable according to the current evidence, and it is reevaluated when relevant new evidence, perspectives, or tools of inquiry become available.

Exhibit 1.1. Summary of Reflective Judgment Stages, Cont'd.

Concept of justification: Beliefs are justified probabilistically on the basis of a variety of interpretive considerations, such as the weight of the evidence, the explanatory value of the interpretations, the risk of erroneous conclusions, consequences of alternative judgments, and the interrelationships of these factors. Conclusions are defended as representing the most complete, plausible, or compelling understanding of an issue on the basis of the available evidence.

"One can judge an argument by how well thought-out the positions are,
what kinds of reasoning and evidence are used to support it, and how consistent
the way one argues on this topic is as compared with other topics."

Those whose reasoning is characteristic of the early stages (Stages 1, 2, and 3) assume that knowledge is gained either by direct, personal observation or through the word of an authority figure; they assume that knowledge thus gained is absolutely correct and certain. People who hold these assumptions do not differentiate between well- and ill-structured problems, viewing all problems as though they were defined with a high degree of certainty and completeness. We refer to this type of reasoning as pre-reflective; it is exemplified in the excerpt from the interview with the high school student presented near the beginning of this chapter. By contrast, reasoning more typical of the middle stages (Stages 4 and 5) recognizes that knowledge claims about ill-structured problems contain elements of uncertainty; thus there is an understanding that some situations are truly problematic. The difficulty is in understanding how judgments ought to be made in light of this uncertainty. Individuals who hold the assumptions of Stages 4 or 5 typically argue that, while judgments ought to be based on evidence, evaluation is individualistic and idiosyncratic. While they acknowledge differences between well- and ill-structured problems (a developmental advance over the earlier stages), they are often at a loss when asked to solve ill-structured problems because they don't know how to deal with the inherent ambiguity of such problems. We refer to this type of reasoning as quasi-reflective; it is illustrated by the interview with the college student described near the beginning of this chapter.

Stages 6 and 7 represent the most advanced sets of assumptions identified to date that are used in solving ill-structured problems; they are exemplified by the excerpt from the interview with the graduate student. These stages reflect the epistemic assumption that one's understanding of the world is not "given" but must be actively constructed and that knowledge must be understood in relationship to the context in which it was generated. An additional assumption is that some interpretations or knowledge claims may be judged as more plausible than others. Thus, while absolute truth will never be ascertained with complete certainty, some views may be evaluated as more reasonable explanations. This view presumes that judgments must not only be grounded in relevant data but that they must also be evaluated to determine their validity. Criteria that might be used in making such evaluations include conceptual soundness, coherence, degree of fit with the data, meaningfulness, usefulness, and parsimony. We refer to this type of reasoning as truly reflective thinking. (In Chapter Three, we offer a detailed description of each of the seven stages of the Reflective Judgment Model, along with examples of reasoning that are characteristic of each of these stages.)

In summary, the Reflective Judgment Model postulates that reflective judgment is the outcome of a developmental progression. While one must have both knowledge and reasoning skill to engage in reflective thinking, true reflective thinking presupposes that individuals hold the epistemic assumptions that allow them to understand and accept real uncertainty. Similarly, while individuals may reason well or poorly about well-structured problems, they engage in reflective thinking (as defined here) only while they are considering ill-structured problems. Further, the ability to engage in reflective thinking must be assessed in relationship to ill-structured problems. (Assessment issues are discussed in detail in Chapters Four and Five.)

Summary

This chapter began with three excerpts that illustrate different ways people approach and resolve complex and controversial issues; in the context of the Reflective Judgment Model, they exemplify pre-reflective, quasi-reflective, and reflective thinking. Our work on reflective thinking is grounded in Dewey's (1933, 1938) definition of this concept, especially his astute observation that uncertainty is a characteristic of the search for knowledge. Reflective judgments are made by examining and evaluating relevant information, opinion, and available explanations (the process of reflective thinking), then constructing a plausible solution for the problem at hand, acknowledging that the solution itself is open to further evaluation and scrutiny. Although this process is not assumed to yield absolute truth, it provides a means of discovering errors and omissions in problem solving and therefore is likely to lead to more accurate, adequate, and well-grounded solutions. In other words, engaging in reflective thinking that culminates in a reflective judgment helps people become better problem solvers.

Reflective thinking is related to but not synonymous with critical thinking because critical thinking involves many types of reasoning, including deductive and inductive logic about well-structured problems. In addition, critical thinking is typically characterized as a set of skills that can be acquired through the learning of increasingly complex behavior or rules. We take a different approach, suggesting instead that the development of reflective judgment is the outcome of an interaction between the individual's conceptual skills and environments that promote or inhibit the acquisition of these skills.

More specifically, where the Reflective Judgment Model departs most dramatically from most models of critical thinking is in its insistence that the ability to engage in reflective thinking cannot be understood without considering the cognitive characteristics (specifically, the epistemic assumptions) of the developing person. The Reflective Judgment Model hypothesizes that six sets of epistemic assumptions and associated reasoning strategies typically precede the assumptions and strategies that are associated with true reflective thinking.

Further, we emphasize the importance of epistemic assumptions in the development of reflective judgment. To the extent that reflective judgment is called for only in those situations in which there is real uncertainty, assumptions about what can be known and how a person can know are critical. These are the assumptions that develop as the person becomes able to differentiate and coordinate increasingly complex cognitive skills.

These assumptions are associated with many higher-order educational goals. For example: "Students need to learn . . . to be able to state why a question or argument is significant and for whom; what the difference is between developing and justifying a position and merely asserting one; and how to develop and provide warrants for their own interpretations and judgments" (Association of American Colleges, 1991, p. 14).

These are educational goals and cognitive skills of no small consequence, and they are clearly associated with the desirable attributes of an educated person. However, as noted here, the development of such skills is associated with the development of the individual's epistemic assumptions. These assumptions not only affect how individuals will approach the task of defending a judgment but also how they will respond in learning environments designed to teach these skills. It is for these reasons that we devote the remainder of this book to the examination of theoretical, research, and educational issues that inform our understanding of the process of assisting students in becoming better able to make reflective judgments.

Chapter Two

Creating a New
Theoretical Model
of Reflective Judgment

In Chapter One we introduced the Reflective Judgment Model, noting that it describes a developmental progression in people's assumptions about how and what they can know. We suggested that this progression can be broken down into seven stages and that each stage can be characterized by a network of assumptions that has its own logical coherence. In this chapter, we first discuss several concepts that underlie developmental stage theories and show how these apply to the Reflective Judgment Model. These concepts in turn provide the foundation for teaching students to think and judge reflectively.

Those who are not familiar with developmental models may wonder what we mean by the term *stage;* those who are familiar with the developmental literature may wonder why we use this term in light of the criticism of the concept in the professional literature. Others may be impatient with the seemingly technical theoretical questions addressed here and wonder about the implications of these issues for teaching students to make more reflective judgments. We will try to address each of these questions in the remainder of this chapter.

We believe that the theoretical assumptions on which the Reflective Judgment Model is grounded merit attention because of their implications for both educational practice and research. For example, many educators teach critical thinking skills using a traditional learning theory approach, emphasizing specific techniques of analysis and learned rules (Ennis, 1985a; Glaser, 1985; Lipman, 1985), and documenting their efforts accordingly. Developmental approaches, particularly those based on developmental stage models, are grounded in the students' own internal "rules" for making sense of their experiences and thus have different implications for teaching and evaluating critical thinking. We think such assumptions should be stated as explicitly as possible, and we attempt to do so here and throughout this book.

Next, we introduce a more recent conceptualization of stage-related development. Although Fischer's (1980) skill theory model was developed independently, it complements the Reflective Judgment Model to an extraordinary degree and has greatly stimulated our thinking about the nature and course of development. Fischer's model has had remarkable explanatory value in interpreting the findings from research on the Reflective Judgment Model and in richly informing our discussion of applications to education.

In the last section of this chapter, we compare the Reflective Judgment Model with other models of adult intellectual development. This comparison includes both its predecessors from the early 1970s (including William Perry's well-known scheme of intellectual and ethical development) and its contemporaries in the mid-1990s, and it notes points of concordance as well as points of departure. Our purpose here is not to present a detailed critique of related theories in the field but to provide a historical and contemporary context for the Reflective Judgment Model, showing how it evolved from existing models of intellectual development and how it is related to current models in the field.

Concepts Associated with Developmental Stage Theories

The issue of whether cognitive growth is stagelike is controversial in developmental psychology and education (Brainard, 1978; Fischer, 1980; Fischer and Bullock, 1981; Flavell, 1971;

Schaie, 1977–78). As Flavell (1982b) has noted, the terms *development* and *developmental stage* seem to apply more naturally to childhood than adulthood. Further, many developmentalists suggest that both the importance of individual differences and the influence of the environment increase with age and, reciprocally, that the homogeneity associated with stagelike development decreases with age (Fischer and Silvern, 1985; McCall, 1981). Nevertheless, we refer to the seven reflective judgment levels as stages for reasons given below. Here, we address the question of what we mean by stages and why we have chosen to use the term.

Although there is considerable debate about the nature of stages, several characteristics are commonly associated with the concept. These are drawn to a great extent from the work of Jean Piaget ([1956] 1974), who studied and wrote extensively about intellectual development in children and adolescents. Since many of the assumptions on which the Reflective Judgment Model is based are drawn from Piaget's work, we will briefly digress from our discussion of reflective judgment to review those assumptions.

Piagetian Assumptions of Stage-Related Development

Based on his studies in biology, Piaget (1960, 1970, [1956] 1974; Ginsberg and Opper, 1969) thought that human intellectual functioning is characterized by two functions: organization and adaptation. For Piaget, organization referred to the tendency of all biological systems to organize basic components into higher-order systems. He thought that intellectual development follows the same principle: over time and with appropriate environmental stimuli, humans tend to organize simple categories or structures into more complex, integrated, and complete structures.

Further, Piaget claimed that these categories are shaped as individuals adapt to the stimuli provided by the environment. This adaptation occurs through the joint functions of what he called assimilation and accommodation. Assimilation is the process through which current structures are used to interpret environmental stimuli. If this process existed in isolation, the organism and its structures would not change. However, it is balanced by accommodation, through which structures change in response to environmental demands. One of the authors of this book observed an example of these functions in the early language acquisition of her son. Mother and son were traveling in the car. To entertain the two-year-old, Mom was pointing out and naming animals: *horse, dog, sheep, cow,* and so on. The son seemed to be able to label only two categories of animals: all big animals he called *cow,* and all small animals he labeled *dog.* When Mom pointed to a sheep and said the word *sheep,* the son regularly said *dog;* he gave the same response when she pointed to a cat. Similarly, when Mother pointed to a horse and said *horse,* her son regularly said *cow.* In Piaget's terms, the child was assimilating the animals to his own two-category language structure. This went on for many miles; every time the son misnamed an animal, his mother again gave the correct name. When they stopped for gas, there happened to be a sheep in a pen nearby, and they walked over to look at it. Mom again said *sheep* for probably the twentieth time. This time the son looked at the animal for quite a while; Mom again said *sheep.* This time the son said *sheep.* In Piaget's terms, the boy had accommodated to the demands of the environment, and his language structure expanded accordingly. College students who learn to use the technical language and sophisticated concepts of a discipline are also changing their language and thought structures to accommodate finer and more complex distinctions. Similarly, students who are asked to explain the factual basis for divergent views on a topic may also have to accommodate their structures of knowledge to those that recognize the role of evidence in making judgments.

According to Piaget, the two processes of assimilation and accommodation continue throughout life and account for changes in the conceptual structures people use to understand the world. Intellectual development is assumed to evolve over time as people adapt to the environment and organized experience; thus intellectual capacity is not assumed to be a static characteristic of people.

Along with the tendency of individuals to adapt to the

environment, Piaget also observed that cognitive structures change in regular ways and that individuals at different ages exhibit qualitatively different ways of responding to the environment. (Piaget attributed this to the use of different cognitive structures.) These structures provide the framework through which individuals interpret experience. Piaget referred to these structures as stages when they become stable or equilibrated.

Based on the work of Piaget and others (notably Kohlberg, 1969), Flavell (1963, 1971, 1977) has argued that stage models generally assume that there are qualitatively different structures that are organized into logically coherent systems or stages and that these stages appear in an invariant sequence. He has also suggested that the concept of stage implies that development is abrupt and that there is discontinuity between stages. We concur with those who have taken issue with the idea that the concept of stage implies radical discontinuity — for example, that a person operates exclusively within only one stage structure at a time (Fischer and Bullock, 1981; Fischer, 1983; Rest, 1979). (Research on this question is presented in Chapter Six.)

The Meaning of Stages in the Reflective Judgment Model

What does the term *stage* mean in the Reflective Judgment Model? Are the Reflective Judgment stages organized structures? Are they characterized by qualitatively different forms of thinking? Do they appear in an invariant sequence? We will begin with the least controversial claim about the stage properties of this model, that the Reflective Judgment stages are *organized*. If this is so, according to Flavell's (1971) criteria, two or more elements are interrelated, these organizations are relatively stable, and they form the basis of apparently unrelated acts. In the research to date on the Reflective Judgment Model, we have found remarkably consistent interrelationships between individuals' assumptions about the nature of knowledge and how they justify beliefs in the face of uncertainty. This connection between epistemology and concepts of justification strongly suggests an interrelated network of assumptions and approaches to justification as people reason about ill-structured problems.

The connections between epistemological assumptions and justification also appear to have an internal logic, although the logic may not be apparent to the casual observer. Rather, the organization is implicit in the structure of the belief system. For example, if an individual has only a single category with which to classify knowledge (for instance, knowledge is based on direct observation), then it is not only illogical but impossible for the individual to justify his or her beliefs by reference to the probability that one view of a phenomenon is more accurate than another. Further, the assumption that "what is observed is what is true" reflects other underlying beliefs that may initially appear to be unrelated, such as a belief in the word of an authority figure and a belief that justification is unnecessary. Each stage in the Reflective Judgment Model is similarly characterized by a network of assumptions that may at first seem unrelated. To use another example, an individual might suggest that the views of authority figures represent their own biases, that no view of an issue is better than any other view, and that everyone has the right to his or her own opinion. Underlying this belief system appear to be the following assumptions: knowledge is ultimately subjective, it is not understood with certainty, and there is no rational way to discover it completely. Using this logic, it is consistent to conclude that authorities' claims to know simply reflect their own subjective biases. (See Chapter Three for a more thorough discussion of the internal logic of beliefs at each stage of the Reflective Judgment Model.)

Further, responses from the Reflective Judgment Interview (the standard measure used in this line of research) are quite consistent across domains as divergent as science and history. Correlations between individuals' responses to different problems are generally moderate to high, and familiarity with content has only minimally affected Reflective Judgment scores. These results suggest that networks of assumptions in the Reflective Judgment Model are moderately robust and show more consistency than one would predict without a stage model. Similarly, assumptions are relatively stable over short periods of time without explicit educational interventions designed to promote or support development. In Piaget's terms, individuals seem to be assimilating problem solving in different domains to the same set of assumptions or structures (that is, stages), and accommodation to higher stages appears to take place slowly. In these ways, the Reflective Judgment stages appear to be organized. (Data from studies reporting stage properties are presented in Chapters Five and Six.)

Flavell's second criterion, as noted above, is that the different forms of thinking are *qualitatively different*. The qualitative differences between stages of the Reflective Judgment Model were introduced in Chapter One and are discussed in detail in Chapter Three, so discussion of this criterion will not be repeated here. One observation will suffice: there is a qualitative difference in the assumptions of a person who believes that authorities are the source of all knowledge and that knowledge thus gained needs no further analysis and one who believes that knowledge must be constructed by integrating evidence as well as expert opinion into a reasonable conjecture.

The third major criterion of stage models noted above is that the different forms of thinking appear in an *invariant sequence*. The seven stages of the Reflective Judgment Model do appear to form such a sequence (though not as predicted using a simple stage model where there is radical discontinuity between stages). That is, the advances of a prior stage appear to lay the groundwork for movement to the subsequent stage. Although different people may progress at different rates and as a result of different experiences, when they move from Stage A to Stage C, they do not typically skip the intervening Stage B.

From a research perspective, invariance is a claim that is difficult to confirm or disconfirm since the time between measurements, as well as measurement error, does not allow the researcher to trace all changes in the individual's thinking or track them precisely and completely. For example, an individual's use of reasoning at a given stage may not be documented because data collections were scheduled before and after that type of reasoning stage became a prominent feature of the person's thinking. Nevertheless, longitudinal data do provide a picture — however incomplete — of qualitative changes in reasoning over time. Data from longitudinal studies support the sequentiality of the seven Reflective Judgment stages, and are reviewed in Chapter Six. In general, when development in reflective judgment is observed over time, it appears in a sequential fashion. Davison (1979) developed a test of sequentiality in developmental stage models that has also been applied to data from longitudinal studies of reflective judgment. In all cases, the results of this test support the sequentiality of the Reflective Judgment stages.

Another method that has been used to evaluate the sequential relationships between the stages utilizes a Guttman scale of a cumulative sequence of comprehension tasks. Using this approach, Kitchener, Lynch, Fischer, and Wood (1993) tested individuals' comprehension of Reflective Judgment Stages 2 through 7. They found that individuals could not comprehend the meaning of higher stages if they did not comprehend the meaning of the preceding stages. This study provides further support for the sequentiality of the reflective judgment stages.

In summary, we concur with Piaget's guiding principle that individuals develop (here, that their assumptions about knowledge develop) as they attempt to organize and adapt to the environment. We use the term *stage* in the Reflective Judgment Model because of the consistency between the defining characteristics of stage models and the evidence that has been gathered over the last fifteen years on the Reflective Judgment Model. For the seven stages of the model, we have (1) explicated the logical relationships between the components of each stage that reflect an underlying (organized) structure, (2) shown the qualitative differences between these sets of assumptions, and (3) documented sequential changes in the emergence of these assumptions. It is our conclusion that a stage model, as defined here, provides a useful framework for describing the development of reflective judgment.

Fischer's Model of Cognitive Development

One issue associated with stage models that was not addressed in most of the early research on the Reflective Judgment Model

---

Note: This section is based on King (1985) and Kitchener and Fischer (1990).

is whether there is discontinuity in development, that is, whether abrupt changes are associated with the acquisition of a new stage. Most of the data on the Reflective Judgment Model suggest that this is a gradual process. Work by Fischer (1980) provides an explanation for these findings and suggests how development occurs between stages. We believe this model has important implications for educators concerned with promoting reflective thinking.

Fischer and his associates (Fischer, 1980; Fischer and Canfield, 1986; Fischer and Kenny, 1986; Fischer, Hand, and Russell, 1984) argue that at a micro-developmental level, the complexity of information a person can process affects the level of differentiation and integration of assumptions the person uses when approaching a problem. Fischer and others (Case, 1985) postulate that between infancy and adulthood individuals progress through a series of levels or stages of "increasingly complex cognitive control" (Fischer, 1980, p. 485). According to Fischer and Farrar (1987), seven developmental levels emerge when people are between two and thirty years of age; these levels are characterized by qualitative differences in the skill structures an individual can control. The changes in skill structure provide the foundation not only for the changes observed in the ability to think reflectively but also for changes that are associated with more mature moral judgment, more complex conceptions of the self, and more sophisticated concepts of relationships (Kitchener, 1982).

According to Fischer's theory, two aspects of development must be taken into account when individual change is considered (Fischer and Pipp, 1984). The first, *optimal level,* addresses the major cognitive shifts that people show over a long period of time. The second, *skill acquisition,* describes how people learn specific skills both between and within levels.

Optimal Level. Optimal level is defined as "the upper limit of the person's general information-processing capacity" (Kitchener and Fischer, 1990, p. 54). Although individual performance may vary widely depending upon the context, it does not exceed an optimal level of complexity when a person is involved in independent problem solving. Fischer and Pipp (1984) argue that optimal level increases with a person's age and is marked by periods of relatively abrupt or fast growth followed by periods of relative stability. According to this model, although there may not be discontinuity in the strict sense of the word, there should be evidence of rapid growth as a new skill level emerges over time.

Each period of relatively fast growth, called a spurt, marks the emergence of a new developmental level that is characterized by a qualitatively different structure. Each spurt is then followed by a plateau, at which time skills are generalized to new domains. In terms of the Reflective Judgment Model, a spurt marks the emergence of a new stage, characterized by a new epistemology and a new form of justification. According to Fischer, a person's best performance in a familiar domain improves sharply when a new level is emerging. During the plateau, the new skill structure is elaborated and applied in new areas. For this reason, the plateau period should not be considered a period of developmental stasis.

Fischer and his colleagues (Lamborn and Fischer, 1988) have called the difference between the optimal and functional levels a person's developmental range. They note that the concept of developmental range leads beyond standard stage characterization of the individual's thinking in terms of a single point on a developmental scale to a range of stages within which the individual may operate, depending on prior experience and the environment in which the performance occurs. This range is charted in Figure 2.1.

The seven developmental levels in Fischer's model directly correspond to the seven Reflective Judgment stages (King, 1985; Kitchener and Fischer, 1990). (Six additional levels emerge during the first two years of life but are not discussed here since they apply to very young children.) We hypothesize that the assumptions associated with each Reflective Judgment stage develop concurrently with the corresponding skill level shown in Table 2.1.

During childhood, the skills that emerge involve concrete representations of people, objects, or occasions; these characterize

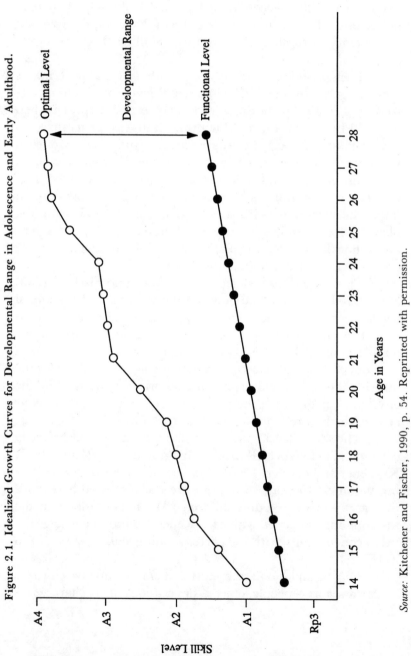

Figure 2.1. Idealized Growth Curves for Developmental Range in Adolescence and Early Adulthood.

Source: Kitchener and Fischer, 1990, p. 54. Reprinted with permission.

Table 2.1. Fischer's Skill Levels and Stages of Reflective Judgment.

Skill level	Reflective judgment stage
Representational 1 Single representation: concrete instances of knowing.	*Stage 1* Knowing is limited to single concrete observations: what a person observes is true.
Representational 2 Representational mapping: two concrete representations can be coordinated with each other.	*Stage 2* Two categories for knowing: right answers and wrong answers. Good authorities have knowledge; bad authorities lack knowledge.
Representational 3 Representational system: several aspects of two concrete representations can be coordinated.	*Stage 3* In some areas, knowledge is certain and authorities have that knowledge. In other areas, knowledge is temporarily uncertain. Only personal beliefs can be known.
Representational 4 = Abstract 1 Two systems of representational systems can be constructed; these are the same as a single abstraction.	*Stage 4* Concept that knowledge is unknown in several specific cases leads to the abstract generalization that knowledge is uncertain.
Abstract 2 Abstract mapping: abstractions can be coordinated with each other.	*Stage 5* Knowledge is uncertain and must be understood within a context; thus justification is context specific.
Abstract 3 Abstract system: several aspects of two abstractions can be coordinated.	*Stage 6* Knowledge is uncertain but constructed by comparing evidence and opinion on different sides of an issue or across contexts.
Abstract 4 = a principle Systems of abstract systems can be constructed; these are the same as a single principle.	*Stage 7* Knowledge is the outcome of a process of reasonable inquiry. This view is equivalent to a general principle that is consistent across domains.

Source: Based on Table 1, pp. 50–51 in Kitchener and Fischer (1990). Reprinted with permission.

the representational tier. With the emergence of each new level, children are able to construct more complex relations between concrete representations. At the first representational level, individuals can work only with single concrete representations about what they know. For example, in the domain of family relationships, a child understands her mother as simply "my mommy." In terms of the Reflective Judgment Model, concepts of knowledge are very simple and concrete—knowing, for example, that certain animals (apes, say) exist.

The second level is called representational mapping because children can relate two concrete representations to each other. In terms of family relations, a child might understand that her mother is also her daddy's wife. In Reflective Judgment terms, a person might understand that apes exist and that an authority figure says it is silly to think that people came from apes.

At the third level, two or more representational mappings are coordinated to produce a simple representational system. In keeping with the family relations example, a child might describe her mommy as *also* her father's wife *and* as her aunt's sister *and* as her grandmother's daughter. In terms of the Reflective Judgment Model, representational mapping corresponds to the third stage of reflective judgment. These skills allow for understanding more complex relations, such as why a priest and a biology professor might say different things about evolution.

At the fourth level, two or more representational systems are related to produce a new kind of thinking, single abstractions; this forms the first level of the abstract tier. It represents the ability to construct and operate on intangible (hence, more abstract) categories. Fischer estimates that this level emerges in early adolescence. In terms of family relations, an adolescent might construct the concept of a traditional nuclear family in which all members have different roles. In terms of the Reflective Judgment Model, in a single abstraction about knowledge, a person can coordinate the concrete observations that different people draw different conclusions on the basis of their own circumstances or biases. From this coordination emerges the beginning awareness of abstractions such as knowledge, evidence, and argument.

As occurred earlier with representations, after an adolescent can use single abstractions, she or he can later relate single abstractions to each other, which forms the fifth level, abstract mapping. In terms of family relations, the person might be able to relate the concept of mothers in traditional nuclear families to mothers in families where the parents are divorced, noting how the roles are similar and different. In the Reflective Judgment Model, an abstract concept of justification can be related to an abstract concept of knowledge. This appears to be the basis of an individual's ability to understand how different rules of inquiry used in gathering and evaluating evidence can lead people to different conclusions about what they know.

At the sixth level, which is posited to emerge initially in young adulthood, individuals can combine abstract mappings into abstract systems. In the family relations example, at this level, a person is able to relate multiple types of families (single-parent, blended, nuclear, extended) and family roles to each other. In terms of the Reflective Judgment Model, this ability allows the individual to consider and evaluate information from several sides of an issue and allows initial comparisons between differing perspectives or contexts (systems, in Fischer's terms), a skill that is required for the familiar "compare and contrast" college assignments. The development of these abilities is significant because it provides the underlying form for intellectual development beyond relativism.

The final reorganization predicted by Fischer's model, at the seventh level, is called a system of abstract systems. At this level, two or more abstract systems are related to form a principle. With respect to families, the principle might be that a concept of family is broader than blood relationships or proximity of the living situation; it involves a special bond between individuals with long-term commitments to each other. With respect to the Reflective Judgment Model, one such principle is that knowledge is the outcome of a process of inquiry that can produce compelling conclusions.

While optimal level specifies the upper limit in the complexity of skill that an individual can control, Fischer (1980) claims that actual functioning at the upper limit requires that performance be induced and supported by the environment. Opportunities to practice the skill, the difficulty of the task, and the assessment procedure can all affect an individual's performance. Thus, spurts in performance are evident only under optimal environmental conditions, when individuals have had an opportunity to master a skill and when there is active encouragement, training, or other forms of tangible assistance (contextual support) for high-level performance. Under these conditions, development appears to be stagelike, and performance shows rapid improvement as a new stage or level is emerging. However, since opportunities for practice and an optimal environment are not typically consistent across domains, development often appears uneven. In other words, whether or not a person is actually able to produce a response at his or her optimal level depends upon the domain, the practice and feedback the person has had with the skill involved, and the context in which the person is asked to perform the skill. For example, college students may have the capacity to perform abstract mappings, such as relating a speaker's beliefs to the evidence the person presents about an issue. However, whether college students actually exhibit that capacity by evidencing Stage 5 reasoning depends on the kinds of opportunities they have had to practice abstract mappings on reasoning about ill-structured problems and on the environmental support (expectations, consistent feedback) for this form of reasoning. That is, whether students develop these skills depends on whether professors, advisers, hall directors, and others who touch their lives expect, ask for, and model Stage 5 responses.

Skill Acquisition. The second aspect of development that Fischer (1980) highlights is skill acquisition, which describes how a person learns or acquires individual skills. New skills are constructed through a sequence of micro-developmental steps between levels. Fischer (1980) has identified a set of transformation rules that specify how particular skills are transformed into later ones. The individual acquiring or generalizing a skill proceeds through many small steps specified by a set of rules before the spurt in performance that marks the emergence of a new level can be observed. The stages in the Reflective Judgment Model capture only large jumps between levels, not the smaller micro-developmental steps described by this process.

Skill development often appears to proceed gradually and somewhat haphazardly. Life events may or may not place two skills in relation to each other in a person's experience, so the impetus for development is not experienced. For example, an individual may not be challenged to try to make sense of discrepancies between the competing views of different authorities because he or she has not previously been asked to compare or contrast such views. When the juxtaposition does occur, as may happen in an educational setting, it stimulates the person to work out a coordination of the skills. As the skills are coordinated across levels, they are transformed into new skills. Without challenges that span different types of skills, a person's existing skill level will probably not change or develop into higher-order skills.

Further, under ordinary circumstances, most environments do not provide cues or support for high-level performance, especially not about issues of knowing. As a result, people do not typically perform at their optimal level but at their lower, functional level. Improvement in functional level is usually slow and gradual, with performance remaining far below optimal level and varying widely across domains. Moreover, as Fischer, Hand, and Russell (1984) have noted, our understanding of optimal level is hampered by the fact that most assessment instruments (including the Reflective Judgment Interview) measure functional level rather than optimal level.

Fischer's model provides a modification of earlier formulations of the stage concept that has been useful in guiding our thinking about research as well as about educational interventions (see Chapter Nine). Initial research has provided evidence for differences in functional and optimal levels in reflective judgment, suggesting that more abrupt developmental spurts may be observed when the environmental context supports high-level performance (such as providing opportunities for practice) but that more continuous development is observed when the environment is not as supportive (Kitchener, Lynch, Fischer, and Wood, 1993).

These concepts have important implications for education since they imply that individuals cannot understand or manipulate concepts that are beyond their optimal level. They can, however, understand concepts at their functional level, as well as those that are between the two levels. We present data in Chapter Six suggesting that while the functional level of most undergraduate students is between Stages 3 and 4, they may be able to comprehend Stage 5 concepts (Kitchener, Lynch, Fischer, and Wood, 1993). If educators expect students to operate at higher levels without providing them with opportunities to practice and without giving them clear feedback about the nature of their performance, students will probably experience frustration and perhaps not master the desired skills. These issues are addressed further in Chapter Nine, along with specific suggestions for promoting reflective thinking among college students.

Prior Models of Epistemological Development

The Reflective Judgment Model was not the first to suggest that people's assumptions about knowledge change over the course of their lifetime; the works of Perry (1968) and Broughton (1975) were its major predecessors. These early models of epistemological development greatly stimulated our thinking about the intellectual development in adulthood, especially during the college years.

Perry's Scheme of Intellectual and Ethical Development

William Perry (1968, 1981) is credited with being the first to observe that underlying assumptions about knowledge and learning make a difference in the reasoning of college students. Based on a sample of undergraduates from Harvard and Radcliffe who were interviewed at the end of each academic year, Perry characterized students' intellectual and ethical development by describing a progression of nine different points of view, which he called positions. These positions traced the evolution of students' thinking about knowledge, truth, and values and their own responsibilities for their beliefs and actions, and they appeared to develop sequentially. (See King, 1978, for a summary and early critique of Perry's model.)

Perry observed that the college students in his sample initially used discrete, absolute, and authority-based categories to understand people, knowledge, and values (positions 1 and 2) and that the students did not perceive legitimate conflicts about knowledge. He coined the term *dualistic* to describe this approach. Positions 3 and 4, which he called multiplicity, reflect more complex assumptions as students begin to acknowledge multiple answers to complex questions. This makes decision making confusing since authorities with single answers are rejected as sources of truth. Perry identified a major change in epistemological outlook in positions 5 and 6, which he called relativism. He hypothesized that here students had begun to see knowledge as contextual and to acknowledge that theories were not necessarily true but were metaphors that allowed interpretation. Evaluations of ideas were then evaluated as "right" and "wrong" within a particular context or setting. He noted that in the face of such relativity of values, students were confronted with the existential responsibility for making a decision.

Perry called the last three positions (7 through 9) "commitment in relativism." He argued that when students working within a relativistic frame of reference were faced with the need to make decisions about issues such as marriage, religion, or career, they did so by making a leap of faith or by an affirmation from within. Such decisions do not reflect cognitive development or change in underlying epistemology beyond relativism. The knowing inherent in such choices, Perry (1981) suggested, is an act of personal commitment.

John Broughton's Model

Broughton's (1975) work on the development of natural epistemology parallels Perry's by arguing that each person constructs a view of self, reality, and knowledge. Like Perry, Broughton suggested that in the earliest stages (which he presumed are characteristic of childhood), individuals view knowledge dogmatically and concretely, assuming that reality and truth exist absolutely. He also observed that later, in adolescence, there emerges a relativistic epistemology, in which an objective reality is denied and individuals claim that values and choices are relative. Unlike Perry, however, Broughton argued that relativism is superseded by what he called a new objective epistemology based on the principles of methodology. This approach is in turn replaced by a form of dialectical materialism in which the self creates rational knowledge through an active, social process, according to Broughton (1978). Broughton's model differs from Perry's in two ways: first, he suggested that there is epistemological development after relativism; second, his data suggest that the earliest stages are much more characteristic of children than they are of college students.

Differences Between Prior Models
and the Reflective Judgment Model

While the Reflective Judgment Model was built on the work of both Perry and Broughton (as well as the work of Harvey, Hunt, and Schroder, 1961, and Loevinger, 1976), it differs from them both. First, the Reflective Judgment Model focuses explicitly on the relationship between epistemology and judgment at each point in the developmental sequence. Although Perry (1968, 1981) described this relationship in detail in the early positions, the nature of judgment was less clearly articulated in the later positions, where he turned to metaphors of existential responsibility and to identity development. Presuming that even those who hold a relativistic epistemology must at some point make judgments about the problems they face, we chose to focus on the form of those judgments in the Reflective Judgment Model.

Second, like Broughton, we hypothesized that people hold epistemological positions beyond relativism; we saw examples of such stances in our interviews with graduate students and university faculty. Similarly, we agree with Broughton that the earliest epistemological perspectives are not characteristic of college students but of the views of children and early adolescents. Although some college students maintain authority-based epistemological views, the move beyond authority-based knowledge to a knowledge base that allows for multiple perspectives is more characteristic of college students, as is shown in Chapter Six.

Contemporary Models of Epistemological Development

More recently, other researchers have also described changes in epistemological assumptions as important characteristics of late adolescent and adult thinking, and they have argued that changes in epistemological assumptions mark major differences in the thinking of adolescents and college-educated adults (Baxter Magolda, 1992; Basseches, 1984a, 1984b, 1986; Kramer, 1983, 1989; Kuhn, 1990; LaBouvie-Vief, 1982; Sinnott, 1984, 1989). Most of these researchers have noted the shift from absolutism to relativism in middle to late adolescence. Kramer (1983, 1989) notes three common themes in the writing of those working in the area of the development of adult thinking. First, most of the authors observed that late adolescents seem to struggle with a new awareness that there are mutually incompatible systems of knowledge and that one's conceptual tools influence the knowledge one has about those systems. Kramer describes this realization as the emergence of an understanding of the relativistic, nonabsolute nature of knowledge.

Second, Kramer notes that most authors identified an increased awareness of contradiction as another characteristic that differentiates adolescent and adult thinking. In some ways, this observation is really a presupposition of the first, since it is based on the recognition that conflicting viewpoints exist about most issues. Once faced with contradiction, the individual must be concerned with how to organize knowledge. It is this concern that seems to propel him or her into relativism.

Finally, Kramer (1983, p. 93) suggests that recent formulations imply that after relativism, individuals integrate or synthesize contradictions into an "overriding more inclusive whole made up of two or more formally consistent systems." In other words, many authors have observed that after relativism, new rules emerge that allow for a comparison, evaluation, or synthesis of apparently contradictory alternatives into

a set of rules based on relationships *between* the elements. Similarly, Moshman and Lukin (1989) have suggested that as individuals reflect on contradictions and the limits of knowing, they
see the possibility of rational coordination of theory and data,
allowing progress toward more defensible claims about truth
and knowledge.

While these theories share the view that there is epistemological development that supersedes a relativistic stance, they
differ in their observations about the *nature* of that development.
Kramer notes that each of these theories includes the observation that adults conceptually coordinate what earlier appeared
to be contradictions of facts and values in order to allow some
judgments on matters of fact. Basseches (1984a, 1984b), Broughton (1975), and Kramer (1989), for example, all suggest that
a dialectical framework best characterizes this movement. While
they do not agree on the precise description of this epistemic
stance, they generally agree that the more advanced stance is
characterized by wholeness, by the relationships between parts,
and by the assumption that knowledge changes.

Differences Between Contemporary Models and the Reflective Judgment Model

Much of what the authors discussed in the preceding section
have observed is consistent with the Reflective Judgment Model
and provides additional support for the claim that post-relativistic
epistemological assumptions emerge after relativism. Two characteristics, however, set the Reflective Judgment Model apart
from its predecessors as well as from other contemporary models.
First, most other models (for example, Basseches, 1984a, 1984b;
Broughton, 1978; Kramer, 1989; Labouvie-Vief, 1982; Sinnott,
1989) have attempted to characterize the general form of adolescent and adult thinking according to the basic premises of Piaget's description of concrete and formal operations (Piaget and
Inhelder, 1969). Thus, the focus of their inquiry has been on
formal reasoning as a description of mature reasoning used by
adults and on whether other forms of thinking supersede formal reasoning.

Although this is a laudable undertaking, it has not been the focus of theory building or research on the Reflective Judgment Model, because we see the development of formal operations as different from reflective judgment (P.M. King, 1977, 1986). Formal operations are defined as the ability to operate both deductively and inductively on propositions (Inhelder and Piaget, 1958) and as such is a model of logical reasoning (King, 1986; Kitchener and Kitchener, 1981). The focus of the Reflective Judgment Model has been in a different intellectual domain, the development of epistemological assumptions. We have found that the ability to reason using either deductive or inductive logic does not account for differences in epistemological assumptions, even at early levels.

While some authors have focused on the role of epistemic assumptions in interpersonal relationships (Sinnott, 1984) and empathy (Benack, 1984), only recently have others (Kuhn, 1990; Sinnott, 1989) turned their attention to the role of epistemic assumptions in problem solving. What sets the Reflective Judgment Model apart from other comparable models are the observations that epistemic assumptions affect the way individuals resolve ill-structured problems and that true reflective thinking occurs only when people are engaged in thinking about problems that involve real uncertainty.

This comparison has focused on conceptual differences between the Reflective Judgment Model and other contemporary models of adult intellectual development. One other distinction is noteworthy: the Reflective Judgment Model has an extensive research base that has enabled us to test the theoretical assumptions presented here. In fact, Pascarella and Terenzini (1991, p. 123) describe this model as "perhaps the best known and most extensively studied" model of adult cognitive development. This research, from which the model itself was derived and refined, serves as the centerpiece of the remainder of this book.

Summary

In this chapter, we first considered the meaning of the term *stage* in the Reflective Judgment Model (based initially on the work of Jean Piaget and more recently on that of Kurt Fischer, who offers a more detailed description of the process of moving between levels or stages). Our purpose here was to show how these assumptions about development lay the groundwork for educational practices based on stage-related models of development. To summarize, when we refer to Reflective Judgment stages, we are referring to sets of assumptions about knowledge and justification of beliefs about ill-structured problems that tend to develop in relationship to each other. We have identified seven distinct, qualitatively different sets of assumptions. There is a strong relationship between concepts of knowledge and concepts of justification in each set, although for some people, the development of one may lag behind or precede the other. The consistency with which people reason across domains is quite remarkable, even when the domains are as different as nutrition and ancient history. These types of consistencies lead us to conclude that there is a cognitive structure within which people reason at any particular point in time. We have also found that the sets of assumptions develop sequentially, with the later stages growing out of and building on the earlier stages, which suggests a pattern in the emergence of cognitive structures. These consistencies and patterns conform to Flavell's (1971) definition of stage-related development as applied to the Reflective Judgment Model. Specific data on this issue are provided in Chapter Six.

Both Piaget and Fischer serve to remind us that learning to think reflectively involves more than learning discrete skills. Educators who use a developmental framework to teach reflective thinking need to take into consideration the assumptions their students are currently using to make sense of their experience. They also need to consider each student's developmental range, or the range of stages from the ones typically used by the student to the most advanced stage at which the student can function, understanding that how students reason at any given time (that is, which set of stage assumptions they use) depends in large part on the characteristics of the learning environment, including the cognitive and emotional supports and challenges. We examine these characteristics in detail in Chapter Nine.

In this chapter we also compared our observations about the development of epistemological assumptions with those made by others studying epistemological perspectives in adolescents and young adults. Three aspects of the Reflective Judgment Model make it unique in this domain. First, we have identified seven distinct steps of epistemological development. Second, we suggest that the development of epistemological assumptions is inherently tied to the way people justify their beliefs when they are faced with ill-structured problems. Last, and perhaps most distinctively, we provide extensive empirical support for our claims; results from this extended program of research are presented in Chapters Five through Eight.

Chapter Three

The Seven Stages
of Reflective Judgment

In this chapter we describe the seven stages, or patterns, of responding to ill-structured problems that constitute the Reflective Judgment Model, explain the internal structure of each stage, and show how each stage builds on the skills of the prior stage and lays the foundation for successive stages. While the reasoning characteristic of some stages is not reflective and may seem simply illogical or intellectually sloppy, our purpose here is not to critique each pattern but to show its internal logic — in particular, how the way a person reasons to and defends a conclusion is intrinsically related to other assumptions the person holds about the process of knowing. For example, among individuals who make the argument that there is uncertainty about a given problem simply because so many unknown variables are involved, we can anticipate the general structure of their responses to the following: how they will explain the basis for

Note: The examples used in this chapter are drawn from transcripts coded only by educational level. As a result, an attempt was made to equalize the use of male and female pronouns to reflect the overall gender balance in the samples from which the transcripts were taken. The examples have also undergone minor editing to make them more readable.

their judgment ("it's just personal preference"), why experts disagree ("because they're just biased"), and whether we can know for sure about this issue ("of course not" — because of the uncertainty). It is easier to understand the issues and problems that individuals raise when asked to justify their beliefs about ill-structured problems if one first understands the network of epistemological assumptions that affect their reasoning, as well as the relationship between the assumptions. (In acknowledging this consistency, we are not assuming that individuals are "in" only one stage at a time, a point addressed in Chapter Two.)

In addition to showing the relationships between the major concepts *within* stages, in this chapter we also articulate the relationships *between* stages. Why are the seven stages of the Reflective Judgment Model ordered in the sequence described here? This question is pertinent to any model that suggests that development occurs in a predictable order. In the case of the Reflective Judgment Model, we offer two arguments. First, the higher stages are progressively more complex, differentiated, and abstract, and the components of which they are composed become interrelated more systematically at each successive stage. Second, there is a natural logic to the progression. Much like the idea that people cannot understand the number two before they understand the number one, we argue that individuals cannot understand multiple abstract views of knowledge before they understand single, concrete views of knowledge. This chapter attempts to articulate how one stage builds on the natural logic of prior stages and how in successive stages, the underlying structure becomes more differentiated, integrated, and organized.

As we describe the stages, we also incorporate excerpts showing how various individuals we have interviewed responded to ill-structured problems, including their assumptions about what and how they knew. Our purpose here is not only to share some of what we heard people say as they struggled to resolve ill-structured problems but to help readers understand how the Reflective Judgment stages were derived from the responses of the interviewees. We hope the model will help readers understand and perhaps appreciate the perspectives of those who hold different assumptions about knowledge and the process of knowing, such as the assumptions students use to make decisions about ill-structured problems.

Development of the Reflective Judgment Model

The Reflective Judgment Model identifies a framework through which a person perceives and attempts to solve an ill-structured problem, focusing on the person's concept of knowledge and process of justification. Most individuals do not explicitly refer to these concepts as they explain their responses to problems. Rather, the stage descriptions are our abstractions of the assumptions and reasoning styles that are apparent in an individual's reasoning. We adopted what Loevinger and Wessler (1970) call a bootstrapping method to develop the model by using theoretical accounts of the nature and development of reasoning to understand and interpret the way people solve ill-structured problems, and then using these natural accounts to revise the theory.

In constructing the Reflective Judgment stage descriptions, we began by examining the scoring rules describing Perry's (1970) positions of intellectual and ethical development in college students that were developed by Knefelkamp (1974) and Widick (1975). As discussed in Chapter One, because of our interest in the relationship between epistemology and justification and our belief that there were structural and epistemic aspects that superseded relativism in Perry's (1970) model, the scoring rules addressing ethical and identity concerns were omitted and the remainder were revised. The works of Popper (1969), Lakatos (1970), Dewey (1916, 1933, 1938), Broughton (1975), and Harvey, Hunt, and Schroder (1961) were used initially to postulate epistemological assumptions that might underlie Stages 6 and 7 and further clarify the relationship between epistemology and justification. The model was then pilot tested on individuals ranging from sixteen to thirty-four years of age. Their responses were used to elaborate principles of justification for each stage and to further refine assumptions about knowledge, particularly at the upper stages. A revised set of scoring rules was then constructed (see King, 1977, or Kitchener, 1977–78). For each stage of the model, these rules included a description of the epistemological assumptions, the role of authority, the nature of decision making, the use of evidence, the extent to which knowledge is seen as true or right, and the reasons for differences in points of view. These scoring rules were used for the first study of reflective judgment (Kitchener & King, 1981). This refined model was further tested in several cross-sectional and longitudinal studies, which are described in Chapter Six. In 1985 the scoring system was again revised on the basis of extensive longitudinal data and served to further clarify the previous stage descriptions (Kitchener & King, 1985).

What has emerged from this process are descriptions of seven qualitatively different networks of concepts that affect ill-structured problem solving. In the remainder of this chapter, descriptions of the network of assumptions and their interrelationships are described for each of the seven Reflective Judgment stages. Examples are included to illustrate the ways that individuals who participated in the Reflective Judgment Interview (RJI) process expressed these concepts.

Pre-Reflective Thinking (Stages 1, 2, and 3)

As indicated in Chapter One, we have labeled the reasoning of Stages 1, 2, and 3 of the model as *pre-reflective*. Individuals reasoning with pre-reflective assumptions do not acknowledge — or in some cases even perceive — that knowledge is uncertain. As a result, they do not understand that real problems exist for which there may not be an absolutely correct answer. Further, they do not use evidence to reason toward a conclusion. Rather, even when they give reasons, the reasons often do not appear logically connected to the issue under discussion.

Stage 1

Stage 1 is characterized by a concrete, single-category belief system: "What I have seen is true." This represents a "copy" view of knowledge. Typically, it is expressed in the belief that there is an absolute correspondence between what is seen or perceived and what is. For example, "I have seen a picture of the Devil, so I know the Devil is real"; or "I have seen posters of evolution, so I know we evolved." Knowledge is seen as absolute and predetermined, and the existence of legitimate alternatives is denied. Such a view of knowledge implies that beliefs do not require justification since one must only observe to know. As a result, knowledge and belief are not distinguished; they are simply assumed to exist. Beliefs are not consciously constructed; they are simply held and are not open to criticism or doubt. Inquiry as a process is not perceived.

The internal logic of Stage 1 appears to be that since knowledge is absolute, controversies do not exist, and thus belief is not problematic. A person using Stage 1 reasoning either sees and believes or holds a belief by following tradition or social convention, without perceiving the need or value of examining the reasons for holding the belief. Both reflect what Fischer (1980) calls a *single representational skill,* the ability to use single, undifferentiated concrete categories (see Table 2.1). Since knowing is limited to concrete instances, individuals using Stage 1 assumptions cannot relate two different views of the same issue, which is a prerequisite for defining issues as problematic. At this stage, individuals understand knowledge as something concrete, not as an abstraction.

Because reasoning is so concrete, it is difficult to provide examples of reasoning about knowledge at this level since knowledge itself is an abstract concept. In the above example about the Devil, both the concept of reality and the concept of knowing are abstractions; these words are more abstract than the individual's ability to know at this level. The view of knowledge and concept of justification for Stage 1 are described next. Each is illustrated with an excerpt from an RJI transcript.

Stage 1 View of Knowledge. Knowledge is assumed to exist absolutely and concretely; it is not understood as an abstraction. It can be obtained with certainty by direct observation.

In the following example, the assumption is made that one knows by reading the newspapers. What exists in the newspapers is assumed to be true. (Again, *I* represents the interviewer in the dialogue, and *R* the respondent.)

I: On what do you base that point of view [that news reporting is an objective reporting of the facts]?

R: Mostly, I hear it and believe it because I figure if it's on the news, it's got to be true or they wouldn't put it on.

Stage 1 Concept of Justification. Beliefs need no justification since there is assumed to be an absolute correspondence between what is believed to be true and what is true. No alternatives are perceived.

In the following example, the individual denies the discrepancy between her belief that the Egyptians built the pyramids and the contradictory data presented in a film she has seen. She does not provide a justification for her beliefs; she simply holds them.

R: There's that movie *Chariot of the Gods.* In a way that conflicts with my beliefs; in another way, it never said someone else built the pyramids. I think the Egyptians built the pyramids just like we build beautiful churches.

At Stage 1, beliefs are undifferentiated: what the individual believes to be true is not differentiated from what authorities say is true. The views are totally interrelated. As illustrated by the pyramid example above, the conflict inherent in alternative views is not acknowledged. Beliefs and facts are not distinguished, and evidence is not compelling; thus, when one is faced with discrepant data, as in the above example, the discrepancies are denied. Individuals using these assumptions appear unable to separate what happened from what they want to believe happened. Consequently, they do not know how to respond when faced with ill-structured problems, such as those posed in the Reflective Judgment Interview (see Resource A and Table 5.1). In responding to the questions posed in the interview, individuals using Stage 1 assumptions typically use disjointed facts and/or opinions without acknowledging the differences between them. For example, in response to a problem that poses two alternative views about the building of the pyramids, one high school student made the following comments: "I think the Egyptians did it because I think people were pretty smart. It's just that no one had any way to write it down. . . . Like Rome fell—maybe Egypt fell too." Apparently, the concepts necessary to see and understand the discrepancy posed in the interview were not available to this individual.

The seeming inability to differentiate one's own beliefs from the evidence for those beliefs that we have observed in some younger interviewees parallels observations Kuhn (1989) has made about the development of scientific reasoning in children. She notes that her youngest subjects, who were sixth graders, vacillated between preconceived theories and evidence as a basis for their beliefs and used biased reasoning strategies that attempted to bring them into alignment with each other. For example, they would use the same evidence differently when evaluating their own beliefs and other less-favored beliefs. Kuhn concludes, as we have, that this melding of evidence and beliefs results from the inability of those in this age group to differentiate between theory and evidence.

Summary of Stage 1. The thinking characteristic of Stage 1 is the epitome of cognitive simplicity. The thinking appears naive and egocentric because of an apparent failure to differentiate categories that to others are clearly distinct, such as the failure to understand that two people can disagree about an issue. In fact, the admission of alternatives lays the groundwork for the progression to the next developmental level.

In our complex society, such simplicity of outlook has only been observed occasionally and then only in the youngest samples tested, who were high school students (Kitchener & King, 1981). Even in a sample of high school freshmen in the lower academic third of their class, no person's RJI score was a pure Stage 1 (McKinney, 1985). The foregoing examples were drawn from interviews that also showed evidence of Stage 2 reasoning; thus they may reflect initial aspects of that level. The assumptions characteristic of Stage 1 are probably only typical of young children who are unable to articulate responses to the issues posed in the RJI.

Closed frameworks such as this are challenged when a person experiences diversity of opinion, different points of view, or differences in religion or culture (a point noted by Perry, 1970). Even young children may find themselves at odds with their parents or friends over the perceptions of events and experiences. Such experiences juxtapose alternative representations of an issue, leading individuals to work out new coordination between them or, perhaps, to retreat into what Belenky, Clinchy, Goldberger, and Tarule (1986) have labeled "silence," a kind of autism in which individuals are confused and overwhelmed by the world. By contrast, those who admit that alternative views exist must also acknowledge that questions for which they have no ready answers also exist. Seeking answers elsewhere, even from authorities, forces movement beyond the single-category system of Stage 1.

Stage 2

Stage 2 is characterized by the belief that there is a true reality that can be known with certainty but is not known by everyone. Certain knowledge is seen as the domain of authorities who are presumed to know the truth, such as a scientist, teacher, or religious leader. Others who disagree with these authorities are therefore wrong. This belief system reflects what Perry (1970) called a dualistic epistemology. Although the existence of alternative views is now acknowledged, belief in absolute knowledge is still maintained. One's own view and the views of "good" authorities are seen as right, while others' views are seen as wrong, ignorant, misled, uninformed, maliciously motivated, and so on.

The admission that truth may not be directly and immediately known by oneself allows for the possibility that someone else may have the truth. This change allows for a separation of the self from what is true or known. The belief that not everyone may know the truth reflects a further differentiation of beliefs into right beliefs and wrong beliefs. The ability to classify beliefs as right or wrong represents an advancement over Stage 1: individuals who hold Stage 2 assumptions are not only able to differentiate between several concrete concepts, but they are able to relate those concepts to each other in an elementary fashion.

The ability to differentiate between beliefs also allows individuals to perceive that for some issues there are differences of opinion, which is a prerequisite for understanding that some problems are ill structured. As a result, individuals are able to accommodate views that differ from their own and also to acknowledge the possibility that not all questions have preconceived answers. These acknowledged differences in opinion are, however, explained as errors that result from being ignorant, misled, or misinformed. Since individuals working within this perspective hold the view that, ultimately, truth can be known with absolute certainty, they do not recognize that the problems posed in the RJI are ill structured. In other words, they assume that absolutely right or wrong answers exist for all problems.

If a question arises for which individuals do not have a preexisting belief they face a dilemma. Justification conceived of as the process of rationally defending one's beliefs by reference to evaluated evidence is not understood by these individuals because it is an abstract process beyond this conceptual framework. However, because they can coordinate two representations of an issue simultaneously (see Chapter Two), they must have some way to choose between them. Individuals using Stage 2 assumptions do this by jumping to another conceptual dichotomy, good and bad authorities, and seek the right answer from a "good" authority. Evidence, whether supportive or contradictory, is not seen as relevant. As Inhelder and Piaget (1958, p. 346) noted, the adolescent's mind at this point is not inclined to "subjugate its ideas to the analysis of facts." Because evidence is not used to disconfirm beliefs, individuals may hold to their own views even in light of disconfirming evidence, as was the case with Kuhn's (1989) youngest subjects. Defending one's point of view is not done to explain the reasons for beliefs but rather to show (by stating them) that one's own beliefs are right and those who believe otherwise are wrong.

What appears to underlie the Stage 2 belief system is the ability to relate two or more concrete instances, what Fischer (1980) calls a *representational mapping skill*. This skill reflects the ability to differentiate between Stage 1 categories as well as the ability to relate them to each other. The individual is thus able to differentiate right answers about an issue such as food additives from wrong answers about the issue and to attribute right answers to good authorities and wrong answers to bad (that is, wrong) authorities. In this perspective, the individual (as in Stage 1) considers knowing in relationship to concrete issues and not as an abstraction. Similarly, the individual understands truth concretely as the right answer about a particular issue rather than as an abstract concept. We turn now to the view of knowledge and concept of justification for Stage 2, illustrating each with an example.

Stage 2 View of Knowledge. Knowledge is assumed to be absolutely certain or certain but not immediately available. Knowledge is available directly through the senses (such as in direct observation) or via authority figures.

The following example illustrates belief in absolutely certain knowledge about one issue as well as the acknowledgement that there are other—albeit, wrong—beliefs about the same issue.

I: Can you ever know for sure that your position on this issue is correct?

R: Well, some people believe that we evolved from apes and that's the way they want to believe. But I would never believe that way and nobody could talk me out of the way I believe because I believe the way that it's told in the Bible.

I: In this case, then, is one view right and one point of view wrong?

R: Well I think the evolved one is wrong.

Stage 2 Concept of Justification. Beliefs are either unexamined and unjustified or justified by their correspondence with the beliefs of an authority figure, such as a teacher or parent. Most issues are assumed to have a right answer, so there is little or no conflict in making decisions about disputed issues.

Individuals who express this point of view explain that there is a "right" way to believe, thus express little or no conflict in making decisions about controversial issues, and often try to align evidence with their beliefs by distorting the evidence. When they do perceive differences in views — for example, between two scientists — they assume that the differences can be resolved simply. To continue with the example, they may argue that the scientists differ because one did an experiment incorrectly.

In the preceding example, the respondent justified his belief in a religious explanation for creation by an implicit reference to authority, referring to the way "it's told." In the following example, the respondent explicitly acknowledges the authority of teachers as the sources of her views.

I: How do you decide?

R: I decide what goes along with my views.

I: Where do your views come from?

R: My teachers and how I've been brought up. As you grow up, you automatically get certain views.

Summary of Stage 2. When individuals whose beliefs are categorized as right or wrong find that they do not know the right answer, they seek the right answer from authority figures whom they assume do know the truth. This dualistic epistemology of Stage 2 reflects an increased differentiation and coordination of simple, concrete categories that allow individuals to acknowledge that there are alternative conceptions of issues and to seek the source of their beliefs outside themselves. Although the views of Stage 2 reflect greater differentiation and integration than those of Stage 1, they often appear more dogmatic than naive because of an insistence on the existence of right and wrong answers and a deference to authority as the basis for belief.

Stage 3

Knowing in Stage 3 is characterized by the belief that in some areas even authorities may not currently have the truth. However, the belief that knowledge will be manifest in concrete data at some future point is maintained. Thus, the understanding of truth, knowledge, and evidence remains concrete and situation bound. For example, a person might argue that we may not currently know how the pyramids were built because we have not yet discovered pictures showing them being built.

In some areas (those in which authorities know the right answers), beliefs continue to be justified via the word of an authority. However, in other areas (those in which authorities still do not know the answers), there is no way to justify knowledge claims. When asked to justify their beliefs in the latter areas, individuals who hold Stage 3 assumptions rely on their personal opinion, explaining that until future developments show the truth, they decide on the basis of what "feels right" at the moment — a rather whimsical basis for judgment.

Stage 3 reflects a further differentiation and intercoordination of Stage 2 categories into simple concrete systems: those areas in which we know that right and wrong answers exist and authorities hold the right answers and those areas in which we do not yet have right answers and no one currently knows the right answers. Diverse points of view, different conceptions of the same problem, discrepant data, and so on are incorporated by the system as areas of temporary uncertainty. This reflects a move beyond the view that "the world is how authorities tell me it is" to the view that "in some areas authorities don't know the truth, and people can therefore believe what they want to believe." Differences of opinion are assumed to result from not knowing the answers with certainty.

Evidence, understood concretely as a reflection of "what really happened" or "the truth," now becomes the harbinger of knowing absolutely in the future. Because individuals maintain the belief that truth will be manifest in concrete data at a future point, they claim that the use of probabilistic evidence to substantiate belief is arbitrary and that interpretation of evidence is illegitimate. These claims reflect their concrete understanding of evidence, which they assume points directly to the truth or the right answer. Individuals using Stage 3 reasoning frequently suggest that interpretations of evidence, including those made by authorities, merely reflect the bias of those claiming to interpret the data. For example, one interviewee worried that authorities were "getting away with a lot of stuff," and since the truth was unknown, no one could catch them. He offered the following explanation: "I know there can be bias in scientific studies on both sides. Until they take it [a chemical additive] off the market, no one is going to do an accurate, reliable study. After they take it off, somebody unbiased is going to do an accurate study. Then they will know."

Such assumptions do not reflect an understanding of evidence as an abstraction, a relational concept in which an inference provides an intermediate step between the evidence and the conclusion. As a result, while people who are using a Stage 3 conceptual framework may refer to factual information that supports their opinion, when challenged, they admit that other views are equally credible. The Stage 3 view of knowledge and concept of justification are summarized and illustrated below.

Stage 3 View of Knowledge. Knowledge is assumed to be absolutely certain or temporarily uncertain. In areas of temporary uncertainty, only personal beliefs can be known until absolute knowledge is obtained. In areas of absolute certainty, knowledge is obtained from authorities.

In the following example, the respondent expresses the belief that currently our knowledge is uncertain, but at a later point, with the concrete appearance of spacemen, knowledge will be available.

I: Is one right and one wrong?

R: If spacemen come back, I guess one view is right, and if they don't, I guess the other one is right. A lot of people say time will tell. Right now it's guesswork. Later, it will be knowledge.

Stage 3 Concept of Justification. In areas in which answers exist, beliefs are justified by reference to authorities' views. In areas in which answers do not exist, beliefs are defended as personal opinion because the link between evidence and beliefs is unclear.

In the following example, the respondent evaluates evidence by its apparent agreement with what she believes rather than by any external criteria.

I: What counts as good evidence?

R: Something that agrees with me. If I really don't believe it, I really don't take it as concrete fact. If I don't think they looked at the whole picture or if I heard from a better source, then I'd tend to take the other as fact.

Summary of Stage 3. Acknowledging that knowledge is temporarily uncertain in some areas reflects an increased differentiation and integration of categories of thought. While this allows individuals to recognize that true problems for which there are currently no absolute answers do exist, these individuals often appear confused when asked to make decisions about such problems. Confusion stems from the need to make decisions without absolutely certain knowledge and without understanding that belief and evidence are separate entities that must be coordinated in the process of justifying beliefs. To the outsider, such views often appear arbitrary, unjustified, or unstable.

The breakdown of the Stage 3 epistemology, as with other stages, is inherent in its structure. In the admission that in some cases knowledge is temporarily uncertain lies the potential for recognizing that uncertainty is an inherent part of the process of knowing. In addition, the dissonance created by holding unjustified beliefs in light of being asked for justification may lead an individual to seek a clearer relationship between evidence and belief. As the person who holds Stage 3 assumptions meets increasingly diverse areas of uncertainty and diversity while concomitantly being asked for justification of beliefs, movement toward Stage 4 is encouraged.

Quasi-Reflective Thinking (Stages 4 and 5)

As discussed in Chapter One, the reasoning associated with Stages 4 and 5 was labeled *quasi-reflective*. Individuals using the assumptions associated with these stages recognize that some problems are ill structured and that knowledge claims about them contain an element of uncertainty. As a result, they understand that some issues are truly problematic. Although they use evidence, they do not understand how evidence entails a conclusion; thus, they have difficulty when they are asked to draw a reasoned conclusion or to justify their beliefs.

Stage 4

Stage 4 is characterized by the belief that one cannot know with certainty. The generalization reflects an advancement over the Stage 3 assumption that uncertainty is temporary. In fact, Dove (1990) independently analyzed responses to the RJI to see whether respondents identified the uncertainty that was intrinsic to each problem. He found that those who scored at Stages 4 and 5 identified uncertainty as an issue significantly more often than did those who scored below Stage 4.

Stage 4 also marks the emergence of knowledge understood as an abstraction, not limited to concrete instances. That is, not knowing for certain about issues such as food additives or the building of the pyramids is combined with a new understanding that knowing is also uncertain about many other issues that cut across disciplines; this realization helps form an abstract, intangible category, knowledge that is uncertain. Justification is also initially understood as an *abstraction* at Stage 4: it is understood as a process that involves giving reasons as an essential part of an argument. The two abstractions, knowledge and justification, are, however, poorly differentiated. Because justification is not yet fully related to knowing, knowing is understood as idiosyncratic to the individual. The logic that results from these assumptions appears as follows: because neither evidence nor evaluations of evidence are certain, any judgment about the evidence is idiosyncratic to the person making the judgment.

Since individuals who hold Stage 4 assumptions have an initial understanding of justification as an abstraction, they begin to understand the need to relate evidence to belief, and they start to separate beliefs and evidence for those beliefs. However, they relate the two idiosyncratically and sporadically, failing to distinguish between considering evidence for a belief, evaluating the belief in light of that evidence, and basing a belief on that evaluation. Rather, they choose evidence that fits their prior beliefs (a strategy Baron, 1988, refers to as irrational belief persistence) and presume that others do the same. As a result, they often dismiss the views of authorities as biased, assuming that experts evaluate evidence the same way they themselves do or that experts' opinions are no different from their own.

Fischer, Hand, and Russell (1984) have noted that initial abstractions are quite primitive and undifferentiated. Thus it is not uncommon for individuals to have difficulty differentiating abstract concepts such as evidence and belief. As a consequence, individuals may see that evidence contradicts their own opinion but still hold to the opinion without attempting to resolve the contradiction. Similarly, although they may acknowledge that opinions do not form a sufficient basis for developing an argument, they are not consistent in their use of evidence for this purpose. Internally, the argument appears to be that if knowledge is uncertain and there are no external criteria for evaluation, then someone can choose when and how to use evidence and when not to do so. People using Stage 4 assumptions do not reason that evidence entails a conclusion but use personal beliefs to choose the evidence used to support preconceived beliefs.

Kuhn (1989) observed similar reasoning difficulties in the students she interviewed about scientific problems. She postulates that in order to coordinate theory and evidence, individuals need to identify the two as distinct entities. Her data suggest, however, that even college students are limited in their ability to differentiate between and, therefore, to coordinate the two concepts. Kuhn argues that in order to evaluate evidence for a theory, the evidence must be encoded and represented separately from the theory. To coordinate the two, a person must

mentally "bracket" or set the theory aside in order to evaluate
the evidence for it. If initial abstract concepts remain poorly
differentiated, then individuals using Stage 4 reasoning are probably unable to separately encode the theory (or their belief about
it) and the evidence for the theory; thus they cannot perform
the necessary mental operations that would allow them to evaluate the theory on its merits. As a result, when they attempt to
construct a solution for an ill-structured problem, individuals
using Stage 4 assumptions shift their focus (Fischer, 1980) from
one piece of evidence to another. The connection between the
pieces of evidence appears to be temporal rather than conceptual. For example, evidence sometimes appears to be used in
the order in which it occurs to a person rather than used with
the intent of making a coherent argument; in such cases, the
logic of the argument appears incomplete and idiosyncratic.
Even the person making the argument from a Stage 4 perspective appears aware that his or her conclusions are tenuous and
assumes that others' conclusions are as well. Next we summarize the view of knowledge and concept of justification for Stage
4 and provide illustrations of each.

Stage 4 View of Knowledge. Knowledge is uncertain and knowledge claims are idiosyncratic to the individual since situational
variables (such as incorrect reporting of data, data lost over time,
or disparities in access to information) dictate that knowing always involves an element of ambiguity.

   In the following example, the individual says that "we'll
never know" for sure because of a situational variable ("no one
was there") and acknowledges the dilemma of trying to know
without authoritative knowledge.

R: I'd be more inclined to believe it [evolution] if they had
proof. It's just like the pyramids. I don't think we'll ever know.
People will come up with different interpretations because people differ. Who are you going to ask? Because no one was there.

   Based on their view of knowledge, individuals arguing
from a Stage 4 perspective claim to know what is right for them

but are unwilling to make judgments about others' behavior or ideas. This led to Perry's (1970) classic observation that individuals using this epistemology frequently argue that everyone has the right to her or his own opinion. Such a claim is based on the following concept of justification.

Stage 4 Concept of Justification. Beliefs are justified by giving reasons and using evidence, but the arguments and choice of evidence are idiosyncratic — for example, choosing evidence that fits an established belief.

In the following example, the individual reflects upon the idiosyncratic nature of his own judgments. He appears to have been taught steps to develop a rational argument but interprets them as a lesson in "biased writing."

R: I suppose when I've written philosophy papers, it's a matter of just trying to prove my own point without even trying to give any feasibility to counterarguments. It's pushing my point of view — then bringing up counterarguments and then doing my best to overcome that argument and show it can't stand up. That's the most biased writing I've done.

Another person noted the total subjectivity of judgment when individuals deal with the uncertainty of knowing. She stated, "Well, the thing about this is that anybody can be a judge, but even your decision is an opinion."

Summary of Stage 4. Because individuals using Stage 4 assumptions see knowing and justification as idiosyncratic, they do not acknowledge qualitative differences between the opinions of experts and their own opinions or between different experts' opinions. Each is understood as limited by the same handicaps as are others' personal opinions.

The major development that characterizes Stage 4 is the recognition that in some areas knowledge will never be certain. Even though evidence may exist about an issue, it offers no certainty; thus any conclusions must be idiosyncratic. Nevertheless, the ability to understand knowledge and justification as ab-

stractions marks an important step in the development of rationality because knowing must be understood as an abstraction before it can be understood as a process and because justification must be understood as giving reasons before knowing
and justification can be linked in the inquiry process. While considered judgment and unconsidered belief are not fully differentiated in Stage 4, acknowledging that giving reasons for beliefs
is an essential part of an argument marks an initial step toward
evaluating ideas against a public standard. Similarly, while there
may be no way to rationally adjudicate between alternative conceptions of an issue, the assumption that all points of view are
idiosyncratic allows individuals a new tolerance of alternative
perspectives and of the people holding them. At the same time,
when faced with well-reasoned arguments that are different from
their own, these individuals are also faced with the inherent contradictions in their own thinking: everyone has the right to his
or her own opinion, but others' views must be somehow inadequate (even wrong) since they are arguing against them. Ultimately, these individuals are forced to seek new ways to justify
their knowing and to begin to take on the characteristics of Stage
5 thinking that will help them resolve these contradictions.

Stage 5

Stage 5 is distinguished by the belief that while people may not
know directly or with certainty, they may know within a context based on subjective interpretations of evidence, a belief they
sometimes call relativism. Since knowledge is filtered through
the perceptions of the person making the interpretation, what
is known is always limited by the perspective of the knower.

Underlying the concept of knowing in Stage 5 is the ability to relate two abstractions — for example, how scientists study
chemical additives to how beliefs are justified about the safety
of those additives, or how historians study evidence about the
building of the pyramids to how beliefs are justified about such
questions. Fischer (1980) refers to the ability to relate two abstractions as *abstract mapping skills*. As Fischer, Hand, and Russell (1984) note, with the ability to relate two abstractions comes

the ability to compare and contrast them. Through the contrasts, abstractions are further differentiated from each other; through the comparisons, the abstractions are integrated in new ways. In particular, with Stage 5 skills, individuals can differentiate and integrate the elements surrounding an event with the interpretation of that event. They can better differentiate and integrate knowing and justification, unconsidered claims and considered evaluation, the opinions of authorities and the opinions of self, and so forth. These skills allow for a broader, more interconnected view of problems that is not limited by the idiosyncratic justifications of Stage 4. This more complex view is based on a fuller understanding of justification in relationship to interpretations within a particular perspective.

Stage 5 knowing remains context bound since the individual has not as yet developed the ability to relate several abstractions into a system that allows comparisons across different contexts: for example, comparing knowing and justification about issues in science to knowing and justification about issues in the social sciences. When the individual is faced with ill-structured problems, this limitation leaves him or her unable to weigh evidence for competing views beyond the perspective each allows or to otherwise integrate perspectives and draw conclusions beyond limited relationships.

The major accomplishment of this stage is that the ability to relate two abstractions allows individuals to relate evidence and arguments to knowing. Those who use Stage 5 assumptions are able to relate and compare evidence and arguments in several contexts even though they appear unable to coordinate evidence and arguments across contexts into a simple system. As in Stage 4, they resolve ill-structured problems by shifting focus. At Stage 5, however, the shift is from examining how knowledge is justified within one context to how it is justified within another context. As a result, individuals frequently appear to be giving a balanced picture of an issue or problem rather than offering a justification for their own beliefs.

Kuhn (1989) has suggested that two skills are necessary to coordinate theory and evidence, the recognition that there are alternative theories and the recognition that some evidence does not support a particular theory. Both are present in Stage 5 reasoning. What is missing is the ability to coordinate the two in a well-reasoned argument. What follows are summaries of the view of knowledge and the concept of justification for Stage 5. Examples of each are used as illustrations.

Stage 5 View of Knowledge. Knowledge is contextual and subjective because it is filtered through a person's perceptions and criteria for judgment. Only interpretations of evidence, events, or issues may be known.

In the following example, the respondent notes that she can never know for sure that one point of view or another about creation is correct. Rather, she notes the context within which each must be understood.

R: I don't feel I really know that God created me from nothing, and I really don't know the evolution view. There is a realm of the unknown about either side of this.

I: If you wanted to come to a decision, how would you go about it?

R: I would work to find more data tracing what we do know about evolution and how people actually did evolve. I would see if I could find a scientific inquiry that would lead to a clear pattern of evolution. If I did back it up, I still wouldn't know because I wouldn't know if a driving force, a God, created the original man or the end of the trace. I'd have a really hard time knowing the actuality of one or another. On the other hand, I'd have a really hard time knowing that man was created out of nothing by a divine being. To know that, I could have faith.

Because individuals using Stage 5 reasoning claim that all knowing is contextual, they frequently suggest that terms such as *right* and *wrong* are inappropriate for evaluating views. For example, one person noted, "I wouldn't say that one person is wrong and another person is right. Each person, I think, has their own truth." Different views are seen as potentially legitimate interpretations of issues.

Stage 5 Concept of Justification. Beliefs are justified within a particular context by the rules of inquiry for that context and by context-specific interpretations of evidence. Specific beliefs are assumed to be context specific or are balanced against other interpretations, which complicates and sometimes delays conclusions.

In the previous example, the respondent acknowledges that different rules of justification (faith and scientific evidence) exist for each point of view, yet she never really resolves the issue (either in the excerpt provided or in the remainder of the discussion of the topic). In the following example, the interviewee states that he cannot offer an integrated point of view but decides somewhat mechanically on rules that seem appropriate for the historical problem in question, the building of the Egyptian pyramids.

R: On that particular problem I need to be more acquainted with what goes into building pyramids to take a point of view. So I'd tend to go with the first point of view, that the Egyptians built the pyramids, because it is the simplest explanation at this point; you'd have to come up with some far-out explanation of who built the pyramids if the Egyptians didn't. When you are uncertain about both, take the simplest explanation. . . . I'd say the historical point of view also gave a purpose. It tries to give an explanation of how the Egyptians built the pyramids, so I feel since the first theory tries to make an explanation, I'd be more inclined to accept the first one.

Summary of Stage 5. The acceptance of knowledge as contextual, which results in legitimately different conclusions, leads the individual using Stage 5 assumptions to identify ways of knowing that allow for interpretations. These ways of knowing are rules of evidence that, when understood, provide the individual with ways to begin to make judgments without risking a return to the dogmatism of earlier stages. Complexity is manifest in the greater differentiation of contexts, in the awareness that different perspectives rely on different types of evidence, and in the ability to use evidence to reason logically within a particular context. What is missing is the ability to compare and contrast evidence across contexts.

Paradoxically, while individuals are immersed in balancing one point of view against another, they are learning the initial rules of synthesis that will move their reasoning beyond this stage. In the act of trying on one frame of reference after another lies the formation of new and larger categories, for example, how these frames of reference are themselves similar and different.

Reflective Thinking (Stages 6 and 7)

We use the label *reflective* to describe the reasoning characteristic of Stages 6 and 7 of the Reflective Judgment Model. People who reason with the assumptions of these stages argue that knowledge is not a "given" but must be actively constructed and that claims of knowledge must be understood in relation to the context in which they were generated. Furthermore, those reasoning with Stage 6 or 7 assumptions argue that while judgments must be grounded in relevant data, conclusions should remain open to reevaluation. As we noted in Chapter One, we believe that this kind of reasoning has the characteristics of thinking Dewey (1933) called reflective thinking or reflective judgment.

Stage 6

Stage 6 is characterized by the belief that knowing is a process that requires action on the part of the knower; the spectator view of the knower that characterizes earlier thinking will no longer suffice. There is an initial recognition that ill-structured problems require solutions that must be constructed and that even experts are involved in a similar process. While the Stage 5 skill of balancing one view against another helps an individual understand issues more fully, this by itself does not lead to a resolution of a problem. The discordance between the task of arriving at a decision about ill-structured problems and the epistemology of Stage 5 leads the individual to approach the task differently, either by abstracting the common elements from different perspectives into a new perspective or by looking for ways to integrate the elements into a more inclusive framework. The major development of Stage 6 is the recognition that problems that are complexly understood (for example, understanding that a problem can be approached from multiple perspectives, incorporating multiple kinds of evidence) require some kind of thinking action before a resolution can be constructed.

Individuals using Stage 6 reasoning maintain that knowledge is uncertain and must be understood in relationship to context and evidence. However, they also argue that some judgments or beliefs may nevertheless be evaluated by using criteria such as the plausibility of an argument and the utility of a solution. This claim is based on principles of evaluation that allow them to draw conclusions across perspectives because by using Stage 6 skills they can compare and relate the properties of two different views of the same issue. For example, knowing and justification about the advantages and disadvantages of chemical additives can be compared and contrasted with knowing and justification about the advantages and disadvantages of nuclear energy, combining them into system that allows for common elements (such as health risks and environmental concerns) to be identified. The identification of common elements allows judgment to be drawn. In other words, knowing and justification can be coordinated, thus allowing cross-domain comparisons and conclusions to be drawn.

Integrating abstract mappings into a system is an improvement over Stage 5 abilities and reflects what Fischer (1980) calls *abstract system skills*. Individuals are able to coordinate the subtle similarities and differences of abstract relationships into intangible systems (Fischer & Kenny, 1986). They can compare the evidence for and against the safety of food additives, for example, frequently differentiating between factors such as the type of chemical, the purpose for which it is being used, and general circumstances of food distribution and shelf-life and also construct qualified conclusions about the merits of a particular point of view about the additives. Thus, while individuals using Stage 6 assumptions will usually reject the terms *right* and *wrong* when evaluating arguments, they will suggest that one view is better, explaining that the other view has less evidence, that it is less appropriate or less compelling for the particular situation at hand, and so on. The ability to draw conclusions across perspectives reflects the beginning of internalized categories of comparison and evaluation. Using Stage 6 reasoning, individuals may rely on the evaluated opinions of authorities, now understood and valued as experts who have investigated the issue more thoroughly or who have special competencies. Reliance on the opinions of experts does not reflect a return to earlier authority-bound beliefs but rather the ability to differentiate between the judgments made by experts and those made by laypeople. On occasion, people using Stage 6 reasoning will explicitly note that they evaluate the expertise, opinions, and conclusions of experts. One graduate student, for example, suggested that she based her opinion about chemical additives on the "credibility of the people I hear reports from."

Stage 6 View of Knowledge. Knowledge is constructed into individual conclusions about ill-structured problems on the basis of information from a variety of sources. Interpretations that are based on evaluations of evidence across contexts and on the evaluated opinions of reputable others can be known.

In the following excerpt, the respondent notes the limits of knowing, which suggests that she has evaluated the credibility of sources, and cautiously offers a personal evaluation of the evidence and argument.

R: I think if the FDA is convinced that the risk is high enough [to ban the use of a particular chemical additive], then in my mind that tends to increase the likelihood that it might cause cancer. If cyclamates cause cancer in rats or something, obviously they could cause cancer in humans, but there's no way I can verify these things firsthand. All I know is what I read in the paper, what I hear at [school]. To the extent that people who are saying these things have some credibility, it increases the likelihood in my mind that these are some of the things that may cause cancer.

I: Do you think you'll ever be able to say which is the better position?

R: Well, the one that says they do cause cancer would be the most valid one from my point of view.

Stage 6 Concept of Justification. Beliefs are justified by comparing evidence and opinion from different perspectives on an issue or across different contexts and by constructing solutions that are evaluated by criteria such as the weight of the evidence, the utility of the solution, and the pragmatic need for action.

In the following example, the respondent both states and illustrates the advantage and limits of Stage 6 thinking. He claims that one view is more compelling, but only for himself as an individual. Unlike in Stage 4, he makes a decision based on the compelling nature of the evidence rather than for his own idiosyncratic reasons. The example illustrates the problem of making knowledge claims while simultaneously understanding and appreciating the origins of different points of view.

I: Could you say that a person [who holds a different point of view] is wrong?

R: No. You cannot say, "you are stupid or wrong" to someone. But I think if you push them far enough, they, too, would have to admit their argument is based on assumptions that are empirically falsifiable. It's a problem that all social science statements carry with them. There are no absolutes.

I: Can you say one is better and one is worse?

R: I would say it's more compelling for me. I'd never say it's more compelling universally because everybody has a subjective bias. It has to be from an individual perspective.

Summary of Stage Six. The inadequacy of purely contextual and subjective knowing becomes apparent in Stage 6. Ill-structured problems that press the individual to look for shared meaning across contexts do exist. Further, those who reason from this perspective assert — and demonstrate — that solutions to such problems must be constructed rather than simply found. Making comparisons and observing relationships across domains provide an initial basis for rationally formulating conclusions. However, because individuals using Stage 6 reasoning fail to understand the larger system of knowing in which such comparisons and conclusions are embedded, conclusions remain limited and situational.

In the process of evaluating and endorsing the views of experts or constructing tentative, personal conclusions, individuals appear to develop what Harvey, Hunt, and Schroder (1961, p. 91) call "abstract internal referents" of validity and probability. These are used to develop a more general system of knowing that provides the basis for Stage 7 thinking.

Stage 7

Stage 7 is characterized by the belief that while reality is never a given, interpretations of evidence and opinion can be synthesized into epistemically justifiable conjectures about the nature of the problem under consideration. Knowledge is constructed by using skills of critical inquiry or by synthesizing evidence and opinion into cohesive and coherent explanations for beliefs about problems. It is possible, therefore, through critical inquiry or synthesis, to determine that some judgments, whether they are the judgments of experts or one's own, have greater truth value than others or to suggest that a given judgment is a reasonable solution for a problem.

People engaged in the thinking that is characteristic of Stage 7 take on the role of inquirers; they are agents involved in constructing knowledge. They see that the process is an ongoing one in the sense that time, experience, and new data require new constructions and understandings. They are aware that their current knowledge claims may later be superseded by more adequate explanations. At the same time, they are able to claim that the conclusions they are currently drawing are justifiable, believing that other reasonable people who consider the evidence would understand the basis for their conclusions. They often argue that the process of inquiry leads toward better or more complete conjectures about the best solutions for ill-structured problems or the issues under discussion.

The Stage 7 ability to integrate several Stage 6 systems

(knowing and justification about scientific issues, social science issues, and other issues) into a general framework about knowing and justification allows for a generalization of assumptions and a clarity of judgment that were not apparent at Stage 6. Abstract internal referents used to judge individual problems are reintegrated into a general principle: knowledge is constructed through critical inquiry. These referents are illustrated by such phrases as "that which best fits the evidence as I know it" and "that which is discrepant from generally observed processes." The ability to understand the underlying principle is based on what Fischer (1980) calls *systems of abstract system skills:* the mastery of these skills assumes the ability to abstract generalizations about inquiry from frequent participation in the inquiry process.

Thinking in Stage 7 appears to be an improvement over thinking in Stage 6 in its display of intelligent, reflective choice. Judgment demonstrates individuality constrained by reason and a willingness to critique one's own reasoning. Such reasonable judgment is possible because the individual clearly understands the process of knowing as an abstract one and endorses his or her own role in constructing what is known or believed to be true. Contrary to Perry's (1970) most advanced positions, characterized as "commitment in relativism," the idea of being committed to a point of view does not fit here, given the assumption that all conclusions are open to reevaluation based on new information or new interpretations.

Stage 7 View of Knowledge. Knowledge is the outcome of a process of reasonable inquiry in which solutions to ill-structured problems are constructed. The adequacy of those solutions is evaluated in terms of what is most reasonable or probable on the basis of the current evidence and is reevaluated when relevant new evidence, perspectives, or tools of inquiry become available.

While the respondent in the following excerpt acknowledges the problematic nature of knowing, she also suggests that a reasonable conclusion can be drawn on the basis of the available facts.

I: Can you ever say you know for sure about this issue?

R: It [the view that the Egyptians built the pyramids] is very far along the continuum of what is probable.

I: Can you say that one point of view is right and one is wrong?

R: Right and wrong are not comfortable categories to assign to this kind of item. It's more or less likely or reasonable, more or less in keeping with what the facts seem to be.

Stage 7 Concept of Justification. Beliefs are justified probabilistically on the basis of a variety of interpretive considerations, such as the weight of the evidence, the explanatory value of the interpretations, the risk of erroneous conclusions, the consequences of alternative judgments, and the interrelationships of these factors. Conclusions are defended as representing the most complete, plausible, or compelling understanding of an issue on the basis of the available evidence.

In the preceding example, the individual justifies her beliefs on the basis of the most probable interpretation of the evidence. In the following example, the respondent offers a complex reinterpretation of the issue of creation versus evolution that reflects a higher-order synthesis of the issue.

R: These two statements are said to be two different understandings of how things are as they are. There are different ways of understanding each of these. In some ways [one can] see them as opposites; in some ways one can see them as buttressing one another. I tend to favor the one that sees these as complementary statements.

I: How's that?

R: Well, in the first place, many religions of the world have creation stories. For example, one proposes that a divine being created the earth and its people. Some scientifically minded people would like to see that as a metaphor, in other words, that it's not to be taken literally. From my own understanding, it seems in some cases almost as accurate to see the scientific understanding as a metaphor for the myth, which actually has the correct understanding in the sense that the myths are based on experience. That for me is the key for understanding this, the fact that we are here, the fact that we grow, indicates some direction and some possibility, even some purpose, if it can be taken a little bit further. And science, science tends to understand it as humans on top of the scale and something else on down to nothing. Well, in terms of the creation myth, this scientific understanding in a way could be a metaphor because it notes the patterns; its concern is to understand how these patterns develop from one to another into a more highly developed stage in the same way that myth explains the nature of creation and dissolution. It has to do with understanding of cycles, of being part of a cycle, a much larger cycle that man is a very small part of.

Summary of Stage 7. The thinking characteristic of Stage 7 reflects the elements Dewey described as the basis of practical and theoretical judgments. Individuals with fully differentiated abstract categories see the problematic nature of controversies. The dissonance involved in understanding that a true problem exists conversely pushes them to become active inquirers involved in the critique of conclusions that have been reached earlier, as well to become the generators of new hypotheses. Since the methods of criticism and evaluation are applied to the self as well as others, individuals see that the solutions they offer are only hypothetical conjectures about what is, and their own solutions are themselves open to criticism and reevaluation. As Baron (1988, p. 286) notes, the highest stages of reflective judgment encourage "actively open-minded thinking [where] beliefs can always be improved; this encourages openness to alternatives and to counterevidence." Similarly, it is only at Stage 7 that individuals model what Bernstein (1971, p. 222) has suggested is Dewey's concept of intelligent action: "Intelligence consists of a complex set of flexible and growing habits that involve sensitivity, the ability to discern the complexities of a situation, imagination that is exercised in new possibilities and hypotheses, willingness to learn from experience,

fairness and objectivity in judging conflicting values and opinions and the courage to change one's views when it is demanded
by the consequences of our actions and criticisms of others."

Summary

In this chapter we have presented a description of the Reflective Judgment Model of intellectual development, offering a
detailed explanation of each of the seven qualitatively different
approaches we have observed people use when reasoning about
and resolving ill-structured problems. We have explained how
each approach reflects a network of interrelated epistemological assumptions, showing how people who reason according to
the assumptions of each stage have a distinct approach to the
way they develop and defend their beliefs about ill-structured
problems. We have also attempted to explicate the structural
relationships between the stages, showing how each stage both
builds on the foundation of skills associated with the previous
stage and how it also lays the groundwork for the cognitive advances of the subsequent stage. We do not claim that people
use only seven sets of epistemic assumptions to guide the ways
that they defend their beliefs. Rather, we present the seven stages
of the Reflective Judgment Model as the seven approaches to
understanding and resolving ill-structured problems that we have
systematically observed to date. The data base that has informed
these observations is summarized in later chapters.

Throughout the process of developing this model, we re-
lied extensively on individuals' responses to the Reflective Judgment Interview, the instrument we designed to measure reflective
judgment. We turn next to the topic of assessment. In Chapter
Four we argue that assessing reasoning about ill-structured problems has been neglected in research on critical thinking. In Chapter Five, we also provide a detailed description of the interview,
which so richly contributed to our conceptualization of the stage
descriptions presented here.

Chapter Four

Assessing Reasoning Skills

How can a person's reasoning skills be assessed? For example, how can a prospective employer assess an applicant's ability to integrate complex sets of information into meaningful interpretations and identify the implications? In responding to a student's concern about a course, how can an adviser ferret out the assumptions that may be guiding the comment? How can professors who aspire to teach the higher-order thinking skills associated with reflective thinking document their success in doing so? In hiring a resident adviser, how can a hall director evaluate a student's ability to analyze adequately the complex and ambiguous problems that typically arise in the residence hall? How can institutions show prospective parents or legislators that they teach students to think critically? Questions such as these drive the collective need to consider the assessment of reflective thinking.

There are many approaches to assessing "good thinking," whether defined as reasoning skills, logical reasoning, formal reasoning, reflective judgment, problem solving, or critical thinking. These approaches typically represent the specific concepts, elements, or strategies that are central to the particular model of good thinking that a given instrument purports to measure.

The attributes of good thinking measured by these instruments vary widely, from the ability to reason deductively to proficiency in identifying underlying assumptions in an argument. Since the definition of good thinking usually determines (or at least strongly influences) which attributes are measured, it is important for a prospective user of any test of critical thinking to consider carefully whether the definition underlying the measure is consistent with the user's evaluative or educational needs.

In addition to definitional differences, existing measures of critical or reflective thinking also differ in the extent to which they focus on well- or ill-structured problems. (Problems that can be defined completely and solved with certainty are referred to as well structured. See Chapter One for a discussion of these terms.) Some problems focus on strictly logical, deductive reasoning. (We do not mean to imply that all logic problems are well structured. This definition applies to logic problems based on propositional calculus, which is decidable and complete, but not—as Church and Gödel have shown [Rundle, 1972]—to those based on the predicate calculus, which is undecidable and incomplete.) Such problems provide a description of a situation that includes all relevant information necessary for correctly answering the question posed, such as the following: All military men tell the truth. John, a military man, says he was engaged by the president to sell guns to terrorists. The president has been accused of conspiring to sell guns to terrorist nations. On the basis of the statements given above, decide whether the president committed this act.

When the basic elements of the problem are provided (even if finding them requires careful reading) and the problem can be solved with certainty, the problem qualifies as a well-structured one. In well-structured problems, logical reasoning skills such as assumption identification, induction, and deduction are emphasized.

A second kind of well-structured problem involves sorting through and correctly applying complex algorithms. For example: A ship leaves port at noon, sailing north at thirty knots. A second ship leaves port an hour later, sailing east at twenty-five knots. At 3 P.M., how fast is the distance between them changing?

Other kinds of well-structured problems may involve such reading and analysis skills as identifying generalizations that follow from stated evidence and detecting fallacious arguments. It is important to note that well-structured problems may range from very simple to very complex and that they can require the application of skills and knowledge from a variety of disciplines. The unifying principle underlying a well-structured problem is that, given the parameters of the problem, a single answer can be determined to be correct. When the educational goal is to teach this type of reasoning, then a critical thinking test that relies heavily or exclusively on well-structured problems would be appropriate and useful.

However, many major national reports have argued for instructional goals that require a very different type of reasoning. For example, the National Commission on Excellence in Education (1983, p. 7) notes that "For our country to function, citizens must be able to reach some common understandings on complex issues, often on short notice and *on the basis of conflicting or incomplete evidence*" [italics added]. More recently, the Association of American Colleges (1991, p. 14) has called for students to be able "to state why a question or argument is significant and for whom; what the difference is between developing and justifying a position and merely asserting one; and how to develop and provide warrants for their own interpretations and judgments." The skills of deduction and induction are not sufficient for the types of analysis and synthesis called for in these reports, and assessments of this type of reasoning cannot rely on questions that assume a single correct answer. By contrast, assessment of this type of reasoning requires measures that include ill-structured problems in which, by definition, the evidence is conflicting or incomplete.

In this chapter, we first propose a list of desirable features of a measure of reflective thinking that may be used to guide the consumer's evaluation of existing measures or the researcher's development of new measures of reflective thinking. We then examine a range of available measures of critical thinking (broadly defined) and evaluate the extent to which they provide information about the kind of reasoning described in the national reports cited above, that is, how people reason about ill-structured problems. The Reflective Judgment Interview, which was expressly designed to measure reasoning about ill-structured problems, is discussed separately in Chapter Five.

Desirable Features of a Measure of Reflective Thinking

How should reflective thinking be measured? What kind of information do educators, institutional researchers, administrators, personnel officers, and others interested in conducting formal assessments of reflective thinking need? Do existing instruments adequately measure reflective thinking? One way to answer the first of these questions is to attempt to generate a list of desirable features of an instrument designed to measure reflective thinking.

For better or worse, the practical realities of conducting assessments and research are often given more consideration than the conceptual soundness and demonstrated reliability of potential instruments. As a result, the first feature many look for is that the instrument be inexpensive, amenable to large-scale administration, and easy to score. While these are indeed attractive characteristics, they should not be used as the most important criteria in selecting or evaluating a measure of reflective thinking. The risk of using "quick and dirty" instruments is that they may quickly yield superficial, irrelevant, unreliable, or uninterpretable data. If the assessment of reflective thinking is really important, then it must be measured carefully. While doing so may take longer and cost more, the resulting data are more likely to be appropriate for answering the kinds of important questions listed at the beginning of this chapter.

Several criteria for evaluating a measure of reflective thinking, as defined in Chapter One, are suggested below. (The need for an instrument with adequate reliability and validity will be assumed rather than discussed here.) The following section describes other desirable features to consider when evaluating or constructing a measure of reflective thinking.

1. *Ill-structured problems should be the focus of the assessment task.*
   Dewey (1933) made the astute observation that only when

people are faced with real problems do they engage in true reflective thinking. These problems involve doubt about the adequacy of one's current understanding of the issue. Using this definition, well-structured problems will not tap a person's ability to think reflectively and thus are not appropriate. Consequently, one critical component in a measure of reflective thinking is the degree of problem structure in the questions it poses.

2. *The assessment should elicit information about the rationale for a response as well as its content.* This criterion is based on the understanding that different people can arrive at the same answer (that the Egyptians built the pyramids) for a variety of reasons. The reasons offered may indicate the sophistication of the respondent's thinking. For example, some of these reasons may relate directly to the evidence (the presence of ancient Egyptian artifacts in the pyramids) or to the source of information (a popular magazine, friend, or parent). In other words, a measure of the quality of reflective thinking will need to attend to the nature of the justification for the judgment as well as to the judgment itself. As a result, the response format will need to allow the respondents to choose from a variety of justifiable answers (a point also made by McPeck, 1981) or to generate their own answers.

Ennis and Norris (1990) discuss the effects of various test formats in terms of the need to understand individuals' justifications for their decision. For example, they note that machine-scorable tests "ask for judgments but do not also seek the reasoning behind the judgments" (p. 25). Essay tests, by contrast, "can easily ask a student to justify the judgments that the student makes. Informal interviews, though very expensive, are even better, because they enable the tester to seek more justification whenever anything seems unclear. Essay tests only invite justification, but do not provide for further interaction when the student's justification itself is in need of clarification or justification. Interviewing may be the best approach if high quality information is needed on a small number of individuals" (p. 27).

3. *Thinking should be sampled across a variety of issues.* This allows for the evaluation of the consistencies and inconsistencies in the participants' thinking across content areas. Sampling across issues also helps minimize the effects of prior familiarity with one topic, discipline, or area of study.

4. *The content should be generally familiar to a wide range of individuals.* This allows for testing across diverse samples of people who have diverse educational experiences. It also allows participants to respond to issues about which they have some working knowledge rather than issues with which they are unfamiliar. This may have the added benefit of increasing their comfort with the task. (This suggestion does not apply to measures that are specifically developed for administration to those who are expected to have expertise in a given area.)

5. *The content should not constrain the instrument's use to individuals in formal educational settings* (such as college students). To tie the content or scoring of a measure to issues or problems that are unique to the college setting or to specific collegiate events would disallow or confound analyses aimed at determining the effects of college attendance or other life experiences on reflective thinking.

6. *The reading level should be such that it can be used with a wide range of potential test takers.* When a test of reflective thinking also requires high-level reading skills, a low score could indicate poor reading skills, poor thinking skills, or both. Taking reading level into account also allows for the examination of the effects of educational experiences that may stimulate reflective thinking but that do not require complex reading skills (such as movies, lectures, or conversations). It also allows for the evaluation of the development of reflective thinking between groups that may differ in reading level, such as high school and college students or those with and without experience in postsecondary education.

7. *If the measure is based on a model that purports to describe the development of reflective thinking, the theoretical model on which it is based should be validated.* While many models of adult cognition have been proposed during the last decade, few have

been extensively researched and validated (Brabeck, 1984; Commons and others, 1990). The process of validation of developmental claims involves many steps and must include longitudinal data. Models in which validation is lacking or is in the very early stages should be considered preliminary conjectures about development.

This list of desirable features of a measure of reflective thinking is designed to assist researchers, program evaluators, and administrators who must identify or recommend instruments designed to measure reflective thinking. Considering these features may help ensure that selected measures will yield high-quality information about students' *reflective thinking,* not just about other important types of thinking, such as deductive reasoning.

Do Tests of Critical Thinking Measure Reflective Thinking?

To what degree are the skills associated with reflective thinking assessed by existing measures of critical thinking? In addressing this question, we will examine whether these measures include ill-structured problems and if so, how these skills are defined and measured. Two major features of each measure will be considered in this analysis. The first of these is the *definition of thinking* in which the assessment is grounded: does the definition reflect well-structured problems, ill-structured problems, or both? The import of this step is emphasized by Ennis and Norris (1990, p. 11): "It is important to base critical thinking testing and evaluation on an appropriate conception of critical thinking. We cannot just pick any conception, since there is so much resting on the result." Second, we will consider *the nature of the task demands* presented to respondents as an indication of the underlying problem structure of the measure. That is, we will evaluate what respondents are asked to do and how much information they are given. For example, if all necessary information is provided and the respondent's task is to identify the correct answer, then we would conclude that this measure reflects a well-structured orientation.

The organization and choice of measures of reasoning that are included in this analysis follow the general framework used by Pascarella and Terenzini (1991) in their comprehensive review of the effects of college. Their review of students' cognitive skills and intellectual growth includes major sections on Piagetian formal operational reasoning, critical thinking, and postformal reasoning. These three approaches, as well as the measures that are associated with each approach, are discussed in order below.

Assessing Formal Operational Reasoning

Learning to reason abstractly and deductively is a hallmark of Piagetian formal operations. Measures of formal reasoning typically focus on scientific reasoning and involve such elements as hypothetico-deductive reasoning (reasoning from the possible to the actual by disconfirming predetermined hypotheses), propositional thinking (exploring logical relationships between propositions), combinational analysis (identifying relevant variables, both alone and in combination with others), isolation and control of variables, and probability (Flavell, 1963). Many examples of problems that can be solved using formal operational skills are presented and discussed by Inhelder and Piaget (1958). One of their popular tests of the isolation of variables involves examining the oscillation of a pendulum. The respondent's task is to identify which of several variables (length of the string, weight of objects attached to the string, height of the dropping point, and force of the push) accounts for the speed with which the pendulum oscillates. This requires the individual to vary each factor while holding the other three constant, thus isolating the causal variable (the length of the string) and excluding the others. Other tests focus on other aspects of formal reasoning.

In these tests, all necessary information can be obtained by manipulating the objects provided in the experiments, the results are falsifiable and replicable, and they ultimately lead to a single correct answer. Therefore, they measure reasoning about well-structured problems. (For a review of college students' success in solving such problems on formal operations tasks, see P. M. King, 1986.)

Assessing Critical Thinking

The term *critical thinking* has been used extensively to refer to a wide variety of thinking skills (see McMillan, 1987; McPeck, 1981; Paul, 1990). According to Pascarella and Terenzini (1991, p. 118), "critical thinking appears to stress the individual's ability to interpret, evaluate, and make informed judgments about the adequacy of arguments, data, and conclusions." The two measures of critical thinking that have been used most extensively will be reviewed here. These are the Watson-Glaser Critical Thinking Appraisal (CTA) (Watson and Glaser, 1964), and the Cornell Critical Thinking Test (CCTT), developed by Ennis and Millman (1971). The technical and conceptual merits and limitations of the CTA and the CCTT have been extensively reviewed elsewhere (Berger, 1985; Ennis and Norris, 1990; Helmstadter, 1985; King, Wood, and Mines, 1990; McPeck, 198; Modjeski and Michael, 1983). The following discussion focuses only on the question of problem structure within the CTA and the CCTT.

The Watson-Glaser Critical Thinking Appraisal. McPeck (1981) cites Watson and Glaser's CTA as the single most widely used standardized test of critical thinking. In fact, when McMillan (1987) reviewed twenty-seven programs designed to improve the critical thinking of college students several years later, he noted that only four of these studies did *not* use the CTA.

Watson and Glaser (1964) view critical thinking as a composite of three elements: "(1) attitudes of inquiry that involve an ability to recognize the existence of problems and an acceptance of the general need for evidence in support of what is asserted to be true; (2) knowledge of the nature of valid inferences, abstractions, and generalizations in which the weight or accuracy of different kinds of evidence are logically determined; and (3) skills in employing and applying the above attitudes and knowledge" (p. 10). This definition by itself does not indicate which problem structure is appropriate for a measure of critical thinking because the three elements could apply to reasoning about problems of either type.

Researchers who have examined the problem structure of the CTA have offered varying evaluations. For example, Brabeck and Wood (1990) point to the procedure used in developing the test as informative on this point: a jury of experts "agreed unanimously that the key answers . . . are logically correct" (Watson and Glaser, 1952, p. 8). Brabeck and Wood note that the claim of logical correctness is consistent with the definition of well-structured problems. They argue further that, "The problems posed by the WGCTA [CTA] may be considered well structured in that the decision maker (i.e., test taker) is presented with the basic elements of the problem situation, and a single verifiable and correct answer may then be arrived at through logical inference and probabilistic prediction" (p. 136). Using an approach that focused on the CTA subtests (for example, deduction and interpretation), King, Wood, and Mines (1990, p. 169) concluded that the CTA "reflects a combination of well- and ill-structured problems."

In the current analysis, the specific reasoning tasks given to respondents were used to indicate the problem structure of the test. Table 4.1 summarizes the reasoning tasks (what respondents are asked to do) for each subtest of the CTA, along with the corresponding response options (the alternative responses from which the respondents may select an answer). The description of the tasks is taken directly from the instructions for each section of the CTA, Form Zm.

The Inference subtest is perhaps unique in tests of critical thinking because its response options place true and false on a continuum, using "definitely true" and "definitely false" as the scale anchors, with "probably true," "insufficient data," and "probably false" falling between these extremes. The crux of this subtest is the *certainty* with which one judges that a conclusion properly follows from the given information. As Helmstadter (1985, pp. 1347–1348) notes: "Unfortunately, in many items of this subtest the judgment component would seem to depend more on a personality response set related to how much evidence is required before one is convinced of an argument than on an ability to ascertain whether an inference is a valid one." The "personality response set" to which Helmstadter refers assumes

Table 4.1. Task Demands of the
Watson-Glaser Critical Thinking Appraisal.

Subtest	Reasoning task[a]	Response options
Inference	Judge the *degree* of truth or falsity about a conclusion based on stated facts.	*Inference* is definitely true, probably true, insufficient data, probably false, or definitely false
Recognition of Assumptions	Decide whether an assumption is made in a given statement.	*Assumption* is made or not made
Deduction	Judge whether a conclusion necessarily follows from a statement.	*Conclusion* follows or does not follow
Interpretation	Judge whether a conclusion logically follows beyond a reasonable doubt from given information.	*Conclusion* follows or does not follow
Evaluation of Arguments	Judge whether an argument is strong (both important and directly related to the question) or weak.	*Argument* is strong or weak

[a]Based on the instructions for each subtest.
Source: Adapted from Watson and Glaser, 1964.

that evidence is required to convince one of an argument, an assumption that we have shown to be as much related to developmental level as to personal preference — a point also made by Kuhn (1989).

McPeck (1981) raises a more fundamental objection in regard to this subtest, arguing that both the description and the instructions reflect a confusion between a proposition, which may be true or false, and an inference, which may be valid or invalid. He notes further: "Normally, we speak of our knowledge or certainty as possessing degrees, but not truth or falsity" (p. 133). From the perspective of the Reflective Judgment Model, this assumption is held only by those who differentiate between well- and ill-structured problems (Stage 4 and beyond).

A related observation is made by Ennis and Norris (1990, p. 30): "People with different levels of sophistication justifiably give different levels of endorsement to a conclusion. Labeling a conclusion *probably true* instead of *true* constitutes a lesser level of endorsement. Saying that the data are insufficient is no endorsement." From the perspective of the Reflective Judgment Model, willingness to judge a response as "definitely true" is most characteristic of those who reason from a pre-reflective stance (Stages 1, 2, and 3). Those who reason reflectively (Stages 6 and 7) are more likely to say "probably true" to a convincing argument because they acknowledge the limits of knowing, balancing this limitation against the need to make judgments in light of uncertainty. Despite these collective concerns that could result in individual variability, there is, nevertheless, a correct answer to each question in this subtest (Brabeck and Wood, 1990). While the nature of the task itself in the subtest appears to be ill structured, it is scored using well-structured assumptions, thus requiring a well-structured solution to an ill-structured problem.

For each of the other four subtests listed in Table 4.1, the response options are of an either/or nature: the assumption is made or not made, the conclusion follows or does not follow, the argument is strong or weak. This is problematic for the Interpretation subtest, where the directions make specific reference to the criterion of whether a conclusion "follows beyond a reasonable doubt, (even though it may not follow absolutely and necessarily)" (Watson and Glaser, 1964, p. 6). The type of ambiguity or uncertainty that is acknowledged in these instructions is common to ill-structured problems. But despite the fact that individuals differ in specifying just where "reasonable doubt" begins and ends, the only response options are "follows" and "does not follow." These two options do not allow for ambiguity or qualification in making this judgment, suggesting that the problem may be well structured after all. In other words, just as with the Inference subtest, while the reasoning tasks themselves *appear* to reflect an ill-structured orientation, the given response options reframe the response into one that is well structured. (See Chapter Seven for a discussion of studies that have investigated the empirical relationships between the CTA and the RJI.)

The Cornell Critical Thinking Test. In Ennis's (1962) seminal paper on critical thinking, he lamented the lack of careful, systematic attention to the identification of the skills required for judging solutions to complex problems. He was particularly critical of Dewey's (1933) description of thinking, which he claimed, "unfortunately suggest[s] that the problem is solved when the solver thinks it is solved, thus providing a psychological instead of a logical criterion for the solution of a problem" (p. 82). Ennis then set out to offer a definition and a detailed description of the concept of critical thinking. "As a root notion, *critical thinking* is taken to be the correct assessing of statements. Since there are various kinds of statements, various relations between statements and their grounds, and various stages in the process of assessment, we can expect that there will be various ways of going wrong when one attempts to think critically. The following list may be looked upon as a list of specific ways to avoid the pitfalls in assessment" (p. 83).

This definition, especially given its emphasis on "correctness" and the explicit acknowledgement of ways of "going wrong," is consistent with a focus on reasoning about well-structured problems. The list to which Ennis referred describes twelve aspects of critical thinking, such as judging whether a conclusion follows necessarily and judging whether an inductive conclusion is warranted. It also includes three dimensions of critical thinking: logical, criterial, and pragmatic. The reasoning described by the dimensions may "require the thinker to go beyond the data given" (McPeck, 1981, p. 145), such as deciding whether there is enough evidence to support a judgment. As such, these dimensions appear less well structured. More recently, Ennis (1987, p. 10) defined critical thinking as "reasonable, reflective thinking that is focused on deciding what to believe or do" and expanded his description to include twelve abilities and fourteen dispositions.

How are these dimensions of thinking measured? The Cornell Critical Thinking Test was developed by Ennis and

Millman (1971) on the basis of Ennis's original concept of critical thinking. In the test manual, they define critical thinking as "the reasonable assessing of statements" (p. 1). Level Z (which is appropriate for college students) consists of seven sections: (a) deduction (determining whether a statement follows from premises in material that is emotionally loaded), (b) detecting fallaciously ambiguous arguments (such as circularity, nonsupporting emotive language, oversimplification of alternatives), (c) judging the reliability of information and authenticity of sources, (d) judging whether or not a hypothesis or generalization is warranted, (e) choosing useful hypothesis-testing predictions when planning experiments, (f) assumption-finding, identifying a definition that best expresses another person's usage of a term, and (g) assumption-finding, identifying a statement that fills a gap in a deductive argument.

What type of problem structure is reflected in this test? Again, the emphasis is on deductive problems that are defined with a high degree of completeness and characterized by a high degree of problem structure. As McPeck (1981, p. 145) has noted, the test's format (short questions and answers, with multiple-choice response options) "does not permit the comprehensive or circumspect judgments that are required by the concept of critical thinking. . . . The resulting content of the questions is thus indistinguishable from what might be found in any beginning-logic test." Later in his critique of this test (pp. 145–146), McPeck comments on the difficulty of assessing reasoning about ill-structured problems:

> When the questions [on the CCTT] turn from deductive inferences to questions requiring judgments that are more characteristic of critical thinking (for example, those that involve several of Ennis's twelve "aspects" in conjunction with the "dimensional criteria") the items become problematic, in that they admit of more than one correct answer. . . . Valid questions requiring inductive reasoning are difficult to construct in the best circumstances because no matter how much information is provided,

it is usually possible to interpret those data in several reasonable patterns. Moreover, a standardized multiple-choice test is a particularly inept vehicle for posing such questions.

A further clue to the problem structure of this test lies in the amount of information that is provided to the thinker for use in solving the problems. Even in the Inference subtest, a full array of necessary information is provided, making the level of inference quite low. This feature led McPeck (1981) to conclude that the questions measure reading comprehension rather than critical thinking. In summary, each of these factors suggests that the CCTT is a test of reasoning about well-structured problems.

Assessing Postformal Reasoning

Models of postformal reasoning are distinctive in that they attempt to describe how adults reason about problems that are not amenable to solution when only skills of Piagetian formal reasoning are used. As a result, these models are more likely to address ill-structured problem solving. Piagetian formal reasoning (Inhelder and Piaget, 1958) is defined as the ability to reason about the logical structure of propositions and their deductive and inductive relationships. By contrast, postformal reasoning refers to models that embed formal operations in new systems or offer an alternative to formal operations as an end point of cognitive development. While the emergence of such models has generated a great deal of interest among cognitive psychologists (note, for example, the series of books on postformal reasoning edited by Commons and his associates: Commons, Richards, and Armon, 1984; Commons, Sinnott, Richards, and Armon, 1989; Commons and others, 1990), few of these models have been validated on an extensive research base (Brabeck, 1984), and few of the researchers have actively engaged in test construction and refinement. Nevertheless, several are worth considering for their potential to inform our understanding of the assessment of critical thinking. In this section, we will discuss four models that describe aspects of reasoning that have been referred to as postformal (Basseches, 1980; Commons and Richards, 1984; Perkins, 1985; Perry, 1970) and offer our evaluation of the problem structure of the tests designed to assess the aspects(s) of critical thinking that each test emphasizes.

Perry's Scheme of Intellectual and Ethical Development. The model of intellectual development that is probably best known in higher education circles is Perry's (1970) scheme of intellectual and ethical development. (Although Pascarella and Terenzini, 1991, classify Perry's model as postformal, we are not convinced that it meets the criteria given above and view this as a topic for future consideration. See Chapter Two for a discussion of this point.) As noted in Chapter Two, Perry and his associates at Harvard University identified a sequence of nine "positions" or vantage points from which students understand the world, especially how they "construe the nature and origins of knowledge, of value, and of responsibility" (1970, p. 1). According to this sequence, students' thinking evolves from a "dualistic" approach (positions 1 and 2) where discrete, concrete, and absolute categories are used to understand people, knowledge, and values. The next level of development is called "multiplicity" (positions 3 and 4). From this vantage point, multiple perspectives on a given topic are recognized, and all points of view are seen as equally valid. With the third level (positions 5 and 6), "relativism," comes the recognition that knowledge is contextual and relative and that the various perspectives are part of a larger whole, the broader context in which the topic can now be seen. Moreover, with position 6 comes a recognition of the need to make one's own choices in the world. The last three positions (7 through 9) address issues of personal commitment, "commitment in relativism," that indicate individuals' affirmations and responsibilities in a pluralistic world, choices (about marriage, a career, and so on) that help them establish their sense of identity in the process. It is from these last three positions that the issues of ethical development noted in the title of Perry's (1970) book are addressed.

Researchers and others interested in assessing students'

developmental status on the Perry scheme have had to select among a variety of "Perry measures" since there is no standard assessment procedure for the scheme. Such measures include those developed by Baxter Magolda and Porterfield (1988); Clinchy and Zimmerman (1982); Erwin (1983); Knefelkamp (1974); Kurfiss (1988); Mentkowski, Moeser, and Strait (1983); Moore (1982, 1989); and Widick (1975). (For reviews of research on the Perry scheme and its measurement, see Baxter Magolda, 1987, 1992; Baxter Magolda and Porterfield, 1988; Moore, 1982; King, 1978; and Rodgers, 1980). Among these instruments, the two that have been used most frequently are the Measure of Intellectual Development (Knefelkamp, 1974; Widick, 1975) and the Measure of Epistemological Reflection (Baxter Magolda and Porterfield, 1988). Each is discussed below.

The foundation for the current version of the Measure of Intellectual Development (MID) was developed by Knefelkamp (1974) and Widick (1975). According to Moore (1982, p. 1), this version is designed to measure "the intellectual aspect of the Perry model (positions 1–5)" and hence is only scored through position 5. (Earlier versions had been scored across the full range of positions.) The MID consists of a series of short open-ended essays about such topics as decision making, classroom learning, and careers. Respondents are asked to provide a written description of an experience in a specified area (such as best class taken in college, a recent major decision) and to comment upon the experience, including how they feel about it. Trained raters match responses to position descriptions. The questions the MID poses are clearly ill structured and require the respondent to generate a description of his or her own way of thinking about each issue. However, the content of the measure renders it useful only for those in collegiate settings.

The Measure of Epistemological Reflection (MER) was developed by Baxter Magolda and Porterfield (1985, 1988), who used concepts and scoring cues from the Perry scheme in its construction; the MER has subsequently been revised on the basis of extensive information from interviews with college women as well as men. This instrument consists of a series of open-ended questions in six domains: decision making in an educational context, role of the learner in the learning process, role of the instructor in the learning process, role of peers in the learning process, role of evaluation in the learning process, and nature of knowledge, truth, and reality. For each domain, students are asked to provide written answers to a specific series of questions. Like the MID, the MER is scored through position 5, relativism.

The first domain, decision making, is introduced as follows (Baxter Magolda and Porterfield, 1988, p. 103): "Think about the last time you had to make a major decision about your education in which you had a number of alternatives (e.g., which college to attend, college major, career choice, etc.). What was the nature of the decision?" The follow-up questions are as follows (p. 103): "What alternatives were available to you? How did you feel about these alternatives? How did you go about choosing from the alternatives? What things were the most important considerations in your choice? Please give details."

For the sixth domain, which has the most explicit epistemological focus, the following questions are posed (p. 220): "Sometimes different instructors give different explanations for historical events or scientific phenomena. When two instructors explain the same thing differently, can one be more correct than the other? When two explanations are given for the same situation, how would you go about deciding which explanation to believe? Please give details and examples. Can one ever be sure of which explanation to believe? If so, how? If one can't be sure of which explanation to believe, why not?"

The problems posed in the MER are clearly ill structured, including both personal and intellectual problems. Scoring of the students' written responses is completed by trained raters; this process has been greatly enhanced by the availability of a detailed technical and training manual (Baxter Magolda and Porterfield, 1988). The reliability and validity of the MER are also documented in this publication, providing the necessary information for researchers seeking to evaluate this measure.

Basseches's Model of Dialectical Reasoning. Basseches's model (1980, 1984a, 1984b) is clearly characterized as postformal: Basseches argues that perspective dialectical reasoning builds on and is more powerful than formal operations. Basseches (1989, p. 45) notes, as we have, that formal operations are limited to what he calls "closed-system" problems. He also notes that many of the problems faced in the adult world require thinking that takes into account the changing nature of the world and call for a synthesis of different and sometimes competing perspectives. He characterizes the new kind of thinking that emerges as dialectical, which he defines as "thinking which looks for and recognizes instances of dialectic—developmental transformation occurring via constitutive and interactive relationships" (p. 55).

With this form of thinking, individuals comprehend that change is a fundamental characteristic of the world and that in the face of change they must often think beyond current stereotypes of solutions to develop new, more inclusive conceptions of a problem as well as solutions for the problem. Basseches has identified twenty-four cognitive abilities that comprise dialectical operations; these include an awareness of whole systems, the essential properties of those systems, and their changing nature; an awareness of internal relationships within a system; and an awareness of the fact that relationships are sometimes essential characteristics of objects or persons (for example, being a member of a family is an essential characteristic of a person's identity). Finally, dialectical thinking can reflect upon itself and demonstrates an awareness that qualitative changes can emerge from quantitative ones.

Basseches uses an example of a mother and daughter who are caught in a conflict over differing values to illustrate dialectical reasoning. The mother reflects on the situation, noting that she, too, had values that were different from her mother's and that her own values have changed over time. The mother begins to understand that her daughter's values reflect an integration of the values she tried to share with her daughter as well as of the experiences her daughter has had in the world, experiences the mother has never had. Thus, the daughter learned and transformed the mother's values to make them relevant to her own life. This conception both acknowledges change and constancy and forms a solution for the mother that transcends the conflict.

Basseches (1980, 1984a, 1984b) has used open-ended relatively unstructured interview procedures to measure dialectical reasoning. In one procedure, he asks interviewees to respond
to a series of questions about education, such as "How would
you go about formulating a conception of the nature of education?" (1980, p. 224). In a second procedure, he asks participants to read twelve pairs of arguments from cards, one pair
at a time. On each card are two arguments about a different
topic, such as the family. One of the arguments is dialectical;
the other is not. The participant's task is to explain each of the
paragraphs in his or her own words. Paragraphs are scored for
whether participants comprehend the dialectical and nondialec-
tical passages.

The first method clearly poses an ill-structured problem
since there is no single correct answer to questions about the
nature of education. Although the second format does not directly pose a problem to the participants, it does involve them
in explaining reasoning about ill-structured issues; thus, it measures participants' comprehension of arguments about ill-structured problems. Basseches's method and results are promising
(older, more educated participants are more likely to use and
comprehend dialectical reasoning); however, the method is time-
consuming to administer (two hours) and score (Basseches,
1984a, 1984b; Benack and Basseches, 1989; Irwin and Sheese,
1989). Further, reliability and validity data are minimal since
the measures have been used with very limited samples.

Commons and Richards's General Stage Model. The General
Stage Model (Commons and Richards, 1984; Commons, Richards, and Kuhn, 1982; Richards, 1990; Richards and Commons, 1984) reflects the authors' attempt to describe formally
the general structure of three postformal stages, the systematic,
meta-systematic, and cross-paradigmatic, which they claim are
hierarchically constructed after formal operations. With systematic reasoning, individuals can operate on whole classes and
relations and understand how they generate systems. In meta-
systematic reasoning, cognitions about multiple systems and
their relations can be generated, and in cross-paradigmatic

reasoning, the relations between systems of systems can be generated. The authors argue that these forms of thinking provide the basis of reasoning about relationships between systems and systems of systems in many fields, including moral philosophy, music, mathematics, and science. (This model is among those for which the data base on the development of the three postformal stages is not extensive.)

Richards and Commons (1984) use a set of four complex seriation tasks to measure systematic and meta-systematic reasoning. In each of the tasks, different criteria are used to evaluate the order of given elements. For example, one story uses economic value and another uses weight as a basis for a complex story that involves serial relationships. The task for the participant is to compare the ordering systems in the four tasks and to identify which of the six possible pairs of tasks are the most similar. Respondents are asked to judge on a scale of 0 to 9 how similar or different the orderings are in the stories (Richards, 1990). The problem appears to be ill structured since there are many ways in which the tasks are similar or different. However, from a mathematical perspective, Richards (1990, p. 190) notes that an "ideal performer" acting within a meta-systematic perspective would judge two of the stories as more similar than any other pair of stories. Presumably, the judgment of this ideal performer indicates the correct performance on the tasks, implying that the problem, though difficult, ultimately belongs on the well-structured end of the continuum. This "single correct answer" orientation is also reflected in the emphasis on the solution per se rather than on the rationale for the solution or the process used to arrive at the solution. Thus, while many of the models classified as postformal address ill-structured problem solving, one cannot assume that because the model is postformal, the assessment will necessarily focus on ill-structured problems: Commons and Richards' model exemplifies a postformal model where the assessment implies a well-structured orientation.

Perkins's Model of Informal Reasoning. The concept of informal reasoning developed by Perkins and his colleages (Perkins 1985; Perkins, Allen, and Hafner, 1983) also explicitly addresses reasoning about ill-structured problems. Even though the research base for this concept is relatively small, it merits inclusion here because of the similarity between the aspects of reasoning it attempts to describe and measure and those of the Reflective Judgment Model. According to Perkins (1985, p. 526): "In informal reasoning, reasons typically occur on both sides of the case, no one line of argument settles the truth of the claim, and no computational procedure assigns the claim a numerical probability. The reasoner must weigh and synthesize to best judge the soundness of the claim."

Informal reasoning is also referred to as everyday reasoning in that it occurs "when a person is deciding which car to buy, which political candidate to vote for, or how to persuade a colleague to adopt a particular position with respect to some burning issue" (Voss, Perkins, and Segal, 1991, p. xiii). These characteristics are clearly consistent with reasoning about ill-structured problems as described by the Reflective Judgment Model.

Perkins (1985) has measured informal reasoning through the use of a ninety-minute interview in which the respondents are presented with a series of "genuinely vexed issues" (p. 564), such as whether violence on television significantly increases the likelihood of violence in real life. In this interview, respondents are asked for an initial judgment on the issue, how confident they are of this judgment, how interested they are in the issue, and how much time they have previously spent thinking about the issue. They are asked to explain their arguments and their reasons for holding them, with several opportunities to elaborate on their statements. In addition, the respondents are asked to state reasons on both sides of the case and to assess the importance of these reasons (Perkins, Farady, and Bushey, 1991, p. 88).

Responses are scored on six scales: (1) number of sentences (a measure of elaboration), (2) number of lines of argument, (3) how many objections were raised to the respondent's own position (a measure of the extent to which each respondent considered the other side of the case), (4) number of times the interviewer prompted the respondent to stay focused on the issue, (5) adequacy of explanation (how well a reason supported a conclusion), and (6) overall quality. The last two scales use a 1 to 5 rating.

As with the definition of thinking, the interview format used by Perkins and his colleagues also appears to be consistent with reasoning about ill-structured problems. Whether it should also be considered a model of postformal reasoning is questionable since it has not been presented as an integrated psychological theory and its developmental basis is not clear. Nevertheless, this measure holds promise for adding to our understanding of reasoning about ill-structured problems.

Summary

How does an instructor, researcher, administrator, or other decision maker evaluate the potential utility of given measures of critical thinking and decide which to use for a specific purpose? Our analysis has suggested that the astute consumer of such measures should begin by carefully examining how critical thinking is defined and measured in any instrument being considered. Whether a given instrument will suffice will probably depend largely on the consistency between the aspects of thinking the individual or institution desires to measure and the operational definition of thinking used in the instrument (a point also noted by Helmstadter, 1985, and Jacoby, Astin, and Ayala, 1987), as well as how appropriate it is for use with the population being assessed. Further, this analysis has also pointed out that many measures of critical thinking actually measure reasoning about well-structured rather than ill-structured problems and that this cannot always be correctly inferred from the type of thinking the test purports to measure.

This chapter has addressed a variety of issues related to the assessment of reflective thinking. Since the attributes of "good thinking" are defined and measured in such a variety of ways, we began with a consideration of what characteristics a measure of reflective thinking and ill-structured problem solving would have in order to provide useful information to teachers, campus administrators, researchers studying educational outcomes, and others. Elements of this list provided a foundation for examining existing measures of critical thinking for the purpose of evaluating their potential as measures of reflective thinking. In particular, we examined the structure of the problems that are provided in each instrument and found that several popular measures of critical thinking focus on reasoning about well-structured rather than ill-structured problems. Thus, they do not serve as suitable measures of reflective thinking.

This discussion of assessment of reflective thinking has focused exclusively on formal assessment instruments because they are typically selected for large-scale assessment projects. Nevertheless, we recognize the value of informal assessment, such as occurs when educators must decide how to respond to individual students. This approach may also yield valuable information about a person's skills in thinking critically and reflectively.

Chapter Five

Assessing Reflective Judgment

"How well can students in my classes explain and defend a point of view about a controversial topic?" "Does our integrated core curriculum enhance these skills?" "Can students on the Academic Honesty Appeals Council and the Student Activities Program Board make reasoned judgments about questions that defy a simple right or wrong answer?" "Does participation in our student leadership seminar help students think more complexly?" "Do seniors in our college reason more reflectively than they did as freshmen? If so, does that hold across majors?" Faculty, student affairs staff members, and institutional researchers alike have a common need as they try to answer questions such as these. They need a way to measure reflective thinking. As discussed in Chapter Four, many existing measures of reasoning skills are unsuited for measuring reflective thinking as discussed in this book because they rely on well-structured problems. For this reason, such measures are not helpful for answering the kinds of questions posed here about students' reasoning skills.

This chapter discusses the assessment of reflective judgment. It focuses primarily on the Reflective Judgment Interview (RJI), which was developed to elicit information regarding individuals' fundamental assumptions about knowledge and how it is gained. The RJI is the instrument that was used to conduct the research on the Reflective Judgment Model reported in Chapters Six, Seven, and Eight of this book.

We begin this chapter by describing the specific structure and process of the RJI, explaining its relevant characteristics, and offering a rationale for several decisions that have guided its development. In order for the reader to better understand how the interview itself works, we next provide verbatim excerpts from two interviews that occurred between an interviewer trained to administer the RJI and a student who responded to the standard RJI questions. Following these interviews, we summarize the data on the psychometric properties of the RJI.

We conclude the chapter with a description of three alternative approaches to assessing reflective judgment. The first was designed to make the assessment process more amenable to large-scale administration. The second approach was designed to examine reflective thinking in the context of specific disciplines. The third was designed to measure both functional and optimal levels of performance in making reflective judgments. Each lays a foundation for new directions in research on the assessment of reflective thinking.

The Reflective Judgment Interview

The primary purpose of the RJI is to elicit ratable data about individuals' fundamental assumptions concerning knowledge and how it is gained. The RJI typically consists of four ill-structured problems and a standard set of follow-up questions. Each question focuses on at least one of the major concepts of the Reflective Judgment Model summarized in Chapter One and described in detail in Chapter Three.

The four standard problems concern a range of issues: how the Egyptian pyramids were built, the objectivity of news reporting, how human beings were created, and the safety of chemical additives in foods. The chemical additives problem is as follows:

> There have been frequent reports about the relationship between chemicals that are added to foods

and the safety of these foods. Some studies indicate that such chemicals can cause cancer, making these foods unsafe to eat. Other studies, however, show that chemical additives are not harmful, and actually make the foods containing them more safe to eat.

In recent research, a fifth problem on the disposal of nuclear waste has also been used. (For a full listing of RJI problems, see Resource A: The Reflective Judgment Interview.) Each problem is defined by two contradictory points of view and is designed to focus on problems in the intellectual domain. The intent in the original choice of problems was to focus specifically on how people reason about intellectual issues. Thus, ill-structured moral, social, and identity problems are not included. Our assumption was that reasoning about other types of issues might have unknown domain-specific characteristics and that including other types of issues might confound the results, making them more difficult to interpret. We concluded that the measurement of reasoning in different domains (such as intellectual and identity development) should rely on independent measures. (See Chapters Seven and Eight for discussions of the empirical data on the relationships between reflective judgment and these other domains.) Consequently, the interviewer is trained to focus on the epistemological aspects of the given problems.

The interview has a semistructured format and is conducted by a trained interviewer. The problems are typically presented in a random or counterbalanced order to control for the effects of order and fatigue. After a problem is read aloud, the interviewer asks the respondent a series of standard probe questions. The interviewer is trained to ask follow-up questions as necessary to clarify or refocus a response. Each question is designed to elicit information about a particular concept of the Reflective Judgment Model, such as the basis for holding a belief or the certainty with which it is held. Table 5.1 lists each of the standard probe questions, along with a description of the purpose of each question. Trained raters evaluate transcripts of the interview for consistency with the Reflective Judgment

Table 5.1. Reflective Judgment Interview
Standard Probe Questions.

Probe question	Purpose
What do you think about these statements?	To allow the participant to share an initial reaction to the problem presented. Most respondents state which point of view is closer to their own (that the Egyptians built the pyramids, that news reporting is biased, and so forth).[a]
How did you come to hold that point of view?	To find out how the respondent arrived at the point of view, and whether and how it has evolved from other positions on the issue.
On what do you base that point of view?	To find out about the basis of the respondent's point of view, such as a personal evaluation of the data, consistency with an expert's point of view, or a specific experience. This provides information about the respondent's concept of justification.
Can you ever know for sure that your position on this issue is correct? How or why not?	To find out about the respondent's assumptions concerning the certainty of knowledge (such as whether issues like this can be known absolutely, what the respondent would do in order to increase the certainty, or why that would not be possible).
When two people differ about matters such as this, is it the case that one opinion is right and one is wrong? If yes, what do you mean by "right"? If no, can you say that one opinion is in some way better than the other? What do you mean by "better"?	To find out how the respondent assesses the adequacy of alternative interpretations; to see if the respondent holds a dichotomous either/or view of the issue (characteristic of the early stages); to allow the participant to give criteria by which she or he evaluates the adequacy of arguments (information that helps differentiate high- from middle-level stage responses).
How is it possible that people have such different points of view about this subject?	To elicit comments about the respondent's understanding of differences in perspectives and opinions (what they are based on and why there is such diversity of opinion about the issue).
How is it possible that experts in the field disagree about this subject?	To elicit comments about the respondent's understanding of how he or she uses the point of view of an expert or authority in making decisions about

Table 5.1. Reflective Judgment Interview
Standard Probe Questions, Cont'd.

Probe question	Purpose
	controversial issues (such as whether experts' views are weighted more heavily than others' views, and why or why not).

[a]If the respondent does not endorse a particular point of view on the first question, the following questions are asked: Could you ever say which was the better position? How/Why not? How would you go about making a decision about this issue? Will we ever know for sure which is the better position? How/Why not?

Source: The Reflective Judgment Interview was originally developed in 1975 by the authors and was copyrighted in King, 1977. Permission to use the instrument is contingent upon the use of certified interviewers and raters.

Scoring Rules (Kitchener and King, 1985). Scoring is designed to reflect whatever stage-characteristic assumptions are evident in the transcripts; these typically range across two adjacent stages. Resource A includes a more detailed description of the procedures for conducting and scoring the Reflective Judgment Interview.

In an interview of this type, the participant is asked to spontaneously produce a response based on his or her existing repertoire of cognitive skills. In this case, participants are asked to express and justify a solution or point of view about a given problem "on the spot." The advantage of these tasks is that they yield rich data about individuals' reasoning styles, such as how they approach the tasks, the processes they use to arrive at a solution, and whether and why they reject alternative solutions. Approaches that use "production" tasks such as these are often preferred for theory construction and validation because the assessment reflects an individual's own approach to the problem rather than an approach that has been provided by the investigator. This interview format yields a more complete and potentially more accurate description of how individuals reason than do other types of formats. (For a discussion of the advantages and disadvantages of production and recognition tasks in developmental assessment, see King, 1990.)

Providing such rich information, however, is a rather demanding and difficult task for the respondents. They are asked to collect their thoughts about the problem quickly, organize them, express them, explain them, and sometimes also defend them against alternatives during the interview. The demanding nature of such an approach sets the stage for learning how individuals *typically* reason about such issues, not how they would reason given the opportunity to think long and hard about them and carefully develop explanations for their views. That is, this format yields more information about how individuals reason on a daily basis than how they think when at their intellectual best. (This distinction is discussed in Chapter Two as a difference between functional and optimal levels of performance.)

Interviewer and rater certification programs were established in 1978 to teach other researchers about the RJI and to increase the comparability of findings across raters, research programs, and studies. These programs certify individuals to conduct or rate the Reflective Judgment Interview; they do not certify participants to train others to do so. Both the RJI and the Reflective Judgment Scoring Rules are copyrighted; permission to use the RJI is dependent upon the use of certified interviewers and raters.

Illustrative Examples of the Reflective Judgment Interview

Following are two verbatim transcripts from two Reflective Judgment Interviews. They include the complete discussion about one of the four standard problems presented to each respondent, or one-quarter of the entire RJI. The first interview was scored as showing pre-reflective thinking; the second shows reflective thinking. (Again, *I* represents the interviewer and *R* the respondent.)

First Sample Interview

I: What do you think about these statements [alternative explanations of the building of the pyramids]?

R: I'm not too sure about alien visitors. I mean, if alien visitors were supposed to help the Egyptians, why wouldn't they come now and help us?

I: So what do you think happened?

R: I think they built them themselves. Used ropes and pulleys and stuff like that.

I: How did you come to hold that point of view? Have you always thought that?

R: I never heard of alien visitors, so I assume that they couldn't have.

I: Is there anything else on which you base your point of view that the Egyptians built them by themselves?

R: Just from learning in school and stuff like that.

I: OK. Anything else?

R: No.

I: Can you ever know for sure that your position is correct?

R: Not unless it's proven.

I: And how could it be proven?

R: I really don't know.

I: Do you think it might be proven some day?

R: Yes.

I: When people differ about this matter of how the pyramids were built, is it the case that one opinion is right and one is wrong?

R: Not really. They could both be partially right and partially wrong. I mean, divided up.

I: Could you explain what you mean?

R: Well, OK. People say alien visitors could have, but not left anything behind to show that they have been. Some people say that if they were here, they would have left something behind. So nobody really knows.

I: OK. Do you think we'll know sometime, someday?

R: Yes. Sometime in the future, maybe.

I: Then will some people be right and some people be wrong?

R: Yes.

I: OK. So, once we find out, then you can say people are right or people are wrong?

R: Yes.

I: How is it possible that people can have such different points of view about this?

R: Just, I guess, from what they've learned, from what they've heard, and practically what they believe.

I: And those beliefs come from . . . ?

R: Anywhere. I mean, other people, from what they've read, what their beliefs are, and sometimes religious, and stuff like that.

I: There are two points of view listed on that card. Do you see any way in which those points of view are related? [pause]

R: No.

I: OK. What does it mean when experts in the field disagree about how the pyramids were built?

R: What does it mean?

I: How could it be that people who know a whole lot about the Egyptians and the pyramids would disagree about how the pyramids were built?

R: They really don't know that much, because if they know that much, they would all agree. They really don't, though.

I: OK. So the fact that they disagree means that they don't have all the information?

R: Right. They don't have enough information. They don't have to have it all, but . . .

I: OK. Is there anything else you would like to say about this issue?

R: No.

Second Interview

I: What do you think about these statements [alternative views on the objectivity of news reporting]?

R: I believe this is very interesting from the point of view of experimental psychology. I tend to agree with the latter half of the statement. But I don't, I wouldn't use the same words that seem to give it such a negative connotation.

I: Could you describe your point of view in your own terms then?

R: Any time information is passed through the human head, it is filtered by the human head and the experiences, beliefs, point of view of that human head, and because of that, it comes out biased. Although *biased* has a negative connotation. It's just that it has been operated upon by a human being in order to be involved.

I: How did you come to hold that point of view?

R: Probably because of my major, and this is one of my areas of interest.

I: And what do you base your point of view on?

R: Experiments, some very interesting experiments with bystander reports, and effects of studies of juries and their deliberations, as well as laboratory type of experiments.

I: Given that you say that there's always some filtering that goes on, in this case, how do you decide what to believe goes on in the papers or in the news?

R: I think that it's always possible to, that different reporters will agree on a large number of things, that it's always possible to find out, at least, what happened. There was a traffic accident. You can find out what the physical event was, but you may or may not be able to exactly determine why it happened, or who was at fault, or things like that which do rely on a bit more interpretation.

I: Can you ever know for sure that your point of view is correct on this issue?

R: No, probably not.

I: Why not?

R: Because I don't believe in permanently correct points of view. I don't think there exists any. I don't think there are permanently correct points of view.

I: When people differ on the issue of whether reporting is objective or biased in some ways, is it the case that one opinion is right and one opinion is wrong?

R: No. I think probably in this case, there could be; people could be brought to a compromise. I don't think it would be that hard to bring people to a compromise in this issue. They may be, they may have a semantic problem as much as anything else.

I: For example, if we were to disagree on whether a particular article that we were both reading was objective or biased, would you be able to say that one of us was right and one of us was wrong?

R: I think we might both be right, but we might be focusing on different things. For example, I think both of us would agree if there were a traffic accident, in which case if I said, "There was a traffic accident," I would be right. But if I said that I knew for sure that so-and-so caused it, it would be very likely that I could be wrong, in that aspect of it.

I: So it depends on the aspect that you're looking at, in terms of right and wrong?

R: Yes.

I: On this issue of objectivity in news reporting, can you say that one opinion is better and one opinion is worse?

R: I would judge it in the same way that I judged the other thing. Like I said before, I think the second opinion is better in the sense that it accounts for the experimental evidence that I am aware of. It's not better in any long-lasting, permanent, moral sense.

I: How is it possible that people have such different points of view on this issue?

R: Perhaps in this case, it's an emotional difference as much as an intellectual difference. The words *unbiased* and *objective* lead me to believe that people have strong feelings. They are based on feelings as much as intellectual conversations.

I: What does it mean when the experts disagree on this issue, the journalists themselves?

R: The experts always disagree. It probably comes from the same reasons that normal people disagree. They may have more information, but they can still apply their personal feelings and beliefs and come up with different opinions.

R: Is there anything else you want to add to this one?

I: I don't think so.

Both interviews show how the RJI is conducted and how the interviewer attempts to elicit information about people's assumptions concerning knowledge and how they justify their beliefs. Next, we turn to the psychometric properties of the RJI.

Reliability of the RJI

Reliability of the RJI has been examined by means of various procedures.

Interrater Reliability and Agreement. Since RJI scores are based on the subjective judgments of trained raters, consistency of scores across raters is of primary interest. *Interrater reliability* is the most common index of rater consistency and is typically calculated by using a Pearson's product-moment correlation. Because the size of a correlation is affected by the range of scores being compared, interrater reliability fluctuates as a result of the heterogeneity of scores within samples. *Interrater agreement,* the proportion of instances in which two raters assign the same score to a given protocol, is a more conservative index of consistency across raters because it reflects actual agreement, not simple consistency. As Tinsley and Weiss (1975) have noted, interrater reliability could be high even though the scores between raters were quite discrepant, so long as one rater consistently rated the protocols higher than the other rater. However, such an occurrence would be reflected in low interrater agreement. In most studies that use the RJI, the scores of two raters are considered to be in agreement when they are discrepant by less than one stage.

The interrater reliability and agreement levels reported in all available reflective judgment studies that have used the standard RJI problems and the standard scoring procedures are reported in Resource B: Statistical Tables, Table B5.1. (These studies are reviewed in Chapters Six, Seven, and Eight.) The coefficients reported here are based on the scores each rater first assigned to each transcript (Round 1). (In Round 2, raters blindly rerate transcripts for which the ratings are discrepant.) Because of this procedure, the list of coefficients in Table B5.1 serves as a conservative index of consistency between raters. Interrater reliability (reported in twenty-four of the studies in Table B5.1) has varied widely, usually reflecting the heterogeneity of the sample: the reliability correlations have ranged from .34 in a homogeneous sample of traditional-age African-American college students (King, Taylor, and Ottinger, 1993) to .97 in more heterogeneous samples that ranged from graduate students to college freshmen or high school students (King, Wood, and Mines, 1990; King and others, 1983; Mines, King, Hood, and Wood, 1990). In the list of studies summarized here, the median interrater reliability coefficient was .78. (This calculation is based on studies where an overall reliability was reported; studies that reported only reliabilities for each individual problem were excluded from this analysis.)

The interrater agreement level, the most stringent test of the consistency between raters, was reported in thirty studies listed in Table B5.1 of Resource B and ranged from 53 to 100 percent. The distribution of overall agreement scores (across raters, problems, and subgroups) reported in these studies yielded a median agreement level of 77 percent. Strikingly, almost 40 percent of the studies reported an agreement level of at least 87 percent, and one-quarter reported an agreement level of at least 90 percent, indicating that trained raters can score RJI transcripts with a very high level of consistency. Looking at the low end of the range, only one study reported that the raters were consistent less than two-thirds of the time. Four studies reported an agreement level of less than 70 percent; interestingly, three of these were from samples that included adult students and nonstudent adults. While dramatic differences between traditional-age and adult students have not been found in prior studies comparing these two groups (see Chapter Six), these agreement levels suggest that some raters may be differentially evaluating rating cues in the transcripts from adult students or that older students may be responding in more diverse ways to the interview questions. This matter has not been the topic of deliberate investigation regarding the RJI, however; the pattern of lower-than-average consistency suggests that such investigation may be needed. Wood (1993a) has investigated interrater consistencies in a secondary analysis of the raw data from fifteen studies ($n = 1439$) that used the RJI. He found at least a .9 level of agreement in about 50 percent of the Round 1 scores and in about 80 percent of the Round 2 scores.

Test-Retest Reliability. Test-retest reliability indicates the degree to which respondents' scores remain stable over a relatively short period of time. Two studies have examined the test-retest reliability of the RJI. Sakalys (1984) reported a test-retest reliability of .71 over three months with a sample of twenty-five senior nursing students. The most comprehensive test of short-term change was conducted by Kitchener, Lynch, Fischer, and Wood (1993) who administered two of the standard RJI problems two weeks apart to fifty-two high school, college, and graduate students ranging in age from fourteen to twenty-eight. They obtained a test-retest reliability of .87.

Internal Consistency. How consistent are individuals' scores across the four standard RJI problems? That is, is a person who earns predominantly Stage 3 scores on the chemical additives in foods problem likely to earn scores that are higher, lower, or about the same on the Egyptian pyramids problem? Consistency of responses across problems has been examined in several ways. The single best indicator of overall consistency in responses to different problems is coefficient alpha, the internal consistency coefficient. This statistic is used to determine whether different items (or in this case, the four standard RJI problems) measure the same construct. Interproblem correlations and problem-total correlations have also been extensively used. While these measures mask individual variability across problems, they provide useful information about overall consistency. Each measure is described below.

A listing of the results of these three measures of internal consistency is presented by study in Resource B, Table B5.2. The raters' final scores were used for the analyses. Based on the complete list of reported alpha coefficients, the median reported alpha level across all studies was .77 and ranged from .47 (Glatfelter, 1982) to .99 (Glenn and Eklund, 1991). Retaining only those studies for which the alphas were calculated in a comparable fashion (studies that compared all four standard RJI problems, used the English RJI, used coefficient alpha, and reported an overall score across problems) yields a clearer test of internal consistency; fourteen studies met these criteria. This procedure yielded slightly higher scores: the alphas ranged from .50 (King, Taylor, and Ottinger, 1993) to .96 (Kitchener and King, 1981; Kitchener, King, Wood, and Davison, 1989), and the median scores were .79 and .85. (Two scores are listed since there were an even number of studies and no single median.) Overall, these scores indicate that the RJI has yielded a high level of internal consistency as measured by coefficient alpha. Wood (1993a) also reported a high degree of internal consistency, which he calculated separately by educational level. Using this procedure, he obtained lower alphas for the high school samples; he attributed this to the more restricted range of intellectual skills among these students.

The second measure of consistency across problems noted above, interproblem correlations (problem 1 with 2, 1 with 3, and so on), provides more detailed information on the relationships between specific pairs of RJI problems. These are reported by study in Table B5.2 and summarized in Table B5.3 of Resource B. The correlation of RJI scores for each pair of problems has ranged from very low to very high, typically falling in the high .40s. As noted above, such correlations are directly affected by the heterogeneity of the assigned ratings.

Problem-total correlations (problem 1 with the average of problems 2, 3, and 4; problem 2 with the average of problems 1, 3, and 4; and so forth) indicate the consistency between the scores assigned for one problem and the scores assigned to the other three problems. These correlations have been moderate to high, averaging in the mid-.60s. No problem has consistently had a higher or lower problem-total correlation than any other problem; in fact, the four problems are remarkably consistent in this regard. Thus, while the question of differences in performance between problems from differing content areas continues to interest some researchers, such differences would not be expected on the basis of the available empirical evidence summarized here.

Only one study (Kitchener, King, Wood, and Davison, 1989) has reported whether individuals (not just groups) were consistent in their use of stage reasoning across problems. Rather than using the mean score for each problem (which masks variability), this study examined each participant's modal RJI score (the stage score most frequently assigned by the raters) and found that the score was consistent across problems 75 percent of the time. The remainder of the time, the modes were discrepant by no more than one stage. This analysis offers further evidence of a relatively high rate of consistency in epistemic assumptions across the four standard RJI problems.

Summary of Reliability Findings. The patterns across the three types of reliability reported in this section — interrater reliability and agreement, test-retest reliability, and internal consistency — indicate that the RJI is a reliable measure of reflective thinking. Interrater reliability and agreement coefficients have averaged in the high .70s, and almost half of the studies reviewed here reported agreement levels of at least 80 percent. These figures clearly indicate that trained raters can consistently assign Reflective Judgment Model stage scores to RJI transcripts. In addition, both studies in which the test-retest reliability of the RJI has been evaluated have also indicated acceptable (.71) to strong (.87) levels of consistency of ratings between intervals of relatively short duration.

The three sets of statistics used to determine internal consistency each indicate a relatively high level of reliability. The reported alpha coefficients were typically in the high .70s to mid- .80s, depending on which group of studies was included in this analysis. The interproblem correlations were lower, averaging in the high .40s. In the studies that evaluated the problem-total correlations, these correlations clustered in the mid-.60s. The most notable finding in the internal consistency data was that no consistent pattern of differences across problems was found (at least using this means of aggregating the data across studies). That is, each of the four RJI problems appeared to "pull its own weight" in terms of its contribution to the RJI as a whole. In light of this rather high level of internal consistency, several researchers have successfully used fewer than all four of the RJI problems (the researchers are listed in Resource B, Table B5.1), making the test administration faster and less expensive.

These three reliability coefficients indicate that the RJI

is a reliable instrument that is suitable for decision making about groups of people; those interested in using it for purposes of individual decision making (such as counseling or advising) should do so cautiously.

Implications for Use of the Reflective Judgment Interview

The RJI has proved to be an effective tool for eliciting information concerning people's underlying assumptions about knowledge, how it is gained, and the basis for the certainty (or uncertainty) of their knowledge claims. The interviews yield rich information about how people approach and resolve ill-structured problems, from the factors that inform their points of view to whether they are genuinely confused about how to use evidence to construct an interpretation, or whether they are unable to arrive at a judgment for fear that doing so denies an appreciation for other perspectives.

For those interested in measuring reflective judgment, especially those who require or prefer production rather than recognition tasks (such as those who are interested in learning how individuals arrive at or defend a point of view or whose research questions require in-depth questioning of individuals' experiences), the RJI can provide useful information about respondents' reasoning styles. Researchers who are responsible for the assessment of educational outcomes on college campuses might consider using the RJI to track changes in reflective judgment among selected cohorts of students. Such a study might be especially useful at the institutional level if other educational experiences that are intended to enhance students' reflective thinking (such as participation in Great Ideas or honors courses or serving as a resident assistant or peer career counselor) were concurrently examined. If resources were not available to conduct the full four-problem RJI, the reliabilities reported here are high enough to justify the use of fewer problems in the interview. For example, within the time frame of a one-hour interview, thirty minutes could be used for students to respond to two RJI problems, leaving thirty minutes for a discussion of experiences that they identify as having affected how they think about such problems. Despite the time and expense required to use an interview format such as that of the RJI, we believe that doing so offers one the opportunity to gather rich material about students' educational experiences. If sponsored by an institution, asking students what and how they are learning or how they are dealing with life's vexing problems can also serve to communicate some important messages to students: that reflective thinking is an institutional value and expectation, that both curricular and cocurricular programs are designed to help students think about life's complicated problems, and foremost, that the quality of their collegiate experience matters. Effectively communicating these messages to students may be as important a contribution to the institution as conducting the study itself.

Alternative Ways of Measuring Reflective Judgment

Although the RJI has been a valuable tool for theory development and has proved to be reliable for research purposes, its design nevertheless has its limitations. For example, it is not amenable to large-scale administration because of the training, time, and expense associated with the interview format. Further, despite the consistency of scores across content areas, some educators and outcomes researchers prefer to use measures that have a closer link to a specific academic discipline. In addition, the RJI in its current form has served as a measure of functional but not optimal level of development. This section will describe recent research projects designed to address these issues.

Reflective Thinking Appraisal

In response to requests from educators and researchers for a measure of reflective judgment that is less expensive and easier to administer and score than the RJI, we are currently developing a new measure, called the Reflective Thinking Appraisal (RTA).*

*This work was sponsored in part by the Fund for the Improvement of Postsecondary Education, Application No. P116B00926, "Assessing Reflective Thinking in Curricular Contexts."

Our goal has been to develop a recognition task that can be scored either optically or through an interactive computerized format. The current version uses a format similar to that of the Defining Issues Test (Rest, 1986). In this approach, respondents read an ill-structured problem and respond to a series of questions that were drawn from the RJI standard probe questions. Respondents are asked to briefly write down their own answer to each question. This step is designed to engage the respondents in thinking about the task by having them produce their own response *de novo*. In the second step, respondents are asked to read several prototypic responses to the question. Their task here is to first identify how similar or dissimilar each prototypic response is to their own way of thinking about the issue and, second, to rank order the top responses that are most similar to the response they generated themselves. The rankings are used to determine an individual's score. This format has been pilot tested with two of the four standard RJI problems; ideally, it could be readily adapted to a variety of discipline-specific problems. (For more detailed information, see Kitchener, King, Wood, and Lynch, 1994). While our hope is that the RTA will provide a reliable, valid, and economical means for assessing reflective judgment, the RJI will still be the instrument of choice for some, depending on the research question or the assessment needs at hand. (For a description of the development of the RTA, see King, Wood, Kitchener, and Lynch, 1994.)

Discipline-Specific RJI Problems

Because faculty are often interested in how students reason about problems within their own disciplines, we have also been testing discipline-specific problems within the standard interview format (Kitchener, King, Wood, and Lynch, 1994). Discipline-specific problems have been developed and tested in three areas: business, chemistry, and psychology. Most of the problems have been constructed in conjunction with faculty members in their respective disciplines. The following examples were constructed by business faculty and chemistry faculty, respectively.

There has been considerable debate over the current size of the federal debt. Some economists and government officials claim that a large federal debt is damaging the economy. Others argue that the economy cannot be improved by reducing the federal debt.

Some scientists claim that the world is warming and base their claims on meteorological data compiled over the past century. Others say that factors such as changes in thermometer design and the growth of "urban heat islands" may bias the data and so create a spurious warming trend.

Examples of other RJI problems from the three disciplines noted above are given in Resource A. Although these new problems have only been tested in small pilot studies, they have been scored reliably by means of the standard Reflective Judgment Scoring Rules (Kitchener and King, 1985). Average scores on the discipline-specific problems have been almost identical to the scores earned by the same participants on the standard RJI problems.

Although these data must be considered preliminary, they are consistent with earlier data on discipline-based problems used in conjunction with standard RJI problems. For example, using a sample of college students working toward teaching degrees, Hayes (1981) compared scores on two standard RJI problems with scores on problems familiar to education students and found no substantial differences among them. This finding suggests that the RJI taps people's underlying assumptions about knowledge, not the assumptions they hold about a specific discipline. Nevertheless, learning about students' assumptions through the content of a specific discipline may make the findings more meaningful to faculty teaching in that discipline; that is, faculty may use these assumptions to better understand students' questions and comments, as well as their academic accomplishments and shortcomings.

The Prototypic Reflective Judgment Interview

As noted earlier, production tasks are not usually conducive to eliciting a person's optimal level of performance, or the highest stage of thinking of which the participant is capable. As discussed in Chapter Two, Fischer (1980) has suggested that people operate at their optimal level under optimal environmental conditions, particularly when they have had an opportunity to practice a skill and when information regarding contextual cues for high-level performance is provided. As already noted in the discussion of standard assessment procedures, opportunities for practice are not provided as part of the RJI's standard assessment. And since issues of knowing are not typically taught as part of a formal curriculum in educational settings, respondents seldom have had the opportunity to explicitly practice the skills that the RJI is measuring prior to the interview. As a result, the standard RJI does not measure a respondent's optimal level. The study discussed next was designed to examine performance differences by using alternative procedures for making assessments about reflective judgment skills.

Kitchener, Lynch, Fischer, and Wood (1993) investigated whether individuals would score higher in reflective judgment if they had the opportunity for practice and were provided with contextual cues than they would score when standard RJI assessment procedures were used. The researchers also tested Fischer's hypothesis (Fischer, Hand, and Russell, 1984; Fischer, Pipp, and Bullock, 1984) that spurts in performance on cognitive skills occur between ages fourteen and fifteen, eighteen and twenty, and twenty-three and twenty-five. They reasoned that if developmental spurts are identifiable at those ages and if reasoning is assessed under more supportive testing conditions, the spurts should coincide with the earliest emergence of Reflective Judgment Stages 5, 6, and 7.

To test these hypotheses, a new measure was constructed, the Prototypic Reflective Judgment Interview (PRJI). In this procedure, participants were presented with a statement that represents a prototypic response for Reflective Judgment Stages

2 through 7, yielding six prototypic statements for each of two standard RJI problems (pyramids and chemicals). The respondents' task was to read each of the statements, one at a time, and summarize it in their own words. For example, a Stage 5 prototypic summary statement from the chemicals problem follows:

> I am on the side that chemicals in food cause cancer, but we can never know this without a doubt. There is evidence on both sides of the issue. On the one hand, there is evidence relating certain chemicals to cancer, and on the other hand, there is evidence that certain chemicals in foods prevent things like food poisoning. People look at the evidence differently because of their own perspective, so what they conclude is relative to their perspective.

To provide contextual cues about important aspects to consider, interviewers asked the respondents a series of questions about the statement — for example, whether it asserted that knowledge could be had with certainty. After responding to the questions, participants were asked to reread the statement and then summarize it in their own words.

The sample for this study consisted of 156 participants, ages fourteen to twenty-eight. Two-thirds of the sample constituted the experimental group, who responded to the chemicals and pyramids problems in the RJI and then completed the PRJI. The remaining third of the sample, the control group, completed only the standard RJI. All participants were retested on both measures two weeks later. Those who were administered the PRJI were also given a homework assignment during the two-week internal: they were asked to study and think about two general prototypic statements that did not make reference to either the chemicals or pyramids problem. One of these statements was coded at the highest stage the participants had accurately comprehended in the first interview, and the second statement represented the next highest stage. This procedure, along with the initial interview, provided at least minimal opportunity for practice; the summary statements, along with the interviewer's questions, were designed to provide contextual support.

The scores for the experimental group were significantly higher (over half a stage) on the PRJI than on the RJI, supporting Fischer's prediction. In addition, these participants scored significantly higher at the second than at the first testing on the PRJI. This difference could not be attributed to the test-retest condition itself. In this study, the practice and the contextual cues for higher-level reasoning were found to have a positive effect on participants' Reflective Judgment scores.

Since the RJI at the first testing provided an estimate of functional level and the PRJI at the second testing provided an estimate of optimal level, it was predicted that the scores on these two measures would differ the most under these two conditions. The differences between scores on the RJI at the first testing and the PRJI at the second testing ranged between 70 percent of a stage in the high school group to nearly a full stage for the graduate students. These data support the interpretation that the RJI is a measure of functional level and that it does not tap respondents' highest level of functioning because it provides neither environmental support for high-level performance nor opportunities for practice. Further, these data support Fischer's hypothesis that individuals operate within a developmental range and that a specific score for any person will depend on opportunities for practice and the contextual cues that support high-level learning.

Evidence for developmental spurts was found in this study among those who took the PRJI (where they were provided with the contextual support and the opportunity for practice). Significant increases in scores were obtained only for those between ages eighteen and twenty and between ages twenty-three and twenty-five or twenty-six (the latter was a mixed age group due to sample size). These spurts were also found to correspond with the initial ability to understand and articulate reasoning at Reflective Judgment Stages 6 and 7, respectively. Furthermore, there was some evidence that there may be a developmental spurt between the ages of fourteen and fifteen. By contrast, no evidence for spurts was found for the RJI, again documenting the idea already introduced that assessment procedures do affect the picture of development that is generated. Finally, among individuals younger than age twenty-three, there was a ceiling on performance: even with support and practice, these students did not accurately paraphrase the statements that reflected Stage 7 reasoning.

Summary

This chapter opened with a series of questions posed by faculty, student affairs staff, and institutional researchers; answering any of these questions requires a way to measure reflective thinking. In describing the format and rationale for the Reflective Judgment Interview, we have identified the types of questions that have successfully elicited information about individuals' assumptions concerning knowledge, how beliefs are justified, and the certainty with which people claim to know. We encourage educators to ask their students questions about ill-structured problems, including the kinds of questions asked in the RJI: What do you think about this issue? On what do you base your point of view? Can you ever know for sure that your position is correct? How is it possible that people have such different points of view about this subject? Is one answer in any way better than another? Doing this not only sets the stage for an interesting discussion, but it helps communicate the expectation that students will wrestle with and attempt to answer such questions. Further, for those with a sensitivity to the types of developmental differences described in the Reflective Judgment Model, students' responses to such questions provide an initial indication of whether their reasoning styles evidence pre-reflective, quasi-reflective, or reflective thinking. Such informal assessments can help educators decide how to structure the classes and other educational programs they offer (such as those described in Chapter Nine).

　　　Formal assessments for research purposes require a more systematic evaluation with a reliable instrument. The reliability of the RJI has been tested in several ways. The resulting data indicate that the RJI is a highly reliable measure of reflective thinking as defined by the Reflective Judgment Model.

Acknowledging that the RJI is also very time-consuming and expensive to administer, we concluded the chapter with a look at alternative ways of assessing reflective thinking. We started with a description of our work (with Phillip Wood and Cindy Lynch) in developing a new instrument to measure reflective thinking, the Reflective Thinking Appraisal. Our goal is to develop a reliable measure of reflective thinking that will be amenable to large-scale administration and thus be available to help answer a variety of questions about the development of reflective thinking from late adolescence into adulthood, including the effectiveness of selected educational practices designed to assist students in making reflective judgments.

The chapter concluded with the discussion of a study that investigated the effects of various assessment conditions on the measurement of developmental level. Kitchener, Lynch, Fischer, and Wood (1993) used the RJI to measure functional level of development, and designed another task (PRJI) to yield information about a higher level of functioning, the optimal level (Fischer, 1980). They found that providing contextual support and the opportunity for practice positively affected individuals' reflective judgment scores. This is good news indeed for educators who intentionally design learning environments to provide appropriate contextual support and opportunities for practice. The same study also lays the groundwork for a variety of possible follow-up studies on ways of providing contextual support that enable individuals to perform closer to their optimal level of development. The new insights about the nature of development and its assessment provided in this study have the potential to richly inform researchers and educators who are interested in measuring reflective thinking and thereby enable them to better understand and promote reflective thinking in their students.

Chapter Six

Research on the
Reflective Judgment Model

with Phillip K. Wood

Being able to think critically is one of the major hallmarks of an educated person and an attribute that commonly appears in statements of educational goals at both the secondary and college levels. Further, educational environments provide many opportunities to assist students in learning how to improve their thinking skills, including reasoning about problems that do not have single, verifiable answers. This is particularly true at the college level, where students are exposed to contrasting perspectives on a multiplicity of ill-structured problems in both academic and social environments and where there are (or should be) many opportunities to learn to reason more complexly and effectively.

The consistency between reflective thinking as a goal of education and the type of thinking described by the Reflective Judgment Model leads us to the major questions of this chapter: (1) Does reflective judgment develop between late adolescence and middle adulthood? (2) How do high school, college, and graduate students reason about ill-structured problems? (3) Does students' reasoning improve with additional exposure to and involvement in higher education? (4) Do adult learners differ from traditional-age students in their reflective thinking? (5) How does the reasoning of adults who have not participated in higher education compare to the reasoning of those who have earned a college degree? (6) Are there gender or cross-cultural differences in the development of reflective thinking? In this chapter, we turn to the research that has been conducted on the Reflective Judgment Model, presenting the results of both longitudinal and cross-sectional research that collectively inform our understanding of these questions.

Research on changes in thinking that are associated with age and educational experiences, including development in reflective thinking, is of interest to different groups of people for different reasons. For example, such research is important to developmental psychologists who seek to understand the nature and the mechanisms of cognitive development through the adult years. Those with institutional studies responsibilities are interested in such research because one index of an institution's effectiveness in promoting reflective thinking is whether its graduating seniors consistently show more proficiency in critical thinking than they did as entering freshmen. College faculty and student affairs staff look to research on the development of reflective thinking because of the insights it can offer for helping them better educate students to value and demonstrate good thinking skills. We believe the following data will be of interest to all three groups.

Research on changes that are associated with age, such as those described by the Reflective Judgment Model, requires comparisons of individuals at different ages. However, age alone would not be expected to lead to higher scores: there is no reason to believe that the passage of time alone should influence the development of reflective thinking unless it corresponds to some other intervening event (such as neurological maturation or age-related involvement in an intellectually stimulating environment). Since educational institutions attempt to involve students in the acquisition, analysis, and utilization of knowledge, improvement in students' ability to make more reflective judgments can reasonably be expected, and the failure to find such changes would be disturbing.

To date, more than 1,700 individuals representing a wide

variety of student and nonstudent subgroups, have participated in the Reflective Judgment Interview (RJI). This number includes almost 200 people who have taken part in longitudinal studies, over 150 high school students, 1,100 college students (both traditional-age and adult samples), and about 200 graduate students. In addition, more than 150 nonstudent adults have been tested. The results help us understand how students reason about ill-structured problems, whether their reasoning changes over time, and whether improvement in the ability to make reflective judgments is associated with participation in higher education. In this chapter, we examine the patterns of scores that have emerged from both longitudinal and cross-sectional studies as they pertain to the development of reflective thinking, particularly in the context of higher education. In considering these results, readers are reminded that the RJI measures how students typically function, not how they might function under optimal learning and testing conditions. (The RJI and its properties are described in detail in Chapter Five.)

We begin our description of research on the Reflective Judgment Model by looking at those studies that have attempted to ascertain whether the ability to make reflective judgments develops over time, particularly between late adolescence and middle adulthood. Charting the changes in individuals' reasoning requires longitudinal data. Such data are essential for the validation of any developmental model because they indicate whether people change in a manner consistent with the description and sequence proposed by the model. Further, they allow a stricter test of the impact of educational experiences than do cross-sectional studies (at least among the particular cohorts tested). Despite the importance of longitudinal research for the study of intellectual development, most of the existing models of adult cognitive development lack a longitudinal data base (Brabeck, 1984), an observation that, unfortunately, is still true today. The Reflective Judgment Model is an exception to this pattern.

We first examine the results of a ten-year longitudinal study of the development of reflective judgment that was an outgrowth of the original Kitchener and King (1981) study. This study covers the longest span of years and the most testings of any group of individuals to date, providing the strongest basis for evaluating the developmental properties of the model. Following these, we describe additional longitudinal studies of shorter duration that used the Reflective Judgment Model. In the second half of this chapter, we review the cross-sectional studies; these are discussed separately for each of the following groups: high school students, traditional-age college students, nontraditional-age college students, and nonstudent adults. We conclude this chapter by reviewing the research on gender differences and cross-cultural differences in reflective judgment. Because of the length of this chapter and because some readers may wish to be selective in their reading of various portions of the research summarized here, the concluding summary is more detailed than that offered for other chapters.

Ten-Year Longitudinal Study of Reflective Judgment

The ten-year longitudinal study noted above traced the development of the reflective thinking of eighty individuals from 1977 to 1987. During this decade, these individuals generously contributed their time (up to four hours per testing) and candidly shared with us the means by which they arrived at conclusions about vexing problems. As a result, we now have a picture of their development from the psychologist's equivalent of a zoom lens, taking periodic snapshots of their reasoning every few years. Since these individuals ranged between sixteen and twenty-eight years of age at the first testing, reviewing their progress provides an overview of the development in reflective thinking during early adulthood. In addition, since most of the participants in the sample were engaged in some aspect of formal education at the same time, this study offers insights into their intellectual journeys during this time and provides an initial assessment of whether involvement in higher education leads to higher levels of reflective judgment. The results document changes in participants' reflective thinking based on their assumptions about knowledge, the certainty with which they said they knew, and how they justified their beliefs.

The study began with a cross-sectional investigation of

three groups of students who differed by age and educational level (King, 1977; Kitchener, 1977–78; Kitchener and King, 1981). The original sample included twenty high school juniors, forty college juniors, and twenty third-year doctoral students. The rationale here was that the different ways of reasoning described by the Reflective Judgment Model should be apparent when tested with students from a wide range of educational levels and that a finding of no differences across these groups would raise serious questions about the model and/or its measurement. The high school students were enrolled in two school districts in communities in or near the Minneapolis metropolitan area; the college students were enrolled in either the College of Liberal Arts or the College of Agriculture at the University of Minnesota; and the doctoral students were liberal arts majors at the same university. The younger two groups were matched to the graduate sample by gender (half female, half male) and by academic aptitude (based on scores from the Minnesota Scholastic Aptitude Test). This matching was designed to serve as a check against the possibility that any obtained group differences in reflective judgment might be a function of differences in academic aptitude.

These individuals were contacted in 1977 and again in 1979, when 74 percent of the original sample was retested (the results are reported in King and others, 1983). The third testing occurred in 1983, with a 69 percent retest rate (see King, Kitchener, Wood, and Davison, 1989; Kitchener, King, Wood, and Davison, 1989). The final attempt to contact all eighty of the men and women who originally participated in the 1977 study was undertaken in 1987. At this time, fifty-six members of the original sample (70 percent) were contacted and agreed to continue their participation. Usable RJI data were obtained for fifty-three of these individuals, or 66 percent of the original sample. (Preliminary findings of the ten-year study are reported in King, Kitchener, and Wood, 1990.) Table 6.1 shows the sample sizes and response rates for each subgroup at each year of testing.

Between 1977 and 1987, a large portion of this sample completed either the educational degree they were pursuing in

Table 6.1. Ten-Year Study:
Sample Size and Response Rate by Group and Year of Testing.

	Educational level in 1977							
	High school juniors		College juniors		Advanced doctoral students		Total	
Year	n	%	n	%	n	%	n	%
1977	20	100	40	100	20	100	80	100
1979	17	85	27	68	15	75	59	74
1983	15[a]	75	27[a]	68	13	65	55	69
1987	13	65	26	65	14	70	53	66

Note: Figures are based on those who completed the Reflective Judgment Interview at each year of testing.

[a]Due to a coding error, the sample sizes for the 1983 high school and college groups listed here are fewer by one than the number we reported in Kitchener, King, Wood, and Davison (1989). This correction does not affect the patterns of results reported there.

1977 or a subsequent degree. Table 6.2 shows the degrees earned by the participants of this study according to subgroup. By 1987, all but one of the former high school students had earned at least a bachelor's degree. Among the former college juniors, 84 percent had completed at least a bachelor's degree; of these college graduates, almost half had also completed a postbaccalaureate degree. By 1987, 80 percent of the former advanced doctoral students had completed the Ph.D. degrees they had been working on in 1977. As the data show, the sample had a rather high level of educational attainment by 1987.

At each testing, the participants were asked to complete several measures, including the RJI. The four standard RJI problems (see Table 5.1) were used at the first, second, and third testings. At the fourth testing, a new problem was added as a check against the possibility that an increase in scores over time might be a function of practice or familiarity with the issues discussed rather than a reflection of development in reasoning. Each problem was rated blindly at each testing; that is, the raters were not informed about ratings that had been assigned at prior testings, about those assigned to other problems at the current time of testing, or about those assigned by the other rater. Raters

Table 6.2. Ten-Year Study: Educational Attainment by 1987.

Highest degree earned by 1987	High school juniors		College juniors		Advanced doctoral students	
	n	*%*	*n*	*%*	*n*	*%*
High school diploma	1	9	4	17	—	—
B.A./B.S.	9	82	11	46	1	7
M.A./M.S.	1	9	3	13	2	13
Professional	—	—	6	25	—	—
Ph.D.	—	—	—	—	12	80
Total	11	100	25	100[a]	15	100

Note: Numbers vary slightly from those in Table 6.1 due to missing data.
[a]Sum of column figures is 101 due to rounding.

were also blind to gender and other demographic characteristics and to group (high school, college, or graduate student) for the first three testings. (By the time of the fourth testing, group membership at the first testing no longer indicated educational level. Further, students from each group had earned high RJI scores at the third testing, so the need for raters to be blind to this information was no longer compelling.)

The other measures that were also administered were Terman's (1973) Concept Mastery Test, a measure of verbal ability; Rest's (1979) Defining Issues Test, a measure of moral judgment; Loevinger and Wessler's (1970) Sentence Completion Test, a measure of ego development, given at the first, second, and third testings only; the Myers-Briggs Type Indicator, a measure of psychological type, given at the fourth testing only; and a background questionnaire on the participants' educational and occupational experiences. (Discussions of the relationships between the RJI and other measures appear in Chapters Seven and Eight.)

Changes in Reflective Thinking Over Time

Conducting longitudinal research presents a variety of challenges. Many participants move (sometimes many times) over a ten-year period; thus, locating former participants may take considerable detective work. Difficulties in locating former participants, combined with life events that interfere with their participation, sometimes result in sample attrition. Participants who are missing or unable to participate at one testing may reappear and be eager to participate in subsequent testings. For example, one of the participants in this study was out of the country during the middle two testing periods but did take part in the fourth testing.

Such sampling problems present subsequent problems for data analysis since not every participant has scores for each testing. The question then becomes whether it is better to evaluate change by looking at the scores of everyone in the sample or just of those people who were present at every testing. If everyone in the sample is included (even if some individuals missed one or more testings), there will be gaps in the data. Where scores are missing, we have no knowledge of whether individuals' scores would have increased, decreased, or stayed the same during specified intervals. On the other hand, if the scores of only the participants who were tested every time are included, the sample size is smaller, and generalizations are in turn limited. Consequently, analyses designed to evaluate changes in Reflective Judgment over the ten years of this study were conducted in three different ways. The first used the most conservative test of a developmental sequence by including only the scores of the thirty-eight people who participated in all four testings (1977, 1979, 1983, *and* 1987). Second, the scores of the thirteen people who had missed only the second or third testing were added to the sample of thirty-eight by estimating their missing scores (missing scores were estimated by averaging the scores that immediately preceded and followed the missing ones); this yielded a sample of fifty-one. Third, the scores of all individuals who had participated in any phase of the study ($n = 80$) were included, without the interpolation of any scores. Since only minor differences in the patterns of results were found in the three types of scores, the following analyses are based on the total sample. (Results based on those with complete data are reported in Resource B, Table B6.1.)

Changes in Group Scores. The three student groups differed in
their reflective judgment levels in 1977: doctoral students scored
significantly higher than college students, who scored significantly higher than high school students. Additionally, differences between these groups remained in subsequent testings:
the former doctoral students scored significantly higher than the
other two groups; moreover, while the RJI scores of both of
the younger two groups increased over time, the patterns of
growth between the two groups was different, and they became
more similar.

Consistent patterns of increasing RJI mean scores were
found for all three groups at each subsequent testing (with the
single exception of the scores for the former doctoral students,
which remained stable between 1979 and 1987). In other words,
with one minor exception, the RJI mean scores of each group
increased with each follow-up testing. These scores are presented
in Table 6.3 and plotted in Figure 6.1. As the ranges of scores
in Table 6.3 illustrate, not only was higher-stage reasoning more
evident over time but lower stage reasoning became less evident. In no case was there a significant decline in scores over
time, and in no case did the increase exceed one and a half stages
between testings. Taken together, these patterns suggest that
the development of reflective thinking as measured by the RJI
evolves slowly and steadily over time among individuals engaged
in educational programs.

The mean RJI scores for the former high school juniors
increased the most dramatically in the ten-year period, from
2.9 to 5.5, a difference of two and a half stages. This increase
in the group mean score reflects a change in epistemic assumptions ranging from Stages 2 and 3 (the stages on which the 1977
score was predominantly based) through Stages 5 and 6 (for the
1987 score), a dramatic metamorphosis in thinking toward making reflective judgments. It is perhaps not coincidental that during the ten years of this study, all but one member of this group
attended and graduated from college.

The ten-year change in mean scores for the former college juniors from 3.8 to 5.1 was not as dramatic but still showed
a steady pattern of development in reflective thinking. The scores

Table 6.3. Ten-Year Study: Reflective Judgment Scores by Group and Time.

| | Educational level in 1977 | | | | | | | | |
| | High school juniors | | | College juniors | | | Doctoral students | | |
Time	M	sd	Range of scores	M	sd	Range of scores	M	sd	Range of scores
1977	2.77	.49	2.17–4.04	3.76	.69	2.46–5.58	5.67	.92	3.83–6.92
1979	3.61	.46	2.83–4.50	4.18	.80	3.21–6.38	6.23	.50	4.97–6.96
1983	4.91	.79	3.46–6.00	4.92	.54	4.12–6.17	6.23	.45	5.21–6.88
1987	5.29	.75	4.12–6.59	5.05	.60	3.96–6.44	6.21	.56	5.06–6.94
Change, 1977–1987	+2.52			+1.29			+.54		

Note: Scores are based on those tested two or more times (1977 plus 1979, 1983, and/or 1987). Sample sizes for each group at each time of testing are given in Table 6.1. The results of a three-way (time × group × gender) General Linear Model were as follows:

Overall model: $F(23,223) = 27.88$, $p < .001$

Time main effect: $F(3,223) = 63.49$, $p < .001$

Group main effect: $F(2,223) = 164.21$, $p < .001$

Gender main effect: $F(1,223) = 4.57$, $p < .05$

Time × group interaction: $F(6,223) = 9.17$, $p < .001$

Time × gender interaction: $F(3,223) = .92$, ns

Group × gender interaction: $F(2,223) = 2.84$, $p = .06$

Time × group × gender interaction: $F(6,223) = .40$, ns

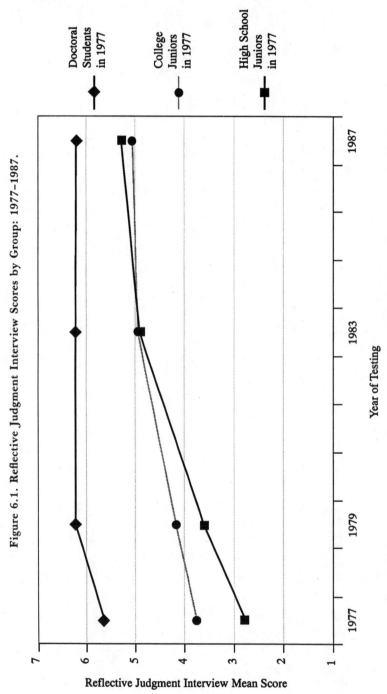

Figure 6.1. Reflective Judgment Interview Scores by Group: 1977–1987.

Note: Scores are based on individuals tested two or more times (1977 plus 1979, 1983, and/or 1987). Sample sizes for each group at each time of testing are given in Table 6.1.

for the former doctoral students are best characterized as stable, changing only from 6.2 to 6.4 over the ten-year period. However, even though this group's mean scores were generally stable, the range of scores shown in Table 6.3 suggests that lower scores were replaced by higher scores, so that by the fourth testing, the entire sample scored close to Stage 6 or 7. The stability in mean scores may reflect a "ceiling effect" on the RJI since the highest possible score, 7.0, can only be earned if all raters consistently rate all responses as Stage 7 over all problems.

Since the 1987 testing included a new problem on the safety of nuclear energy, the correspondence between participants' responses to this problem were compared with their responses to the other problems. If individuals were scoring higher over time as a function of increasing familiarity with the problems, they would be expected to score lower on a less familiar problem. However, differences between the mean score for this problem and the mean scores for the other four problems were negligible, offering no support for the familiarity hypothesis.

Several statistical analyses were run to check for patterns in the mean scores of each group over the ten-year period. First, a three-way General Linear Model (time by group by gender) was run, with the RJI scores used as the dependent variable. (Specific statistical findings for this model are reported in Table 6.3.) Where significant main effects were found, Waller-Duncan K-ratio follow-up t-tests were run. The mean RJI scores across samples increased over time ($p < .001$). These increases were significant between 1977 and 1987, but the overall increase between 1983 and 1987 was not significant.

A time by group interaction ($p < .001$) indicated a disordinal pattern in the RJI scores; that is, as illustrated in Figure 6.1, the amount of growth over time differed by group. In 1977 and 1979, the scores of each successive age/educational group were significantly higher. However, in 1983 and 1987, the ordering of the scores of the former high school and college students was reversed: the scores of the high school students had increased more and actually exceeded those of their older counterparts. The scores of the former doctoral students remained significantly higher than the scores of the other two groups. Since there was such a dramatic increase in the scores of the former high school students, a follow-up ANOVA was conducted only on the two older groups. The time, group, and time by group interactions remained ($p < .01$), indicating that the overall findings of growth over time were not attributable solely to the changes in the former high school students. (Further analyses of group differences, as well as gender differences, are reported below.)

As already noted, the scores of the former high school juniors changed from Stages 2 and 3 in 1977 to Stages 5 and 6 in 1987. The greatest amount of growth for this group occurred between 1979 and 1983; during this four-year period, the average scores changed almost one and a half stages, from 3.9 to 5.3. No other group showed a comparable amount of growth at any point in the study: the average scores of the former college students increased by slightly more than one stage during the ten years of the study (from 3.8 to 5.1), and the mean score of the doctoral students remained stable at Stage 6.

While we can only speculate about the reason for the spurt in the scores of the former high school students, its timing does coincide with their college attendance: 75 percent of the participants in this group entered and completed college between 1979 and 1983. This spurt corresponds to the developmental spurt found among a sample of college students between the ages of eighteen and twenty in the Kitchener, Lynch, Fischer, and Wood (1993) study and is predicted by Fischer's (1980) skill theory model, described in Chapter Two. Thus, the spurt may be due to the influence of being in an educational environment, to maturation, or to both. The premise that the educational environment played a critical role in the development of reflective thinking among the former high school students is supported by an additional finding at the sixth-year testing in 1983. Those who held a bachelor's degree showed significantly more change in their RJI score than did those with only a high school diploma, supporting the contention that there is greater growth in reflective judgment for those who attend and complete college than for those who do not. However, too few of the participants from this group did not attend college for a rigorous test of this hypothesis, so the point remains tentative.

Changes in Individual Scores. Although group data can provide an overview of longitudinal changes, data on individual change over time provide a stronger test. The RJI scores for the entire longitudinal sample in this study (*n* = 71) are listed in Resource B, Table B6.2. These scores are presented in two ways, first as mean scores averaged across all problems and raters. The second index presents each individual's dominant (modal stage score) and subdominant (second most frequently assigned) stage score. The findings presented below on individual changes over time are based on these scores.

The pattern of changes in the RJI scores of the fifty-three individuals who were retested in 1987 gives a full ten-year view of development. (For this purpose, we define change as a difference of at least .1 — for example, a mean score of 5.4 compared to 5.5.) Using this criterion, the RJI scores of 92 percent (*n* = 49) of the sample increased over the ten years of the study. The scores of two individuals (both former doctoral students) decreased over this time, although their modal scores remained stable at Stage 7. There was no change in the scores of the remaining two individuals between 1977 and 1987.

A second set of scores, those of the thirty-eight individuals who participated in all four testings, provides a more detailed picture of the development of reflective judgment. Twenty-six of these individuals (68 percent) had scores that either increased or remained stable between each of the three testing intervals (1977–1979, 1979–1983, *and* 1983–1987), and eleven of the remaining twelve people had only one exception to this pattern (for example, one individual's RJI scores increased between 1977 and 1979, decreased in 1983, and increased in 1987).

This pervasive pattern of upward change in RJI scores over the ten years of this longitudinal study shows that the vast majority of the individuals who participated in the study improved in their ability to make reflective judgments over time. This suggests that the overall changes in mean scores shown in Table 6.3 cannot be attributed to large increases in one subset of the sample (the former high school juniors). Further, the pattern of increasing RJI scores over time clearly indicates the slow, steady emergence of reflective thinking during early adulthood. When individual scores are examined for the dominant and subdominant stages at each time of testing, a sequential (not random) ordering of stages is apparent, and there is consistent evidence of lower-stage usage prior to higher-stage usage. Few examples offer evidence to suggest that stages were skipped. For example, in 1977, one female participant scored at a dominant Stage 2 and a subdominant Stage 3 on the RJI; in 1979, she scored at a dominant Stage 4 and a subdominant Stage 3; in 1983, she scored at a dominant Stage 4 and a subdominant Stage 5; and in 1987 (by which time she had graduated from college), she scored at a dominant Stage 5 and a subdominant Stage 4. Not only had her RJI scores changed over two full stages during the ten years of the study, but the changes had occurred sequentially and gradually.

Variability in Scores Across Stages. Do individuals evidence reasoning that is characteristic of more than one stage of the Reflective Judgment Model at a time? If so, this would be consistent with the complex stage model proposed by Rest (1979), which is described in Chapter Two. If not, how can the variability be characterized? The listing of dominant and subdominant stage usage in Resource B, Table B6.2, informs this question: a subdominant stage was assigned for most individuals in the study; this was almost always an adjacent stage. In only two cases were the ratings limited to a single stage score.

Wood (1993a) has examined this question in more detail in the only existing study to systematically analyze variability in stage reasoning across studies that used the RJI. To do this, he conducted a secondary analysis of RJI scores from fifteen studies that used trained interviewers and raters and for which raw data were available for reanalysis ($n = 1,995$). He calculated the proportion of time each stage was represented in an individual's ratings across the four RJI problems and referred to this as the "percent stage utilization score." To indicate the general patterns in stage utilization as a function of the overall RJI score, he then calculated a series of spline regressions (Darlington, 1990), which predicted each stage utilization on the basis of overall reflective judgment score. The spline regressions for each stage utilization are displayed in Figure 6.2. This figure shows

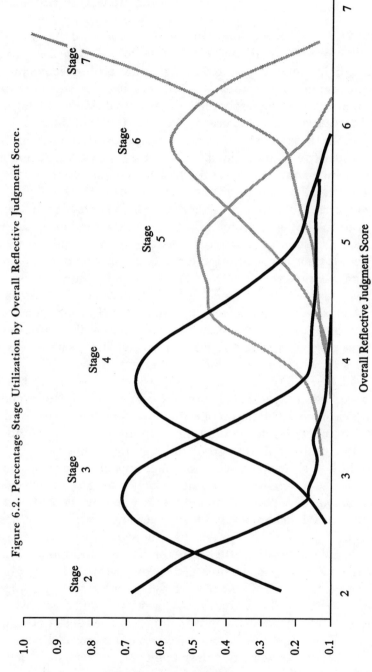

Figure 6.2. Percentage Stage Utilization by Overall Reflective Judgment Score.

that Stage 2 ratings account for about 70 percent of the assigned ratings for individuals whose overall score was Stage 2. By contrast, individuals who scored at higher levels of reflective judgment evidenced reasoning at a wider variety of stages. For example, the line corresponding to an overall score of Stage 3 indicates that, on the average, over two-thirds of the assigned scores for these individuals were at Stage 3, with the remaining scores fairly equally divided between Stages 2 and 4. A similar pattern was found for Stage 4, with the remaining scores being evenly divided between the adjacent stages, or Stages 3 and 5. By contrast, about half the scores for individuals having an overall rating of Stage 5 were at Stage 5, but the remaining scores indicate reasoning characteristic of Stages 3, 4, 6, and 7 as well. Overall, the stage utilization for Stages 5 and 6 cover a wider range of scores than that for Stages 3 and 4. The rather steep curves for the two extreme stages, 2 and 7, may be an artifact of their status as the lowest and highest RJI stages assessed.

The upward progression of overlapping distributions of scores portrayed in Figure 6.2 bears a striking resemblance to Rest's hypothesized graphic presentation of a complex stage model (1979, Figure 6-2.2, p. 66), which he notes depicts "a messier and complicated picture of development" (p. 65). Wood's empirically derived figure offers a more complex picture of the development of concepts of justification than has been described in more traditional cross-group or longitudinal analyses or than would be predicted by a simple stage model of development.

These longitudinal results strongly suggest that the development of reflective thinking as defined by the Reflective Judgment Model unfolds gradually over time, even among those enrolled in educational programs. The sequence of stage usage generally follows the order hypothesized by the model, with higher-stage usage being preceded by lower-stage usage. Regressions appear to be infrequent. Consistent with Figure 6.2, stages are characterized as waves across a mixture of stages, where the peak of a wave is the most commonly used set of assumptions. While there is still an observable pattern to the movement between stages, this developmental movement is better described as the changing shape of the wave rather than as a pattern of uniform steps interspersed with plateaus.

The finding that people commonly use multiple ways of reasoning may give educators a framework for understanding the variability they see within individual students. For example, a student who characteristically approaches problems using Stage 4 assumptions ("all opinions are equally valid as long as they include evidence"; "you can't evaluate opinions") may also surprise an observer with a carefully balanced perspective characteristic of Stage 5 reasoning. As Kroll (1992a) asserts, our educational interventions should be targeted at the leading edge of development, not its central tendency. In other words, educators should teach about and model higher-stage reasoning even when that is not the type of reasoning they may expect students to produce themselves. (This point is elaborated in Chapter Nine.)

Verbatim Examples of Changes over Time. To illustrate the substantive changes in reasoning that the foregoing numbers reflect, we next provide two verbatim examples from the RJI transcripts of participants in this study. As these examples show, changes in reasoning associated with changes in RJI scores do not necessarily reflect a change in the content of a person's basic point of view about an issue (such as whether the Egyptians did or did not build the pyramids or whether news reporting is biased or unbiased). Rather, changes in RJI scores reflect changes in the basis for holding that point of view and the person's assumptions about how she or he could know and understand the topic.

The first example is a response to the creation/evolution problem; it was given by a female high school student who scored at the 76th percentile on a scholastic aptitude test (MSAT). We have included excerpts from her first interview as a high school junior and then from her interview ten years later. (Ratings listed are based on the entire transcript of the problem being discussed, not just the excerpted portions.) This respondent's 1977 rating was dominant Stage 2 and subdominant Stage 3. (As before, *I* represents the interviewer and *R* the respondent.)

I: What do you think about the issue?

R: Like in the Bible, in the beginning God created the earth and everything. I think it's just an idea. How can you describe to people who don't know many things about life? How can you explain to them that they evolved from a lower animal form? You can't. And so I think they tried to put it in a way that they would understand. He (God) thought that was the way they would understand it best. It doesn't really matter how He says it. It is the truth that He is saying. It's not like He's lying or something. It doesn't matter how He says it. It's just that He says it and tries to describe to the people at that time how things came about, in what order, and stuff like that.

I: On what do you base that point of view?

R: A lot of it is our pastor. I used to take a Bible study class with him. There's a lot to it, but I just don't see how people could take such a literal interpretation of the Bible because you just can't take everything literally. Because that's not the way it was meant to be taken.

I: How did you come to hold your point of view?

R: By listening to our pastor and other people and finding mistakes [in the Bible] myself that couldn't always be right.

I: Can you say you know for sure that the literal view presented in the Bible is not correct?

R: Yes, from my science classes and people I've talked to.

I: In this case, can you say that one point of view is right and the other point of view is wrong?

R: I'm tempted to say yes, but I can't because of what people think is truth. I think it's wrong, but you can't tell a great aunt that the Bible is wrong. You just can't say that to them.

I: What does truth mean to you?

R: Truth is like the facts or something like that — what actually took place.

At this point in her life, this young woman held the point of view that the literal creation story was not correct because of what others, such as her pastor, told her. She believed a more literal interpretation of the Bible was wrong but kept her views to herself because of social convention. She held to a concrete view of the truth in her reliance on the "facts." Ten years later, as a college graduate, she offered a different explanation of her views. At this time, her rating was dominant Stage 6, subdominant Stage 7.

I: What do you think about these statements?

R: I tend to stay on the evolution side of it and believe the arguments on evolution as opposed to the creation of the world as it exists today because I think the evidence suggests evolution more than creation. Looking at things like the continental drift, different animals that evolved on different islands, and looking at the fossil records, I have more confidence in that.

I: Can you say you know for sure that we evolved?

R: Yes, I believe I know that for sure, but whether or not we have all of the facts today about evolution, I don't think we do. I think there's always more things being uncovered every day. I don't think we have the full story on it, but I believe that evolution occurred and that it is still occurring.

A decade after her first interview, this young woman continued to hold a similar view about the subject (she still endorsed the evolutionary view), but her rationale for holding it and her understanding of evidence had changed. This time she pointed to a variety of types of evidence she had considered. Further, she was able to reason to a conclusion while also acknowledging that knowledge about evolution grows and changes and that we do not have "the full story on it."

The second example comes from a young man who was also a high school student at the first testing and was responding to the problem about the building of the Egyptian pyramids. He scored at the 86th percentile on a test of scholastic aptitude (MSAT) when in high school. His 1977 rating was dominant Stage 3, subdominant Stage 2.

I: What do you think about this issue?

R: I am a science fiction buff, and I've read books a lot like

Chariot of the Gods, but what they taught us in World History is enough to believe that the Egyptians had all the mathematics and power that they needed to build them. What really proves that point is the way they had their property worked out. Each year the river Nile flows through there. It would flood every year. Well, they would all mark their property off by using special lengths of rope. . . . Everything would be perfect each year because of the perfectionism of their race. Everything worked out exactly. There's no other proof at all of visitors from outer space at that time.

I: Can you know for sure that the Egyptians built the pyramids without help?

R: I cannot. One of the things about me is I can never have a completely closed mind on a subject. So I'll say again that I'm four-fifths sure that they didn't have help, . . . but there's another interesting thing about this: pyramid power. Pyramids have preserving power or something, so maybe there's something more to the pyramids than we think.

I: Can you say that point of view is right and one point of view is wrong?

R: No, I can't because I don't have enough data on it. I don't know for sure; I wasn't living then. There are many different theories you could have about anything, if you don't know anything about it.

   In this excerpt, the young man expressed some awareness that evidence is relevant when solving problems such as this one. Although the evidence he chose was not directly related to the issue, he seemed quite convinced that his "proof" was conclusive. Despite this, he argued that he couldn't know for sure how the pyramids were built because he didn't have enough data. This kind of reasoning (especially the emphasis on the quantity of information without reference to its quality) is typical of individuals whose thinking is in transition between Stages 2 and 3.

   While the content of his point of view had not changed

ten years later, his reasoning was quite different. During this decade, he had graduated from college and had entered a graduate program. By this time, his rating was dominant Stage 7 and subdominant Stage 6.

I: What do you think about these statements?

R: I think the Egyptians did it all on their lonesome, but I would not completely rule out any help. I would like to invoke Occam's Razor here and to say that the most simple theory is generally the true one, as evidenced by the Copernican revolution. And it's just easier for me to believe that the Egyptians did this all by themselves rather than having the highly unlikely event of aliens coming to help them.

I: How did you come to hold that point of view?

R: Again, falling back on Occam's Razor, my general education about how to develop theories and how science has worked has led me to believe that generally the simplest explanation is the true explanation. To extrapolate, the Egyptians were a very sophisticated race as evidenced by the cultural artifacts that they have left in addition to the pyramids. We've also got evidence elsewhere that early civilizations had a very sophisticated means of measuring things like winter and summer solstice — that sort of natural phenomena — as evidenced by Stonehenge. So it seems reasonable to me to expect that the Egyptians could do this one on their own. In addition to their sophistication, they had a large population of slaves. From what little I've read about it in *National Geographic,* they apparently have collected at least some evidence suggesting that it was the sort of human effort which had created the pyramids. On the other hand, there is absolutely no evidence that aliens came to help, no hieroglyphics with UFO saucers and things like that. I would need convincing evidence that in fact that did occur. The circumstantial evidence suggested by people like *Chariots of the Gods* is just not enough.

I: OK. In light of all of that, can you say you know for sure that the Egyptians built the pyramids?

R: No, I cannot because there is no conclusive evidence. . . . I can say that the available evidence points toward the Egyptians building this on their own, so as comparing the two theories, I can say that this one fits the facts better than the other and thus, in relative terms, is more right.

In this excerpt, the respondent still strongly holds his same point of view on the topic but qualifies his assertions in ways that show a change in his assumptions about the certainty with which he holds his beliefs. He also shows how he has synthesized evidence from several sources as the basis for his conclusion and critically evaluates competing perspectives in terms of the quality of the evidence offered. Each of these characteristics is consistent with higher-stage reasoning.

At the end of the same interview, this young man commented on his own developmental processes, noting first that he enjoyed discussing these kinds of issues.

R: I think my education has certainly prepared me to deal with these sorts of issues. It's also given me a set of structured means to go about analyzing a gray area, and I can use that set of evaluation tools in a variety of situations. I think also it's just my natural bent towards liking to discuss stuff. I have friends who have similar bents, and we spend time just choosing sides and really fleshing out an idea.

I: Did you do that in course work as well, or was it more informal?

R: It was more from my friends. Most of my course work was them telling me. You really don't learn discourse in undergrad, and really in the first year of grad school, they're just cranking on you so you don't really learn it there either. But you do learn the tools there, but to use them, it's out in the real world.

This characterization of undergraduate course work, "them telling me," and graduate courses, "they're just cranking on you," is not a flattering portrayal of this man's formal education. How fortunate he was to have (and to have taken advantage of) opportunities to practice using his analytic skills "out in the real world." Rich and diverse opportunities exist on college campuses in both curricular and cocurricular settings for students to be involved in the practical application of their learning, from cooperative education or internship experiences to student organizations and community service projects. This important aspect of a college education may provide a primary incentive for students to grapple with and make difficult choices about issues they define as important. Such conditions for the development of reflective judgment should not be left to chance.

Examination of Gender Differences in the Ten-Year Study

In the last decade, several researchers have proposed new developmental models that include elements they claim are distinctive to or prevalent among women (Baxter Magolda, 1992; Belenky, Clinchy, Goldberger, and Tarule, 1986; Clinchy and Zimmerman, 1982; Gilligan, 1982). In this section, we report the results of our examination of RJI scores by gender in the ten-year study. While these results are by no means conclusive (for example, they vary by the type of analysis and specific subgroups used), they yield some interesting patterns. We begin by examining the results of the three-way (time by group by gender) repeated measures GLM. Gender differences were not found in 1977 or 1979, but a group by gender interaction approached statistical significance in 1983 for those tested all three times. In 1987, when the same three-way GLM was used, the group by gender interaction also approached significance, and a gender main effect ($p < .05$) was obtained, with men scoring higher than women (see Table 6.3 for specific GLM results). (When only the scores of those who participated all four times were used for this analysis, the group by gender interaction and the gender main effect were nonsignificant; see Resource B, Table B6.1.) To better understand these results that suggest different patterns of development for women and for men, we conducted several follow-up analyses.

First, we ran a two-way (group by gender) GLM to see whether this finding could be explained by gender differences on the new problem about the safety of nuclear power. However, both the gender main effect and the group by gender interaction were nonsignificant. We next asked whether men and women had scored differently on any of the four standard RJI problems. Based on a three-way (time by group by gender) repeated measures GLM, no significant gender differences were found for the Egyptian pyramids, news reporting, creation/evolution, or nuclear energy problems. However, for the problem on chemical additives in foods, an inconsistent gender effect was found: among the former high school juniors, men scored about one-third of a stage *lower* than women; among the former college juniors, men scored about half a stage *higher* than women; and among the former doctoral students, the scores were virtually identical. The findings of no difference between the scores of the women and the men on four of the five problems and the inconsistent ordering of scores on the fifth problem offer little support for the hypothesis that the obtained gender differences are attributable to differences on one or more of the four specific problems.

Second, in light of the educational-level differences reported above, we reexamined the data on educational attainment reported in Table 6.2 to see if there were different patterns in educational attainment across gender that might have contributed to these differences. Since the advanced doctoral students had already demonstrated a high level of educational attainment at the time of the first testing, we focused on the former high school and college students. We found that almost half of the men in these two groups (47 percent) had earned postbaccalaureate degrees (M.A., M.D., Ph.D.) by 1987; by contrast, only 15 percent of the women had earned advanced degrees. Since we have already suggested that educational attainment may have a strong influence on reflective judgment, the differences in the educational achievement of the men and women in this sample may have contributed to the gender differences in RJI scores at this time of testing. (Inconsistent patterns of RJI scores by gender have been found in other studies and are reported below.)

Age and Reflective Judgment Level

Another way to examine the development of reflective thinking over time is to examine the relationship between age and RJI scores. To do this, the modal RJI scores of all individuals who had been tested one or more times in the ten-year study were pooled and categorized by their age at the time of testing. For example, all four RJI scores of those participants who were sixteen years old at the time of the first testing and who had participated in all three subsequent testings were entered into these analyses for ages sixteen, eighteen, twenty-two, and twenty-six. By contrast, the score of a participant who was tested only once at age twenty would be entered once under this age category. Ages were then collapsed into five-year intervals. The results of this analysis are shown in Table 6.4.

The modal (or bimodal) reflective judgment stages by age category were as follows: sixteen- to twenty-year-olds, Stage 3; twenty-one- to twenty-five-year-olds, Stage 4; twenty-six- to thirty-year-olds and thirty-one- to thirty-five-year-olds, Stage 5; thirty-six- to forty-year-olds, Stage 6; forty-one-year-olds and

Table 6.4. Ten-Year Study:
Frequency Distribution of RJI Scores by Age.

Age in years[a]	RJI stage scores (%)					
	2	3	4	5	6	7
41 +					50	50
36–40				15	**57**	29
31–35			19	**40**	26	16
26–30			15	**47**	3	35
21–25		17	**51**	17	14	1
16–20	18	**46**	29	6	2	—

*Note: Numbers in bold print indicate the modal Reflective Judgment Model stage(s) for each age category. Some rows total 101 percent due to rounding. Total number of cases = 254.

[a]For ages sixteen to twenty, $n = 55$; for ages twenty-one to twenty-five, $n = 72$; for ages twenty-six to thirty, $n = 60$; for ages thirty-one to thirty-five, $n = 43$; for ages thirty-six to forty, $n = 14$; for ages forty-one and older, $n = 10$.

older, Stages 6 and 7. These findings suggest a strong linear relationship between age and the stage in the Reflective Judgment Model. The modal scores of virtually all of the participants who were tested at age thirty-six or older were at Stage 6 or 7, the stages associated with reflective thinking. Virtually none of the youngest age group and only a handful of those twenty-five and under fell into this category. The emergence of Stage 4 reasoning in these analyses is noteworthy. Recall that the hallmarks of this stage include the acknowledgment of the uncertainty of knowledge, the ability to differentiate between well- and ill-structured problems, and the ability to work with simple abstract concepts (including "evidence" and "knowledge"). These attributes and skills are commonly emphasized in many types of collegiate programs. Stage 4 was the modal score for individuals between the ages of twenty-one and twenty-five, which are the ages at which many traditional-age college students graduate and at which many adult learners are enrolled. Further, recall that virtually all of the former high school group earned an average RJI score of at least 4.0 by the time they were twenty-two years old (in 1983). In other words, by age twenty-two, even those who scored at the earliest stages of the Reflective Judgment Model six years earlier now acknowledged the uncertainty of knowledge and demonstrated their understanding of simple abstract concepts. The progress toward reflective thinking indicated by a shift from Stage 2 to Stage 4 reasoning should not be underestimated: the quasi-reflective reasoning characteristic of Stage 4 is a marked advance over the authority-based, pre-reflective thinking it replaces and lays the foundation for true reflective thinking in later adulthood.

These data suggest that age may be an important factor in the development of reflective thinking. However, the role of age alone should not be overstated on the basis of this study, since members of the sample were actively engaged in a variety of educational pursuits during the decade (that is, this is not a test of simple maturation) and since the sample itself is characterized by a high level of scholastic aptitude and is therefore not representative of adults in general. Whether this progression in scores is due predominantly to age, to education, or to the interaction of the two in this sample remains open to speculation.

Conclusions Drawn

The longitudinal testings of individuals over a decade provided the opportunity to observe long-term changes in their reasoning. In 1977, individuals in each of the three age/educational groups were quite different from their matched counterparts in the other groups. Some of these differences remained intact ten years later (the higher scores of the former doctoral students); others no longer exist (the early differences in RJI scores between the former high school and college students). Over the ten years of the study, most of these individuals were actively involved in earning degrees in higher education, both baccalaureate and postbaccalaureate. To date, no other study of reflective judgment has followed a sample for such an extended period of time; accordingly, no other study has followed a group of high school students through their college years, and no other study has followed advanced doctoral students into middle adulthood. The rich data base that accrued from this study allowed us to begin to answer a variety of questions about the nature of the development of reflective judgment and of the effects of age and education on the ability to think reflectively.

First, however, it should be noted that the sample on which the ten-year study was based is distinctive in several respects. This sample was comprised of white adults from the upper Midwest and was therefore neither geographically nor ethnically representative. While RJI scores from cross-sectional studies (reported later in this chapter) have not been found to differ by region of the country or ethnic background, an unknown bias may be embedded in the homogeneity of this sample. Thus the comparability of this group to other groups is unknown, and the consistently high scores of the doctoral students may reflect not only the demands of doctoral study but a special and unknown characteristic of this particular group of people.

Second, the procedure used to select the high school and

college students (matching them on scholastic aptitude to the graduate students) yielded samples of students at both levels who had unusually high academic aptitude scores. The selection of students who had already shown themselves to be academically successful in 1977 may help account for the high rates of participation in college and postbaccalaureate degree programs until 1987. Nevertheless, in spite of the initial matching, significant differences in reflective judgment levels were found in the three groups. Further, these differences remained over time: the former graduate students started out at a high level and remained there; some of the former college juniors started out at the early or middle stages and progressed to the most advanced stages. The pattern was similar among the former high school students, but for this group, most started out at the early stages and showed evidence of successively higher scores at each time of testing.

The analysis of individual scores over time yielded strong evidence for development in reflective thinking: the observed changes in reasoning over the ten years of this study were clearly consistent with the posited sequence of stages of reasoning outlined in the Reflective Judgment Model. Moreover, the data informed our understanding not only about the nature of the development of reflective thinking among those involved in educational programs but also about the relatively slow pace of its development.

This finding, combined with the observation that individuals evidence reasoning from a variety of stages, serves as a reminder that the ability to think reflectively does not emerge fully formed but develops in a sequential fashion, with earlier stages building on prior stages and laying the foundation for subsequent stages. For example, a student learns to recognize the role of evidence before she composes a compare-and-contrast analysis of two strategies and before she uses the selected strategy to construct a debate-winning argument. Educators have long understood the power of breaking a task into its constituent parts. Since these parts are developmentally ordered as well, educators trying to teach students to think reflectively may want to consider the order in which they ask (or expect) students to put the pieces together. For example, asking students to coordinate a panel discussion so that several points of view on a controversial topic are explained not only presumes that they are aware of (and perhaps appreciate) multiple points of view on the topic but that they understand that people hold different points of view for different reasons. The data presented here suggest that these assumptions should not be taken for granted and, further, that they emerge in a developmentally ordered fashion.

The findings from this study raise new questions about the course and influences of development among college-educated adults. For example, the influence of age, which presumably reflects a range of adult experiences, may have been underestimated in other studies based on shorter retest intervals. While the influence of formal education is consistent with other research (Pascarella and Terenzini, 1991) and may even be gratifying to some college educators, the role of specific collegiate experiences (from participating in debate clubs or departmental honorary societies to taking classes where reflective thinking is an explicit goal to serving in student leadership positions) has not been studied in this regard. Further, the effects of other life experiences (such as changing careers or making decisions about a child's nutritional or medical needs) on reflective thinking are not yet well understood and merit further study.

Other Longitudinal Studies of Reflective Judgment

In this section, we examine the patterns of data found across six other studies in which individuals were tested and then retested after a period of time to see whether their RJI scores had increased, decreased, or stayed the same (Brabeck and Wood, 1990; Polkosnik and Winston, 1989; Sakalys, 1984; Schmidt, 1985; Van Tine, 1990; Welfel and Davison, 1986) plus prior testing of the ten-year sample (King and others, 1983; King, Kitchener, and Wood, 1985; Kitchener, King, Wood, and Davison, 1989). These studies include twelve different samples and a total of 241 individuals, most of whom were tested twice, at intervals of from three or four months to four years.

Table 6.5 provides a descriptive overview of the seven

Table 6.5. Longitudinal Studies of Reflective Judgment.

Sample source	Sample size and educational level at first testing	Age at time 1	Time between testings	RJI scores Time 1 M	SD	Time 2 M	SD	RJ growth over time
Polkosnik and Winston (1989)	16 college students from U. of Georgia	17–23	3 months	3.42	.44	3.44	.49	.02 (ns)
Sakalys (1984)	25 senior female nursing students in a research course at U. of Colorado	25	4 months	3.68	.58	3.87	.61	.19 (ns)
	25 senior female nursing students (control group) from U. of Colorado	25		3.59	.52	3.64	.45	.05 (ns)
	Overall			3.64	.55	3.76	.54	.10[a]
Polkosnik and Winston (1989)	14 college students from U. of Georgia		6 months	3.42	.44	*Time 3* 3.61	.57	.19[b]
Brabeck and Wood (1990)	25 high school females, divided between high- and low-level critical thinkers	18–19	1 year	3.40	.40	3.56	.41	.16[c]
Van Tine (1990)	21 high school freshman from a semirural school district in southern Colorado[d]	14	2 years	2.76	.36	*Time 2* 3.26	.29	.50[e]
King and others (1983)[f]	17 high school juniors from Twin Cities area	18	2 years	2.79	.51	3.61	.46	.82[e]
	27 juniors from U. of Minn.	22		3.75	.72	4.18	.80	.43[e]
	15 advanced doctoral students from U. of Minn.	30		6.03	.63	6.26	.48	.23[e]
Schmidt (1985)	34 traditional-age freshmen from U. of Minn.	18	3 years	3.35	.26	3.56	.29	.20[e]
	11 adult freshmen from U. of Minn.	21		3.47	.39	3.52	.34	.05 (ns)

Study	Sample	N	Years	M	SD	M	SD	Effect
						Time 3		
Welfel and Davison (1986)	13 engineering freshmen from U. of Minn.		Not reported	3.69	.25	4.20	.65	.51[c]
	12 social sciences freshmen from U. of Minn.		4 years	3.56	.31	4.17	.36	.61[c]
	Overall			3.62	.28	4.19	.52	.57[c]
Kitchener, King, Wood, and Davison (1989)[g]	14 high school juniors	18	6 years	2.83	.52	4.99	.82	2.16[a]
	22 college juniors	22		3.72	.72	4.89	.49	1.17[a]
	12 advanced doctoral students	30		6.16	.57	6.27	.39	.12 (ns)
King, Kitchener, and Wood (1990)[h]	10 high school juniors	18	10 years	2.93	.56	5.51	.70	2.58[e]
	17 college juniors	22		3.83	.73	5.14	.66	1.31[c]
	11 advanced doctoral students	30		6.20	.57	6.42	.35	.22[a]

Notes: Data are for seven studies, twelve samples, 241 individuals. The numbers of studies and individuals are based on the first testing only for the Kitchener and King (1981) and the Polkosnik and Winston (1989) samples, even though the samples were retested more than once. Articles are listed in order of length of time between testings.

[a]p < .01.

[b]Polkosnik and Winston (1989) report this as a significant difference (p < .01); however, in an independent analysis of the data reported in Polkosnik (1985), we were unable to replicate the time main effect they report (Wood, 1993a).

[c]p < .05.

[d]Sample originally tested by McKinney (1985).

[e]p < .001.

[f]This is a follow-up study of the original Kitchener and King (1981) sample; the scores include only those of individuals who participated two years later.

[g]This is a follow-up study of the original Kitchener and King (1981) sample; the scores include only those of individuals who participated two, four, and six years later.

[h]This is a follow-up study of the original Kitchener and King (1981) sample; the scores include only those of individuals who participated two, four, six, and ten years later.

longitudinal studies, including sample characteristics of each study, the duration of each study, and how RJI scores changed over time. (This number counts only the first retest of the two samples that were tested more than twice. The four testings of the ten-year study described in the preceding section are counted here as one study but listed separately for each testing to illustrate differences by length of time between testings.) The most noteworthy finding from this group of studies is that *in every sample tested, the scores either stayed the same or increased over time.* Further, with two exceptions, *the mean score increased significantly for all groups tested at one- to four-year intervals.* (The exceptions were the adult college freshmen in Schmidt's [1985] sample and the advanced doctoral students in the Kitchener, King, Wood, and Davison [1989] and the King, Kitchener, and Wood [1990] studies.) These findings offer strong support for the claim that the ability to make reflective judgments changes developmentally over time.

Another noteworthy finding shown in this table is that the amount of change over time appears to be strongly related to the duration of time between testings. For example, the two smallest increases were found in studies of only three or four months' duration (Polkosnik and Winston, 1989; Sakalys, 1984). (Schmidt's [1985] adult freshmen, who were retested after three years with a net gain of .05, are an exception to this pattern.) By contrast, the greatest increase was 2.58 (King, Kitchener, and Wood, 1990), which was found in the ten-year retesting of the group of former high school students discussed earlier in this chapter.

Only the three samples tested over a short period of time showed nonsignificant change. The study of shortest duration in which significant changes were reported was that by Polkosnik and Winston (1989) in their second retest. After six months, they found that the students' scores had increased modestly but significantly over their first-testing scores (a main effect that Wood [1993a] was unable to replicate in an independent analysis of these data). By contrast, studies with at least a year between testings consistently reported significant positive change in RJI mean scores (with the two exceptions noted above).

Although longitudinal data used to validate a developmental model typically focus on increases in functioning over time, "regressions," as indicated by decreases in scores, also provide useful information in understanding changes in intellectual performance over time. Information about the incidence of regressions is reported for several of the studies discussed above (Brabeck and Wood, 1990; King and others, 1983; King, Kitchener, and Wood, 1985; Kitchener, King, Wood, and Davison, 1989; Sakalys, 1984; Schmidt, 1985; Welfel and Davison, 1986). In each of these studies, the proportion of the sample for which the RJI mean score either remained constant or increased ranged from 84 to 100 percent, which is consistent with that found in the ten-year study. The finding that stability rather than development characterized the thinking of some participants at the longitudinal testings suggests that the rate of change across the stages varies across individuals. Of course, the test of this observation would require a study of longer duration, with more than two observations of individuals' reasoning over time.

Because of the short-term duration of Sakalys's study, her data on reversals (Sakalys, 1982) may be used as an estimate of measurement error. In her study, raters were blind to time of testing of the responses being rated; that is, they were unaware of whether a given transcript was from the first or second time of testing. Sakalys reported reversals (downward change of more than .1) in 16 percent of her cases. Since the reported incidence of reversals in all the studies of longer duration occurred less frequently than this and because of the overall low incidence of reversals, observed "regressions" may be considered as measurement errors.

Despite the consistency between these data and the description of intellectual development proposed by the Reflective Judgment Model, alternative explanations that might account for or contribute to increases in reflective judgment scores over time still merit consideration. Since questions regarding both test-retest and internal consistency reliability are addressed in Chapter Five, we focus here on the question of whether the obtained increases in RJI scores over time can be attributed to differences between those who continued their participation in the ten-year longitudinal study and those who were not retested. For example, a person who was keenly aware of reasoning more complexly at the second testing than she was at the first might be more likely to agree to participate in a follow-up interview in order to show her new ways of thinking. By contrast, a person who earned a low RJI score because she did not enjoy explaining or defending her beliefs in detail and found the task too challenging to be enjoyable might be less inclined to continue her participation. Following this logic, any obtained increases in scores might reflect a selection effect on the part of the participants. Several studies have tried to assess whether this selection effect occurred by comparing the scores of participants who dropped out of the study to those of participants who returned for retesting. When such comparisons have been made, the differences between dropouts and ongoing participants were nonsignificant (King and others, 1983; Kitchener, King, Wood, and Davison, 1989; Schmidt, 1983). Another way to approach this question is by looking at the similarity in the patterns of responses between those who participated all four times and those who took part in at least one longitudinal retest. With the few exceptions noted above, these patterns were very similar.

A second alternative explanation is that increases in RJI scores reflect practice or familiarity with the test rather than development in reasoning. It is plausible that those who were interviewed may have given serious thought to one or more of the dilemmas between testings and may even have sought out additional information on the topics, especially if they had already agreed to be retested in the future. To the degree that this happened, taking part in the interview may have indirectly served to stimulate their intellectual development. The only direct evidence of this possibility is reported above from the fourth testing of the sample in ten years. In this study (King, Kitchener, and Wood, 1990), a new problem on the safety of nuclear energy was added to the four standard RJI problems as a test of familiarity. The researchers reasoned that if familiarity with the standard problems accounted for higher scores between testings, then participants would score higher on the standard problems than on the nuclear energy problem. However, no differences were found in participants' scores between problems.

In summary, findings from a number of longitudinal studies offer additional evidence that development in reflective judgment occurs slowly and steadily over time and that the increases in scores are not an artifact of selective participation or practice. Further, these studies show that stability and development are much more common than regression in reflective thinking. Significant increases in RJI scores were reported in all studies of at least a year's duration, predominantly among those involved in collegiate programs. Answers to the questions of whether age or education is the more powerful influence on the ability to make reflective judgments and whether similar growth also occurs among other groups of people will require additional research.

Cross-Sectional Studies of Reflective Judgment

Cross-sectional studies provide an index of levels of reflective thinking across different groups of individuals. We have organized these individuals into ten educational levels that range from early high school to advanced graduate school plus non-student adults. In this section, the results of studies that tested almost fifteen hundred students will be reviewed; these students were from diverse geographical regions of the United States and ranged in age from the teen years to middle adulthood. Data from specific studies are summarized in the text; the interested reader may consult Resource B: Statistical Tables for the findings of each study on which the following summaries are based; there is one table for each major educational level plus one for studies that tested nonstudent adults.

We begin this section with an examination of the RJI scores of high school students, which we then compare with the RJI scores of college students at various levels (such as freshmen and seniors) and with the scores of those who have not only completed college but pursued postbaccalaureate degrees (graduate students). Finally, we contrast the scores of nonstudent adults with the scores from the other groups. Our aim in this section is to provide the reader with a broad overview of how individuals at different age and educational levels think about and resolve ill-structured problems.

Before proceeding with this discussion, we would like to acknowledge that increases in reflective judgment across educational levels should not be attributed solely to the effectiveness of educational institutions; as already noted, age and educational level are frequently confounded in studies that contrast students of different grades or classes. Age brings with it more opportunities for a broad range of life experiences. As students complete more class credits, they also age and face a myriad of life events and personal decisions (such as work experiences, increased family responsibilities, involvement in community organizations, or decisions about health care). Moreover, educational level reflects both a *degree of exposure* to the classes and programs of the institutions and a *degree of success* in mastering the academic demands necessary for advancement to the next educational level. Those who graduate are also the "survivors" of the experience, those who have been successful in negotiating social and institutional systems in support of this goal. Nevertheless, if students at increasingly advanced educational levels do evidence greater skill in reflective thinking, this may also suggest the effectiveness of the educational programs in which the students participated.

Table 6.6 provides a summary of how Reflective Judgment scores differ by educational level. This table was constructed by averaging the RJI mean scores from all available studies* for each educational level to provide a composite view across studies. The mean scores in this table correspond to stages: an RJI mean score of 3.0 indicates that the average stage usage for a given educational level was Stage 3. The table shows that RJI scores increase slowly but steadily from high school to col-

---

*A series of studies on the Reflective Judgment Model used a "modified" version of the RJI (Barone, 1989; Currier, 1989; Liberto, Kelly, Shapiro, and Currier, 1990; Milman, 1988; Montecinos, 1989; Pape and Kelly, 1991). These studies are not reviewed here because they used a nonstandard version of the RJI and/or a nonstandard scoring procedure and did not use trained raters. As a result, it is impossible to interpret their findings or meaningfully compare them to findings from other studies. An additional study by Kitchener and Wood (1987) is not included because the sample consisted of West German university students whose educational levels were not comparable to those of university students in the United States. This study is discussed later in this chapter under cross-culture differences.

Table 6.6. Reflective Judgment Scores by Educational Level.

Educational level	Average RJI score	SD	n
High school			
Grade 9	3.08	.41	57
Grade 10	3.46	.35	15
Grade 11	3.12	.61	33
Grade 12	3.27	.51	67
Average	3.19	.50	172
College (traditional-aged students)			
Freshman	3.63	.53	329
Sophomore	3.57	.43	89
Junior	3.74	.59	159
Senior	3.99	.67	369
Average	3.79	.61	946
College (nontraditional-aged students)			
Freshman	3.57	.42	78
Sophomore	4.30	.59	13
Senior	3.98	.74	46
Average	3.78	.61	137
Graduate			
Master's/Early doctoral	4.62	.81	126
Advanced doctoral	5.27	.89	70
Average	4.76	.85	196

lege and from college to graduate school. Among high school students, the average RJI score is 3.2. Among undergraduate students, the overall score was 3.8 for both traditional-age and adult students. By contrast, the average RJI score among the graduate students, 4.8, was a full stage higher than that for the college students. These scores are graphed in Figure 6.3, which shows the mean score for each level (the middle line) and also the variability within educational level, as reflected by the lines that graph the upper and lower limits of the standard deviation for each educational level. The RJI scores of two-thirds of the samples tested fell within the range of scores indicated by the top and bottom lines on this graph.

It is noteworthy that not only do the mean scores of the samples increase across the educational levels but the amount of variability in responses also increases (indicated in Figure 6.3 by

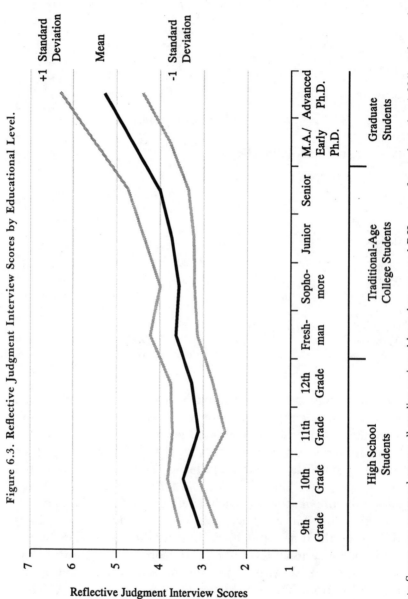

Figure 6.3. Reflective Judgment Interview Scores by Educational Level.

Note: Scores are averaged across all studies reviewed here that reported RJI scores for students ($n = 1,334$) at these educational levels. For specific scores, see Table 6.6.

the wider band of scores at the more advanced levels). This suggests a pattern of mixed success in improving reflective thinking (King and Kitchener, 1993). Although the RJI scores increase, even those who are about to complete a college degree do not consistently evidence reflective thinking. We are not suggesting that these students are not able to think reflectively but that they did not appear to do so in their typical manner of reasoning elicited in the context of the RJI. Further, we acknowledge that higher-level thinking is harder to sustain without ongoing practice and contextual support (Kitchener and Fischer, 1990) and that this factor might also have influenced their scores.

While averaging scores in this manner offers a general picture of the trends in reflective thinking across educational levels, it also masks the variability inherent across samples, even those at the same educational level. While we have aggregated scores within educational level, we recognize that there is a great deal of variability between samples (for example, some control for academic ability and some do not) and that comparisons between educational groups thus constituted should be made cautiously. Nevertheless, our purpose here is to provide a broad view of how students' ability to make reflective judgments differs by educational level, not to provide a specific prediction of students' reasoning based solely on their educational level.

Reflective Thinking Among High School Students

We set the context for an examination of changes in reflective thinking across educational levels by examining the scores of high school students; this group provides relevant information about the levels of reflective thinking that exist prior to the students' enrollment in college. We believe that university faculty and staff need to understand the foundation upon which they have the opportunity to build in teaching students to think reflectively, a foundation that may still be in place during the freshman year of college. Five studies have sampled high school students. (Average RJI mean scores for high school students appear in Resource B, Table B6.3.) About half (five of eleven) of the mean scores for the high school samples were below 3.0. There have been too few studies of tenth and eleventh grade students (one and two, respectively) to be able to draw meaningful conclusions about their reasoning. As a consequence, the fluctuations in scores that appear in Figure 6.3 for tenth and eleventh graders should be interpreted with caution. The mean scores for ninth and twelfth graders are 3.1 and 3.3, respectively, indicating that, on average, high school students tend to hold epistemic assumptions consistent with Stage 3 of the Reflective Judgment Model. Students who hold these assumptions typically maintain that certain truth is ultimately attainable but that in some areas it is not currently available. When faced with uncertainty that they believe is temporary, they are often confused about what to believe. Frequently, they have difficulty relating evidence to their opinion and fall back on a "whimsical" style of reasoning, choosing to simply believe what they want to believe, at least until the truth is known. In other cases, they maintain the belief that authorities have the truth, and they rely on authorities to inform them of what to believe about such dilemmas. (See Chapter Three for a detailed description of reasoning at each stage of the Reflective Judgment Model.)

It should be noted that the scores summarized here are probably not representative of high school students across the United States: of the eleven samples listed in Table B.6.3 in Resource B, seven were from studies that sampled academically talented high school students (Kitchener and King, 1981; Kitchener, Lynch, Fischer, and Wood, 1993;* McKinney, 1985). While such sampling can assist us in comparing high school students with college students by controlling for academic achievement within studies, it may have yielded a pattern of results germane only to academically talented students and not to high school students in general. However, despite the number of studies that attempted to control for the effects of academic ability or achievement, it is noteworthy that the mean score for high

---

*To avoid confusion, the Kitchener, Lynch, Fischer, and Wood (1993) reference will be cited throughout this chapter even though RJI scores are reported there by age rather than by educational level. RJI scores from this study are reported by educational level in Kitchener (1992) and Wood (1993a).

school seniors was almost half a stage lower ($p < .001$) than the mean score for college freshmen. (See Chapter Seven for a discussion of the effects of intellectual ability on reflective judgment.)

Reflective Thinking Among Traditional-Age College Students

Traditional-age college students have been tested in twenty cross-sectional studies ($n = 946$) that have used the standard RJI format and scoring procedure (Bowen, 1989; Brabeck, 1983a; Evans, 1988; Glatfelter, 1982; Kelton and Griffith, 1986; Hayes, 1981; King, J. W., 1986; King and Parker, 1978; King, Taylor, and Ottinger, 1989; King, Wood, and Mines, 1990; Kitchener and King, 1981; Kitchener, Lynch, Fischer, and Wood, 1993; Mines, King, Hood, and Wood, 1990; Nickerson, 1991; Polkosnik, 1985; Sakalys, 1984; Schmidt, 1985; Shoff, 1979; Strange and King, 1981; and Welfel, 1982b). Counting the RJI scores reported for each subsample tested within each study yielded a total of forty-four samples. (These are listed by RJI score in Resource B, Table B6.4.)

Most studies of traditional-age college students that used the RJI have tested freshmen and seniors (twelve and twenty samples, respectively); fewer have tested sophomores (five samples) and juniors (seven samples). In general, the freshman students in these samples evidenced the use of assumptions of Stages 3 and 4 of the Reflective Judgment Model. Both the overall mean score and the median score across all freshman samples ($n = 329$) were 3.6. Only one sample averaged 4.0 or above, and this was a sample of academically talented students (Kitchener, Lynch, Fischer, and Wood, 1993). The means of the remaining samples of freshmen clustered between 3.2 (the lowest score) and 3.5 and between 3.7 and 3.9. The prevalence of Stage 3 reasoning means that like the high school students, many of the college freshmen articulated the belief that absolute truth is only temporarily inaccessible, that knowing is limited to one's personal impressions about the topic (uninformed by evidence), and that most if not all problems are well structured (defined with a high degree of certainty and completeness). However, as is apparent in Figure 6.3, two-thirds of the freshmen reasoned between Stages 3 and 4, suggesting that other freshmen were beginning to accept the concept that uncertainty may be an ongoing characteristic of the knowing process. Consequently, they are beginning to accept the idea that some problems are truly ill structured.

The overall mean score for the college sophomore samples was 3.6 ($n = 89$), the same overall mean as that found for the freshmen. The overall mean score for the juniors ($n = 159$) was slightly higher, 3.7. The highest average mean score among the college student samples was that of the seniors ($n = 369$), 4.0, which is significantly ($p < .001$) higher than the freshman average, by about half a stage. By contrast with the freshman samples, all the senior samples had an RJI mean score of over 3.5, and half had a mean score of 4.0 or higher. In other words, Stage 4 reasoning was used by all the senior samples. The range of scores for the seniors was more variable than that of any other class level—from a low of 3.6 (Glatfelter, 1982) among seniors at a state university in the West to a high of 5.0 (Kelton and Griffith, 1986) among seniors enrolled in a highly selective liberal arts college in the Southeast.

A difference of half a stage between the averaged scores of college freshmen and seniors may not suggest a dramatic metamorphosis in thinking. However, while the numerical difference is small, the development in reasoning that it reflects is nevertheless noteworthy. The Stage 4 reasoning prevalent among the senior samples is clearly more adequate and defensible than the reasoning it replaced. Recall that at Stage 4 comes the acknowledgment that uncertainty is not just a temporary condition of knowing. It is at this stage, too, that students begin to use evidence systematically to support their judgment, a development of no small consequence. As Barry Kroll (1992b) has described this type of development, students are abandoning "ignorant certainty" (characteristic of earlier stage reasoning) in favor of "intelligent confusion." While promoting students' confusion is not a goal typically published in college mission statements, Kroll's observation serves to remind us that intelligent confusion is a developmental advance over ignorant, dogmatic certainty and that it paves the way for more thoughtful, reasoned judgments that may follow. In this sense, then, the development from Stage 3 to Stage 4 reasoning can be hailed as an important step in the process of learning to make reflective judgments.

Nevertheless, the prevalence of Stage 4 reasoning (most apparent among the senior samples) also indicates that many college students are at a loss when asked to defend their answers to ill-structured problems, for Stage 4 has as a major characteristic the assumption that, because there are many possible answers to every question and no absolutely certain way to adjudicate between competing answers, knowledge claims are simply idiosyncratic to the individual. In other words, an answer to an ill-structured problem is seen as merely an opinion. Further, many college students are not demonstrating an ability to articulate the role of evidence in making interpretations (Stage 5) or to defensibly critique their own judgments or explanations as being in some way better than or preferable to alternative explanations (Stage 7), which is a hallmark of reflective thinking. So while college educators can take solace in the observation that upward movement toward being able to make reflective judgments is identifiable across educational levels during the college years, college seniors do not typically articulate concepts that underlie reflective thinking. However, as noted in Chapter Five, Kitchener, Lynch, Fischer, and Wood (1993) found that under certain circumstances, college seniors can demonstrate an understanding of Stage 6 reasoning. Kroll (1992b) also presents convincing evidence that college freshmen can learn to think reflectively in college classes that are structured to stimulate questioning and in which they are expected and encouraged to make thoughtful, reasoned judgments.

The King, Taylor, and Ottinger (1993) study is noteworthy because it also examined the relationship between RJI scores and students' academic standing and graduation status five years later (these data are reported in King, Taylor, and Ottinger, 1993). The sample for this study consisted of 146 African-American students; five years after these students took the RJI, their GPA and graduation status were examined. By means of a stepwise multiple regression procedure, RJI scores were found to predict students' college GPA ($p < .001$). Further, those who had graduated scored significantly higher on the RJI than those who were on academic warning, were suspended, had been dismissed, or had withdrawn from the university.

In light of this body of research on the reflective judgment of college students, it may be helpful to reexamine the educational proposals that currently serve as the foundation for collegiate educational reform. For example, the following observation was made in a major report on curricular reform in higher education: "By attending to the knowledge claims of the major over time and by treating increasingly complex matters from multiple points of view, students discover that nothing is self-evident, that nothing is simply 'there,' that questions and answers are chosen and created—not given—and that they always are framed by context; for that reason, they always are contingent" (Association of American Colleges, 1991, p. 13). This document, *The Challenge of Connecting Learning,* persuasively and eloquently presents a vision of the kind of reasoning that should be associated with the goals of undergraduate liberal education and certainly with the completion of a baccalaureate degree. Underlying it are the assumptions that answers are contingent and knowledge is contextual. These assumptions reflect Reflective Judgment Stage 5 reasoning, which, as shown above, is a full stage above the average RJI score of college seniors.

A second example from the same document illustrates a related discrepancy between educational goals and many students' reasoning: "Students cannot be allowed to be content with the notion that issues may be addressed by any number of equally valid formulations among which they cannot choose. They must learn to discriminate by arguing, and they must realize that arguments exist for the purpose of clarifying and making choices" (Association of American Colleges, 1991, p. 14). In this example, the skills associated with learning to discriminate the valid from the invalid (or less valid) formulations are associated with the upper stages of the Reflective Judgment Model (Stages 6 and 7), as is the ability to make discriminating arguments. And while some college students show an appreciation or understanding of the necessity of making informed, thoughtful choices about ill-structured problems, most college students do not typically evidence high-level reflective thinking. As King

(1992a, p. 8) notes: "Teachers who attempt to teach about this process . . . without attending to students' underlying epistemic assumptions will probably be very frustrated, and their students will probably be dissatisfied as well." Educators who understand their students' epistemic assumptions will be able to make more informed decisions when choosing assignments or activities designed to help students learn about, practice, and improve their reflective thinking skills.

Dings (1989) studied faculty members' perceptions of the epistemic assumptions of college freshmen and seniors (described by the Reflective Judgment Model) and their evaluation of their own assumptions. He found that faculty members considered Stage 2 reasoning to be most descriptive of freshman students, Stage 6 reasoning to be most descriptive of senior students, and Stage 7 to describe their own reasoning. These findings suggest that faculty members are underestimating the cognitive complexity of freshmen and may be overestimating the cognitive skills of seniors. Dings's study raises questions about how educators arrive at assumptions about students' reasoning skills, how they translate these assumptions and expectations about student reasoning skills into assignments and grading criteria, how students understand these expectations, and whether and how discrepancies between educators' assumptions and students' skills are addressed. It also raises the question of the degree of variability teachers expect to see in students' responses. For example, Lynch (1989) found that in using a recognition task, college students could understand information about a stage above where they could produce a response on the RJI. Whether discrepancies such as those found by Dings result in frustration and low performance or whether they serve to challenge students to operate closer to their optimal level remains to be seen. Studies conducted to date have not addressed this question; we encourage further research in this area.

Reflective Thinking Among
Nontraditional-Age College Students

A discussion of differences in reflective thinking across the college years must also take into account the prevalence of adult learners on college campuses, who are now approaching a majority (U.S. Department of Education, 1991). With this demographic change, a correspondence between age and class level can no longer be assumed. RJI mean scores have been reported for five studies that tested nontraditional-age students (Glatfelter, 1982; King, J. W., 1986; Schmidt, 1985; Shoff, 1979; Strange and King, 1981). These are listed in Resource B, Table B6.5. In these studies, a total of 137 adult learners were tested. Such studies are important in informing the question of whether educational level or age has a more potent influence on the development of reflective judgment. Among college students, this question is of particular interest since adult learners have been found to differ from traditional-age college students on such dimensions as learning style, motivation for attending college, and assertiveness (Apps, 1981; Brookfield, 1987; King and Bauer, 1988; Knowles, 1984; Mezirow and Associates 1990). The studies described here examined whether differences in reflective thinking exist as well.

The scores for the freshman adult learners ranged from 3.3, earned by a sample of entering continuing education students whose mean age was twenty-three years (Shoff, 1979), to 3.8, earned by a sample of twenty-two-year-old students (Strange and King, 1981). By contrast, the lowest mean for a sample of college senior adult learners (all over twenty-five years old) was 3.7 (Glatfelter, 1982), which is very close to the highest score for any freshman sample among the nontraditional samples. The highest RJI mean score for an adult college senior sample was 4.4 (Strange and King, 1981), earned by a group of twenty-six-year-old seniors. Adult college seniors scored significantly higher than adult freshmen ($p < .001$).

In contrast to the differences found on other educationally relevant dimensions, adult students do not appear to be dramatically different from their younger counterparts in terms of their reflective thinking. The mean scores by class are remarkably similar to those of traditional-age students at the same class level: the overall mean score for both adult and traditional-age freshmen was 3.6; the overall mean score for both adult and traditional-age seniors was 4.0. However, the range of scores for the adult seniors was narrower (3.74 to 4.41) than that for the traditional-age seniors (3.56 to 5.02). The single small sample of sophomore adult learners scored higher than traditional-age sophomores (4.3 and 3.6, respectively).

Any interpretation of these findings about the reflective thinking of adult learners must take into account the variability in definitions of adult learner that have been used, reflecting a range of age-based criteria. Second, since many adult learners are enrolled part-time, readers are reminded that being a senior reflects a wide range of years of enrollment for many adult learners. Third, there is a much smaller body of research on the reflective thinking of adult learners ($n = 137$ students) compared with that of traditional-age students ($n = 966$ students). These caveats make for more cautious interpretations.

These studies suggest that adult students also hold assumptions about knowledge that limit their ability to make judgments on the basis of critical analysis (at least as measured by the RJI). As discussed at the beginning of this chapter, age alone is not predictive of the ability to think reflectively. But for students who have delayed their pursuit of a college degree, age may be strongly related to other relevant factors, such as readiness to learn or openness to being challenged or to entertaining divergent views, and these students may experience a developmental spurt during college as a result of this combination of factors. The data provide additional support for the argument that attending college plays an important role in the development of reflective thinking, and we encourage further research to help sort out and better understand the relationships between the attitudinal, readiness, and cognitive ability factors so that adult learners can be better served by college faculty and staff in pursuit of this goal.

Reflective Thinking Among Graduate Students

Graduate students have consistently earned the highest RJI scores of any students tested: their assumptions about knowledge and knowing are more consistent with the upper stages of the Reflective Judgment Model. Seven studies have used the

RJI to test a total of 196 graduate students (Brabeck, 1983a; King, Wood, and Mines, 1990; Kitchener and King, 1981; Kitchener, Lynch, Fischer, and Wood, 1993; Kitchener and Wood, 1987; Lawson, 1980; and Mines, King, Hood, and Wood, 1990). Their scores are listed in Resource B, Table B6.6. These studies included both graduate students who were working on a master's degree or were early in their doctoral studies (up to two years) and those who were at an advanced level of doctoral study (more than two years); they have been classified accordingly. (More precise classifications were not possible because of the general way in which several samples were described—for example, as "graduate students." Where graduate samples were not identified by specific degrees, categorizations were based on other indicators of degree completion, such as the number of credits earned or other relevant descriptors.)

The age/educational effect is again apparent for this sample: the early-level graduate students used epistemic assumptions consistent with Stages 4 and 5, and the advanced-level graduate students used assumptions consistent with Stages 5 and 6. Overall, advanced doctoral students scored almost three-quarters of a stage higher ($M = 5.3$) than did graduate students earlier in their programs ($M = 4.6$). It is important to note that students enrolled in graduate programs were the first to consistently demonstrate the use of Stage 5 assumptions on the RJI. Further, only at the advanced doctoral level was there evidence of the consistent use of Stage 6 assumptions on the RJI.

In general, the graduate students evidenced the ability to offer a balanced perspective on a controversial issue, such as understanding why different people might approach a given problem from different perspectives and how that would lead them to focus on different types of evidence. Moreover, at the advanced doctoral level, they evidenced the ability to explain how they arrived at a judgment about an issue, a judgment they defended as more reasonable or more plausible than other alternatives or as the best interpretation of the available evidence. In short, they more consistently demonstrated the ability to make truly reflective judgments.

The attainment of this goal may reflect a variety of factors. For example, graduate admissions committees may select students who have already demonstrated advanced reflective thinking skills. By contrast, the higher scores of the doctoral students could be attributed to the intellectual demands of graduate study, from course assignments to research projects. It may not be coincidental that students who scored at the advanced levels, predominantly doctoral students, were enrolled in educational programs that require the writing of a dissertation. This undertaking frequently demands a careful analysis of an issue that acknowledges competing perspectives, followed by the creative synthesis of ideas and the requirement of taking the responsibility for explaining one's own point of view and defending it in light of competing alternatives.

One study found disciplinary differences in reasoning about ill-structured problems: King, Wood, and Mines (1990) found that graduate students in social science disciplines scored significantly higher on the RJI than did their counterparts who were enrolled in mathematical sciences, a difference that remained significant even when GRE scores were partialed out. These authors suggest that this difference may be a function of the emphasis (or lack thereof) given to ill-structured problems within each discipline. Little is currently known about the specific demands of graduate study that contribute to (or hinder) students' abilities to make reflective judgments. Given the multitude of ill-structured problems that professionals face today and the need to make defensible, reasoned choices about these issues, we encourage more research into ways in which graduate study can be structured to better prepare students to make such judgments.

Reflective Thinking Among Nonstudent Adults

While the preponderance of the research on reflective judgment has focused on students at various educational levels, six studies have examined how adults who are not formally enrolled in educational programs reason about ill-structured problems (Glatfelter, 1982; Glenn and Eklund, 1991; Josephson, 1988; Kelton and Griffith, 1986; J. W. King, 1986; Lawson, 1980). In most cases, the nonstudent adult samples were included as comparison groups with samples of college students, especially adult students; this design provides a control for age when studying educational effects. Eight samples of nonstudent adults have been tested to date ($n = 191$); means are listed in Resource B, Table B6.7. Comparing the RJI scores of those samples in which participants had and had not earned college degrees yielded a very distinct pattern in which those without college degrees consistently scored lower. Further, there was no overlap in the range of mean scores between the samples with and without college degrees: the mean scores for the samples without college degrees ranged from 3.5 to 3.7; the mean scores for the samples with college degrees ranged from 4.0 to 5.2. Even the sample of adults who had been enrolled in a collegiate program but then dropped out of college (Glatfelter, 1982, classified here under those without college degrees) fit this pattern. The two highest mean scores in this group were earned by samples with postbaccalaureate degrees (Glenn and Eklund, 1991; Josephson, 1988).

The strongest contrast between college-educated and non college-educated adults is provided in the Glenn and Eklund (1991) study. These researchers administered the RJI to two groups of participants who were at least sixty-five years old (thus controlling for age) but who differed in terms of their educational attainment. The first group consisted of adults with up to a high school education; their RJI mean score was 3.7, which is about half a stage higher than the overall mean score among high school seniors (3.3) and closer to the average for the college samples (3.8). The second group consisted of retired faculty members with doctorates; the RJI mean score for this group was 5.2, which is comparable to the scores earned by advanced graduate students.

How do various types of life experiences affect reflective thinking? Several provocative findings on the effects of given life experiences on moral development may inform our understanding of the life experiences that affect reflective thinking. In summarizing this research on moral development, Rest (1986, p. 57) notes: "The people who develop in moral judgment are those who love to learn, who seek new challenges, who enjoy intellectually stimulating environments, who are reflective, who make plans and set goals, who take risks, who see themselves in the large social contexts of history and institutions and broad cultural trends, who take responsibility for themselves and their environs." It seems reasonable to assume that the same is true for people who develop in their ability to make reflective judgments.

Research on Gender Differences in Reflective Judgment

Do women and men use comparable sets of assumptions about knowledge when resolving ill-structured problems? This question has frequently been raised in light of the prevalence of models or theories of development that have been derived exclusively or predominantly from male samples (Chickering, 1969; Erikson, 1963; Kohlberg, 1969, 1984; Levinson, 1978; Perry, 1970). The underlying concern here is that such models may not offer accurate or adequate descriptions of the development of women and that research based on these models is inherently biased. Two recent developmental models that address gender-related differences in cognitive development are those of Baxter Magolda (1992) and Belenky, Clinchy, Goldberger, and Tarule (1986). (For analyses of persisting beliefs regarding gender differences in moral development, see Brabeck, 1983b, and Mednick, 1989.) Even though the Reflective Judgment Model was derived from interviews with equal numbers of women and men, questions of gender differences continue to be raised. Most of the studies reviewed in this chapter included both women and men and are used as the basis for our discussion of gender differences in reflective judgment. Studies that tested all-female samples (Brabeck, 1983a; Brabeck and Wood, 1990; Glatfelter, 1982; Hayes, 1981; J. W. King, 1986; Josephson, 1988; Nickerson, 1991; Sakalys, 1984) are not included in this discussion.

In addition to the longitudinal studies based on the original Kitchener and King (1981) study, seventeen other studies that used the RJI included both male and female participants (Bowen, 1989; Evans, 1988; Glenn and Eklund, 1991; Kelton and Griffith, 1986; King, Taylor, and Ottinger, 1993; King,

Wood, and Mines, 1990; Kitchener and Wood, 1987; Kitchener, Lynch, Fischer, and Wood, 1993; Lawson, 1980; McKinney, 1985; Polkosnik and Winston, 1989; Schmidt, 1985; Shoff, 1979; Strange and King, 1981; Van Tine, 1990; Welfel, 1982b; Welfel and Davison, 1986). Four of these were longitudinal retest samples. Of the seventeen studies, three (Evans, 1988; Kelton and Griffith, 1986; Polkosnik and Winston, 1989) did not report whether gender differences were obtained. Of the remaining fourteen studies, seven reported finding no differences by gender.

Of the seven studies that found gender differences, six reported that males scored higher than females (King, Wood, and Mines, 1990; Kitchener and Wood, 1987; Kitchener, Lynch, Fischer and Wood, 1993; Lawson, 1980; Shoff, 1979; Strange and King, 1981). The remaining study (Schmidt, 1985) reported no overall gender main effects but a class by gender interaction: female traditional-age juniors and nontraditional-age freshmen (but not traditional-age freshmen) scored higher than their male counterparts.

The class by gender interactions found by Schmidt (1985) and in our six-year and ten-year follow-up studies suggest that men and women may develop at different rates and that the rates may differ between cohorts of men and women. Wood (1993b) explored whether differential patterns of growth and change exist in the data reported by Kitchener, Lynch, Fischer, and Wood (1993). He found systematic differences in growth spurts between males and females, with males showing more evidence for spurts and sustained growth during the college and graduate student years, while females showed more evidence of dramatic growth in their late teens (eighteen to nineteen) and more moderate increases thereafter. These data suggest that there may be differences in the timing of developmental changes in men and in women. We encourage more research on this possibility.

Baxter Magolda (1992) offers a different perspective on the question of gender differences in intellectual development. This perspective is based on extensive interview data she collected from a cohort of college students over a five-year period. She claims that while there is little evidence for gender-based structural differences in reasoning, gender-related differences do exist *within* epistemological structures. Since the RJI was not designed to elicit such information and since the data reported here have not been scored for this purpose, it cannot be said whether such differences might also exist in the context of the Reflective Judgment Model.

We also offer a word of caution about interpreting these findings because of differences in sampling and in the treatment of related variables. First, the criteria for sample selection varied widely across studies (including high school students matched on academic aptitude to a sample of graduate students, as well as samples of college students selected at random). Second, some reported results accounted for the effects of such factors as academic aptitude while others did not. (For a discussion of the necessary but not sufficient relationship between aptitude and reflective judgment, see Chapter Seven.) It is important to remember that these samples vary on a wide range of variables beyond gender and are not always comparable. Therefore, whether the reported gender differences described above result from differences in factors such as ability, rates of maturation, the timing of developmental spurts, or differential opportunities for involvement in intellectually stimulating environments remains to be seen.

Research on Cross-Cultural Differences in Reflective Judgment

Are the epistemic assumptions and concepts of justification found in samples from the United States unique to this culture, or are they also found in samples from other countries? Only one study has used the RJI to investigate this question with a certified interviewer and certified raters. Kitchener and Wood (1987) tested a sample of forty-eight college students divided evenly between men and women from a traditional German university. (The university is located in what was West Germany.) One-third of the participants were beginning students; one-third were advanced students completing work for the master-diplom or diplom ingenieur degree; and the remainder were doctoral students. The participants' mean ages were twenty, twenty-five, and twenty-nine and a half, respectively. All participants took the German Reflective Judgment Interview (GRJI) as well as the analogies portion of the Intelligenz Struktur Test (IST), which is a measure of verbal ability (Amthauer, 1955). The GRJI was identical to the RJI with two exceptions: it was translated into German, and the creation/evolution problem was omitted since in a pilot study using German participants, this problem did not have salience for the sample. A new problem on the safety of nuclear energy was written for use in this study.

Interrater reliability was .83, and interrater agreement ranged from .79 to 1.00 when calculated separately for each problem; these are comparable to figures for samples from the United States. Similarly, the response patterns of German students conformed to those predicted by the sequential ordering of the Reflective Judgment Model when evaluated by Davison's (1979) test for sequentiality. An educational level by gender ANOVA revealed significant main effects for education: the doctoral students scored significantly higher on the GRJI (5.3) than the two younger groups (4.7) and (4.6). A main effect for gender was also obtained, perhaps reflecting the fact that the men were older than the women, having completed their compulsory military service prior to enrollment. The educational level effect, but not the gender effect, remained significant after covarying out IST scores. While German university students as a group are different in many respects from U.S. students (notably selectivity), the GRJI scores of the doctoral students are comparable to RJI scores of U.S. samples. The scores of the entering and diplom students were higher than those typical of undergraduate samples in the United States but similar to those earned by U.S. postbaccalaureate students.

Although Germany and the United States are both highly industrialized societies, academic socialization differs in the two countries. This was particularly true in the mid-1980s, when the data for this study were collected. If the stages of the Reflective Judgment Model were found to reflect only the influence of academic socialization in the United States (which was not the case here), other concepts of justification and assertions about knowledge or perhaps a different developmental sequence would have been identified in the German sample. This study provides preliminary support for the cross-national applicability of the Reflective Judgment Model. We encourage more research on this topic.

Overview of Research Findings

This chapter has summarized the findings of thirty-three studies of more than seventeen hundred individuals who have taken the RJI. These findings can be used as the basis for answering the six major questions posed at the beginning of the chapter: (1) Does reflective judgment develop between late adolescence and middle adulthood? (2) How do high school, college, and graduate students reason about ill-structured problems? (3) Does students' reasoning improve with additional exposure to and involvement in higher education? (4) Do adult learners differ from traditional-age students in their reflective thinking? (5) How does the reasoning of adults who have not participated in higher education compare to the reasoning of those who have earned a college degree? (6) Are there gender or cross-cultural differences in the development of reflective thinking?

The first of these questions is particularly important because data on changes in reflective thinking over time test the developmental assumptions of the Reflective Judgment Model and are necessary for its validation. Documenting change over time requires longitudinal data on individuals who are tested and retested over time. Although longitudinal data are scarce to nonexistent for most models of adult cognitive development (Brabeck, 1984), for the Reflective Judgment Model, longitudinal data have been collected from 241 individuals in nine studies.

Ten-Year Longitudinal Study of the Development of Reflective Judgment

The ten-year longitudinal study of the development of reflective thinking is not only the study of longest duration but included the most testings (four) and the largest sample size (eighty at the first testing and fifty-three at the fourth testing ten years later). In 1977 (the year of the first testing), the participants in this study were from three educational levels: high school juniors, college juniors, and advanced doctoral students. The students in the younger two groups were matched by gender and academic aptitude to the graduate sample. (This procedure yielded a sample with rather distinctive characteristics.) All were invited to continue their participation in the study again in 1979, 1983, and 1987.

RJI scores differed by group in 1977, with the more advanced students earning successively higher scores. The rate and amount of change over time were found to differ by group: while the scores of the former doctoral students remained relatively stable (at Stages 6 and 7), the scores of the other two groups increased steadily over time. The scores of the former high school students showed the most growth over the decade, about two and one-half stages, from 2.9 to 5.5; the scores of their former college counterparts increased by about a stage, from 3.8 to 5.1. By using a new interview problem in 1987, we determined that these changes were not attributable to familiarity with the standard RJI problems.

Because grouped data mask changes in individual scores, individual mean and modal scores are also reported. The RJI scores of fully 92 percent of the longitudinal sample increased between 1977 and 1987; for over two-thirds of the sample, scores increased or remained stable between each testing interval. The sequence of stage usage generally was found to follow the order hypothesized by the model, with higher-stage usage following lower-stage usage. Few regressions were observed. Individual scores also indicated that most of the participants used reasoning that is characteristic of more than one stage in the Reflective Judgment Model at any given time (see Figure 6.2), with Stages 5 and 6 being the most variable. Individual changes over time are also depicted in verbatim examples from the ten-year longitudinal study. Each transcript illustrates development along at least one dimension of reasoning described by the Reflective Judgment Model.

In the 1987 testing (but not in prior testings), men scored higher than women. In examining the educational attainment of these individuals (excluding those who were already enrolled in doctoral programs in 1977), we found that almost 50 percent of the men but only 15 percent of the women had earned postbaccalaureate degrees. Since graduate programs often require students to make independent judgments grounded in the knowledge base of a discipline, this gender difference may be attributable to the men's higher level of participation in educational programs in which higher-stage reasoning is an explicit goal, in which higher-stage reasoning is taught, or in which students are given feedback on their progress. The larger educational issues raised by this finding, including the effectiveness of graduate programs in teaching students to think reflectively, clearly merit additional research.

Other Longitudinal Studies of Reflective Judgment

The patterns of scores from seven other longitudinal studies in which 241 individuals were tested over time have also been examined. In every sample tested, the scores either stayed the same or increased over time. Further, the amount of change over time was strongly related to the duration of time between testings: the longer the duration, the more growth between testings. These studies provide additional evidence that development in reflective thinking occurs steadily and slowly over time, following the sequence described in the Reflective Judgment Model.

Cross-Sectional Studies of Reflective Judgment

The results from twenty-five cross-sectional studies in which more than fifteen hundred students took the RJI have also been summarized. The students ranged in age from the teen years to middle adulthood and were from diverse geographical regions of the United States. The subsamples within studies have been grouped into ten educational levels that range from early high school to advanced graduate school plus nonstudent adults. Our purpose here is to provide a broad view of how students' ability to make reflective judgments differs by educational level, not to provide a specific prediction of students' reasoning based solely on their educational level. Because of the variability in sampling procedures across studies (for example, some controlled for academic ability and some did not), differences between educational groups should be interpreted cautiously.

The findings from these studies suggest that RJI scores increase slowly but steadily from high school ($M = 3.2$) to college ($M = 3.8$) to graduate school ($M = 4.8$). Among nonstudent adults, the average RJI score for those without a college degree was 3.6; for those with a college degree, the mean RJI score was 4.3. The high school students consistently evidenced the assumptions of the pre-reflective stages of the Reflective Judgment Model — for example, making decisions on the basis of what they "wanted to believe" or "what felt right" or defending beliefs as personal opinions that are not subject to evaluation. Since these assumptions may still be in place at the time of a student's enrollment in college, faculty and staff may also hear such statements. Although such thinking is antithetical to true reflective thinking, we encourage all educators to recognize that these assumptions ring true to some students as a framework for understanding and resolving ill-structured problems and that educators should not assume that these students are aware of the limitations of this framework.

Twenty studies tested a total of 966 traditional-age college students. In general, the freshmen in these samples evidenced the use of Stage 3 and Stage 4 assumptions of the Reflective Judgment Model ($M = 3.6$). The mean RJI score for the seniors was higher ($M = 4.0$), and their scores were more variable. Although the numerical difference between the averaged scores of freshmen and seniors is not large (about half a stage), the qualitative difference in reasoning it reflects is noteworthy. The Stage 4 reasoning prevalent among the senior samples was clearly more adequate and defensible than the Stage 3 reasoning it replaced: with Stage 4 reasoning comes the acknowledgment that uncertainty is not just a temporary condition germane only to a select set of problems but that it is an ongoing characteristic of the knowing process. It is also at this stage that indi-

viduals begin to understand the role of evidence in making judgments. While some educators may see this as so basic that it
need not even be mentioned, the role of evidence (or what constitutes evidence) is not well understood or self-evident to many
college students. While students are beginning to understand
that evidence can be used as a tool in building arguments, they
are also beginning to understand that the relationship between
evidence and judgment is sometimes a complicated one, such
as when the same evidence can be used to build conflicting arguments; this often leaves them feeling confused. Barry Kroll
(1992b) has described this type of development as the abandon-
ment of "ignorant certainty" (the dogmatic approach that is characteristic of earlier stage reasoning) in favor of "intelligent confusion." Kroll's observation should remind educators that the
intelligent confusion students express should not be dismissed
out of hand as merely confused thinking. The questions that
the confusion generates show that students are acknowledging
the complexity of an issue; this acknowledgment paves the way
for more thoughtful, reasoned judgments. In this sense, the development from Stage 3 to Stage 4 reasoning across the college
years should be understood as an important step in the process
of learning to make reflective judgments. Nevertheless, although
the scores of the undergraduate students showed progress toward
the goal of learning to think reflectively, they did not show the
achievement of this goal, as indicated by the prevalence of quasi-
reflective reasoning among the college seniors.

Adult learners in five studies (a total of 137 students) have
taken the RJI; these studies help us understand the relative effects
of educational level and age on the development of reflective
judgment. Contrary to studies that have alerted educators to
differences between traditional- and nontraditional-age students,
these studies revealed that the adult students in the samples were
not dramatically different from their younger counterparts in
terms of their reflective thinking. In fact, despite the variability in the operational definitions of the adult samples, the mean
scores by class were remarkably similar to those of traditional-
age students at the same class level. Again, among the adult
learners, the seniors scored higher than the freshmen, providing

additional support for the positive influence of higher education on reflective thinking. While age alone does not predict
reflective thinking ability, it may be strongly related to other
relevant factors (readiness to learn, openness to being challenged,
prior experience entertaining divergent views); these factors may
help explain the perceived developmental spurt many adult
learners report during college. However, these studies also show
that adult students, too, hold assumptions about knowledge that
limit their ability to make judgments on the basis of critical analysis; their style of reasoning is best characterized as quasi-
reflective. Only samples of advanced graduate students have consistently yielded evidence of reasoning at Stage 5 or above.

A total of 196 graduate students have taken the RJI; their
average RJI score ($M = 4.8$), was a full stage higher than that
of the undergraduate students. Further, early-level graduate students (master's degree students or those who were in the first
two years of doctoral study) used epistemic assumptions consistent with Stages 4 and 5, while advanced-level graduate students (those with more than two years of doctoral study) used
assumptions consistent with Stages 5 and 6. In their interviews,
graduate students tended to offer a balanced perspective on a
controversial issue, explaining why different people might approach a given problem from different perspectives and how that
leads them to focus on different types of evidence. At the advanced doctoral level, students tended to defend their judgments
as more reasonable or more plausible than other alternatives
or as the best interpretation of the available evidence. They also
typically explained how they arrived at their judgment, with
explicit reference to how they sorted and weighed the evidence
in support of this judgment. Such reasoning demonstrates the
ability to make truly reflective judgments. Whether these findings
are a reflection of graduate school selection criteria, the intellectual demands of graduate study, more individualized mentor-
ing, or unknown maturational factors is unclear. What is clear
is that professionals in all fields face a multitude of ill-structured
problems about which they are expected to make defensible, reasoned choices and that graduate programs have the responsibility to help students learn to make reflective judgments. The

data suggest that there is still room for improvement in meeting this goal.

The six studies of 191 adults who were not enrolled in educational programs provide a point of comparison with several of the student samples (especially adult learners) since the inclusion of nonstudent adults provides a control for age when studying educational effects. Adults who had earned a college degree scored consistently higher ($M = 4.3$) than those who had not done so ($M = 3.6$). In one study of adults over age sixty-five (Glenn and Eklund, 1991), the RJI scores of retired college faculty members were found to be slightly higher than the average score of graduate students in other reflective judgment research (see Table 6.6). The retired faculty members were matched on age with adults who had earned a high school diploma but who had not gone to college or graduate school. The scores of this comparison group were higher than those of high school students (their educational-level counterparts, albeit of a much younger age) and close to the average RJI score earned by college students in other studies. One provocative interpretation of these findings is that life experiences outside of formal education are also associated with the development of reflective thinking. While this may seem commonsensical, there is remarkably little evidence pointing to specific types of experiences outside of formal educational settings that foster cognitive development, a topic that merits additional research.

In general, the increases in reflective judgment across educational levels in the cross-sectional studies probably reflect a variety of factors, such as personal maturity, students' level of involvement with academic and cocurricular offerings, students' success in negotiating academic and social systems, or other concurrent life experiences, such as changing family responsibilities and participation in the work force. These increases may also reflect the effectiveness of educational programs designed to teach students to think reflectively and to make reasoned, interpretive arguments. While the cross-sectional studies did not evaluate the impact of specific educational programs on reflective thinking, the strong relationship between educational level and RJI scores does suggest that postsecondary education has been influential in promoting reflective thinking. We encourage research that helps identify which aspects enable or hinder the achievement of this goal.

Research on Gender Differences in Reflective Judgment

Many developmental models have been criticized as gender biased because they were derived exclusively or predominantly from male samples (Chickering, 1969; Erikson, 1963; Kohlberg, 1969; Levinson, 1978; Perry, 1970). In light of the continuing interest in gender-related issues within developmental models, the data on gender differences from studies using the RJI have been reviewed even though the Reflective Judgment Model was derived from interviews with equal numbers of women and men and there was no a priori reason to suspect that such differences exist. Of the seventeen studies that included both males and females (excluding the ten-year study, discussed separately), seven reported differences by gender and seven reported finding no gender differences; three did not report on the matter. Of the seven reporting differences, males scored higher RJI than females in six of the studies, and the seventh study reported a class by gender interaction. While these findings may suggest a trend of higher scores for men, we think such a conclusion is premature in light of the wide variations in sampling used across these studies (for example, some were matched to characteristics such as academic aptitude while others were not). In particular, the reported differences (and *lack* of differences) may be attributable to a variety of factors in addition to gender, such as academic aptitude, leadership opportunities, and different rates of maturation, or differences in the timing of growth spurts, such as those found by Wood (1993b).

Research on Cross-Cultural
Differences in Reflective Judgment

In the one study to date that investigated cross-cultural differences (Kitchener and Wood, 1987), the RJI was adapted for use with German samples. The resulting reflective judgment scores were comparable to those obtained with samples of doctoral students from the United States; the scores of two other groups of young adults were also comparable, though somewhat higher. The significant differences between educational levels remained even after controlling for the effects of verbal aptitude.

Summary

The studies described in this chapter have collectively contributed to the validation of the Reflective Judgment Model and provided a picture of reflective thinking of individuals at different educational levels and in different settings. While the longitudinal studies provide a stricter test of development by following individuals over time to chart their development, the cross-sectional studies provide more diverse samples across different types of students at different types of institutions across the United States.

Overall, the findings from the longitudinal and cross-sectional studies of reflective judgment suggest a slow but steady pattern of development. The general findings from these studies can be summarized as follows: first, people who are engaged in educational activities tend to improve in their reasoning about ill-structured problems. Second, development typically follows the stage-related patterns described by the Reflective Judgment Model. The consistently higher mean scores among older, more highly educated individuals in cross-sectional studies, the consistent increase in mean scores over time in the longitudinal studies, and the more fine-grained analyses of the sequence of changes within individuals support this claim. Third, being in an educational setting seems to facilitate development. Although we cannot identify the specific components of an educational environment that make the difference, cross-sectional comparisons of student and nonstudent adults, comparisons of older adults with and without advanced degrees, as well as longitudinal data on those who completed a college degree and those who did not, all suggest that those who enter college and earn a college degree have higher reflective judgment scores than those who do not.

Understanding intellectual development and its many influences clearly requires careful examination of characteristics of people (such as students' epistemic assumptions) and characteristics of the multiple environments that stimulate, nurture, and challenge them (such as college classrooms and residence halls). Finer-grained analyses of both types of characteristics offer more detailed information on which to base instructional and other educational decisions. Chapter Nine of this book explores such strategies in more detail.

Chapter Seven

Relating Reflective Judgment to Intellectual Development

The development of the intellect has been a major goal — some would say *the* major goal — of American education since the late 1800s (Dewey, 1897, 1933; Rudolph, 1990), and research on intellectual development has been a major focus of both education and psychology. Intellectual development is a broad field of study, and there are many definitions of it, including critical thinking, intelligence, problem solving, and mathematical skill.

The study of reflective thinking also falls into the domain of intellectual development since the intellect is typically defined as involving the ability for rational thought, abstract thinking, and the application of knowledge to new situations. However, the domain extends far beyond the ability to engage in reflective thought, an observation that leads us to one of the central questions of this chapter: What is the relationship between reflective judgment and other aspects of intellectual ability, such as critical thinking, intelligence, and logical reasoning?

The question of what the Reflective Judgment Model has to offer to the vast literature on the development of the intellect is important, for if it is redundant with other definitions of intellectual development, then it has little that is new or insightful to add to our understanding of such development. Clearly,

189

there are more economical and established ways to measure intelligence than using the Reflective Judgment Interview. Unless the RJI is measuring an intellectual capacity that is in some way distinctive, it is only a more time-consuming and expensive way to measure an existing construct. In this chapter, we will explore the relationship between reflective judgment and three other constructs that describe other abilities in the intellectual domain: critical thinking, intelligence, and formal operations. Each has been the subject of substantial theorizing as well as empirical investigation.

Critical Thinking and Reflective Judgment

As noted in Chapters One and Four, there are obvious conceptual similarities between some definitions of critical thinking and reflective judgment. There are also some definitions of critical thinking that differ in substantial ways from the definition of reflective judgment. As we argue in Chapter One, critical thinking is typically defined as logic or as a set of general problem-solving skills, and many definitions focus on the role of formal or informal logic to illuminate basic reasoning skills.

By contrast, those who write about critical thinking within a cognitive psychology tradition tend to be more concerned about the thinking process and how it develops (Benderson, 1990). In addition, most also focus on puzzle solving rather than on ill-structured problems. Although some of the puzzles on which they focus are quite complex, these problems nonetheless call for answers that may be verified as correct or incorrect.

Neither group acknowledges the importance of epistemic assumptions in distinguishing between problem types or the role that these assumptions play in formulating solutions. We agree with Paul (1990) that monologic is insufficient for understanding critical thinking (see Chapter One). Answers for well-structured problems may be decided by means of inductive or deductive reasoning. However, as we have argued, solving ill-structured problems may require not only deductive and inductive problem-solving skills but skills that reflect more advanced epistemic assumptions as well. These epistemic assumptions change over time, especially between late childhood and early adulthood. In this way, our work is consistent with the developmental psychology tradition in assuming that there are age-related developmental differences that should be considered in teaching critical thinking skills to students. As we have already shown in Chapter Six, this contention is supported by data showing that epistemic cognition develops with age and education.

A few researchers have examined the empirical relationship between critical thinking and reflective judgment. In the next section, these studies are reviewed. The reader is reminded that many measures of critical thinking are arguably measures of the skills that are necessary to solve ill-structured problems (See Chapter Four for an explanation of this point.)

Brabeck (1983a) was the first to research the question of whether increases in reflective judgment across educational levels might be due to the attainment of critical thinking skills and, in particular, logical reasoning skills. She sampled women at four educational levels (high school, college sophomore, college senior, and master's levels) who were matched across groups on high and low critical thinking scores. The Watson-Glaser Critical Thinking Appraisal (Watson and Glaser, 1964) was used to measure critical thinking. These four groups were then compared on their RJI scores. Despite the matching, Brabeck found a significant education effect for reflective judgment, with the more advanced students scoring significantly higher than the younger students. In addition, the group with the high critical thinking scores earned higher RJI scores than did the group with the low critical thinking scores. Further, there was significantly higher variability among the RJI scores of the high critical thinking group than the low critical thinking group. While only those scoring high in critical thinking scored above a Stage 4 in reflective judgment, high WGCTA scores did not uniformly lead to high RJI scores. Brabeck (1983a, p. 32) has concluded that the skills that the WGCTA measured may be necessary but not sufficient for high levels of reflective judgment: "while students were able to identify appropriate deductions and inferences, to recognize assumptions, and to evaluate arguments, these are not sufficient to describe processes involved when students justify their own beliefs."

Brabeck and Wood (1990) retested twenty-five high school students from the original Brabeck (1983a) sample one year later on both the RJI and the WGCTA. While they found no significant increase in critical thinking scores, they did find a significant increase in RJI scores. They have suggested that while the development of critical thinking skills may not continue into the early college years, development in reflective judgment clearly does so. This point merits additional research.

Two companion studies (King, Wood, and Mines, 1990; Mines, King, Hood, and Wood, 1990) examined the relationship between the RJI and two measures of critical thinking, the WGCTA and the Cornell Critical Thinking Test (CCTT) (Ennis and Millman, 1971). They sampled undergraduate and graduate students in mathematical and social sciences. The graduate students scored significantly higher than the undergraduates on all three measures; however, on the WGCTA and the CCTT, the educational-level differences could be accounted for by differences in academic aptitude. This was not the case for the RJI, where educational-level effects remained after the effects of academic aptitude were partialed out.

While significant correlations between the measures were obtained, the correlation between the CCTT and the WGCTA was stronger than that between either measure and the RJI. Further, a moderate ($r = .54$, $p < .01$) relationship between the WGCTA and the CCTT remained even after academic aptitude was statistically controlled; the correlations between these two measures and the RJI were low ($r = .27$ for each, $p < .05$). These findings are consistent with the suggestion that the RJI is measuring a different kind of problem solving than are the other two tests. We recognize, however, that the CCTT and the WGCTA are paper-and-pencil recognition tasks, while the RJI is an interview production task and that the formats of the tests may have contributed to some of the differences. In an additional analysis based on this data set, Wood (1990) tested the relationship between the WGCTA composite score and the CCTT composite score and the RJI mean. He found a necessary but not sufficient pattern of response between the RJI and the other two measures.

Taken together, these studies suggest that reflective judgment and critical thinking are related but different constructs. In addition, they suggest that some of the skills necessary to solve well-structured problems that are measured by tests of critical thinking may be necessary but not sufficient for later levels of reflective judgment.

Intelligence and Reflective Judgment

Comparing reflective judgment with intelligence is difficult since it sometimes seems that there are as many definitions of intelligence as there are psychologists. As Sternberg and Powell (1983, p. 341) have observed, "Everyone agrees that intelligence develops, few people agree as to what intelligence is. The problem is confounded in that there is also little consensus as to just what develops or whether the intelligence that develops is the same thing at different ages." Although intelligence may be impossible to define precisely, two conceptions are common in various theoretical models (Sternberg and Powell, 1983). First, intelligence involves the capacity to learn from experience; second, it involves adapting to novel problems and situations in life. Since reflective judgment focuses on the ability to solve ill-structured problems, which are common in adult life, it clearly falls within the second conception of intelligence.

Although intelligence involves the two general capacities just noted, the definition of intelligence has generally remained inferential. That is, psychometricians measure how much children or adults know, what they have learned, or how they perform and then draw inferences about people's intelligence or mental ability on the basis of the outcome of these measures (Lindemann and Matarazzo, 1984). Anastasi (1983, p. 182) suggests that traditional intelligence tests "measure a cluster of intellectual traits demanded in modern, technologically advanced societies." These traits, she argues, are related to success in academic settings and are fostered by participation in schooling.

In addition to the controversy surrounding the definition of intelligence, there has been considerable debate over whether intelligence is a unitary ability or whether it is composed of component abilities. Most current theorists, however, advocate multiple-component models (Lindemann and Matarazzo, 1984). In this regard, the theory that has the clearest implications for the Reflective Judgment Model is the theory of fluid and crystallized intelligence (Horn and Cattell, 1966). Fluid intelligence is defined as those abilities that reflect the influence of biological makeup on intelligence. These abilities are described as flexible and applicable to almost any kind of problem solving. Because they result from biological processes, Horn and Cattell have hypothesized that they are not affected by experience or education.

By contrast, crystallized intelligence is defined as the learned ability to solve problems, make judgments, draw conclusions, and identify relationships (Whitbourne, 1986). It is this aspect of intelligence that seems most closely related to the development of reflective judgment since it includes components that are tied to judgment and problem solving. As Horn (1982) has noted, because crystallized intelligence is so broadly defined, it refers to a huge repertoire of skills that are organized into what he and Cattell called primary abilities (Horn and Cattell, 1966). These include abilities such as verbal comprehension, formal reasoning, general reasoning, and concept formation.

There is no single test of crystallized intelligence. In this line of research, several scales from different intelligence tests are typically used to assess each ability (Whitbourne, 1986). Although measures of crystallized intelligence could theoretically include ill-structured problems, this does not appear to be the case. For example, verbal comprehension items typically tap knowledge about the meaning of words and their relationship to synonyms or antonyms; formal reasoning items assess logical thinking; and items on general reasoning evaluate the ability to solve general well-structured problems, such as those that involve mathematics (see Whitbourne, 1986, for examples). Although some of the problems are quite abstract and involve complex relationships and advanced knowledge, the items on most tests of crystallized intelligence evaluate the amount of information or knowledge available to the individual and the inductive or deductive conclusions that can be drawn on the basis of that information (Kitchener, 1986). Each type of item presumes there are right or wrong answers for the questions. In other words, the problems used to measure crystallized intelligence can usually be solved with a high degree of certainty and do not tap people's epistemic assumptions.

On the other hand, there is a presumption in the trait theory tradition that intelligence develops or at least changes over the life span, with increases in crystallized abilities being apparent until middle age (Horn and Donaldson, 1980; Whitbourne, 1986). Sternberg (1988) has suggested that development in intelligence may occur for several reasons. First, there may be increasing differentiation of abilities, and older people may have more abilities to draw upon. Second, the weights of the factors or their relevance may also change with increasing age; that is, while the number of factors may stay the same, their relative importance within a person's cognitive system may change. Third, although the factor structure itself may not change, the content on which it operates may change as the individual has new experiences and gains additional knowledge.

As discussed in Chapter Six, there is clear evidence that development according to the Reflective Judgment Model occurs between at least age fourteen and the early thirties. Thus, it is possible that development in reflective judgment could be accounted for by the increased differentiation or organization of intelligence factors. Hypothetically, the development of reflective judgment might then be attributed to changes in crystallized intelligence. Unfortunately, this hypothesis cannot be tested directly since adequate tests of all of the factors are not available (Horn, 1982). Further, where tests are available, there have not been studies of these factors and their relationship to reflective judgment.

There are, however, many tests of verbal reasoning, an ability often associated with the verbal comprehension component of crystallized intelligence. Because the RJI relies on verbal production, it would seem that verbal reasoning might contribute strongly to RJI scores and that development in verbal reasoning might account for the changes that are observed in RJI scores. As with other mental ability tests, however, verbal ability is typically measured as if it were a puzzle, using puzzle-solving tasks: there are right answers to the questions posed, and the individual's task is to identify those answers correctly.

If we focus specifically on verbal reasoning, several possible relationships with reflective judgment can be hypothesized. First, it may be that some adults become very adept at solving verbal puzzles but never acknowledge the ambiguity that underlies the solving of ill-structured problems. These adults may reduce ill-structured problems to puzzles that can be handled by deductive or inductive inferences. Second, the skills involved in puzzle solving may be necessary but not sufficient for high levels of development according to the Reflective Judgment Model. Third, although verbal reasoning and reflective judgment are measured in very different ways, it may be that verbal reasoning is the fundamental component of reflective judgment and cannot be distinguished from it. Whatever the relationship, each has different implications for educational programming. For example, if there is no relationship between the two constructs, then they may be seen as two distinct skill domains, each of which requires attention in an educational setting. However, if puzzle solving is a necessary but not sufficient condition for the higher Reflective Judgment stages, then educators need to address the issue of how to sequence skill development in each area.

Several studies have investigated the relationship between Reflective Judgment and verbal reasoning; these are listed by study in Resource B, Table B7.1. Some have used Terman's (1973) Concept Mastery Test (CMT), a measure of verbal reasoning that was designed to assess the reasoning of high-functioning adults. A second group has used either one or several of the verbal subtests of the WISC-R or WAIS-R, which measure the ability to reason inductively about verbal problems. Still others have used measures of scholastic aptitude.

The correlations between CMT scores and RJI scores have generally been low to moderate. (The one exception to this pattern occurred in a Kitchener and King [1981] study, where the correlations for the graduate student sample and the sample as a whole were both .79.) WISC-R and WAIS-R correlations with the RJI score have typically been moderate, ranging from .37 to .55. Correlations between the RJI and measures of scholastic aptitude or academic ability have been lower, from – .17 to .26. The low-to-moderate correlations suggest that traditional measures of verbal ability and scholastic aptitude are measuring constructs that are related to reflective judgment but that can be distinguished from it.

Another way to look at this issue is to ask about the nature of the evolving relationship between verbal reasoning and reflective judgment over time. In other words, since both verbal ability and reflective judgment continue to develop through adolescence and into adulthood, are changes in the ability to make judgments about ill-structured problems simply due to increases in verbal facility (such as increased vocabulary and the ability to identify synonyms correctly)? Two sets of longitudinal studies have looked precisely at this question (King, Kitchener, and Wood, 1990; Kitchener, King, Wood, and Davison, 1989; Welfel and Davison, 1986). (Schmidt [1985] also reported longitudinal data on the relationship between the RJI and the CMT. However, because the CMT was incorrectly scored, results from this study are not included here.) Both sets used the Concept Mastery Test (Terman, 1973) to assess verbal reasoning.

The first study (described in detail in Chapter Six) tested three groups of students at two-, six-, and ten-year intervals on both the RJI and the CMT (King and others, 1983; King, Kitchener, and Wood, 1990; Kitchener, King, Wood, and Davison, 1989). Development over time was observed on both measures, but the amount of development differed by group. At the sixth-year retest (Kitchener, King, Wood, and Davison, 1989; King, Kitchener, and Wood, 1990), the youngest group (who were first tested at age sixteen) showed the largest increase on both measures, while the oldest group (for whom the average age was twenty-eight at the first testing) showed the smallest increase. This pattern was also found at the tenth-year retesting of these samples. The differences in growth may reflect a greater capacity for development in the younger group in both domains, as well as a ceiling effect on the RJI (discussed in Chapter Six). Further, since most members of this group were either in high school or college during the years of the study, this finding may also reflect a beneficial outcome of participation in education. In the absence of a matched cohort of those who were not in school, the improvement in reflective judgment and verbal reasoning cannot be unequivocally attributed to an educational effect. Nevertheless, the dramatic changes in this group are consistent with the fundamental goal of education to promote the development of the intellect in its broadest sense. However, despite the comparable patterns of development over time across the two measures, increases in RJI scores could not be statistically accounted for by changes in CMT scores.

The second longitudinal study first tested twenty-five college students during their freshman year and retested them four years later (Welfel and Davison, 1986). Again, increases in RJI scores over time could not be statistically accounted for by changes in verbal ability, supporting the hypothesis that these are two different but related constructs.

Formal Operations and Reflective Judgment

The third construct from which reflective judgment needs to be distinguished is formal operations. This is especially relevant in light of our earlier assertion (see Chapter Two) that formal operations and reflective judgment represent different intellectual domains. In their treatise on the development of formal operations, Inhelder and Piaget (1958) argued that formal operations provide the foundation on which adolescents build life plans and programs for changing society. By contrast, we have suggested that these tasks involve the resolution of ill-structured problems and, therefore, epistemic cognition.

According to Inhelder and Piaget, formal operations involve integrated, structural relationships between propositions that provide the basis for transforming observations about the real world into abstractions. This transformation allows the mental manipulation of propositions so that variables that are relevant to a problem can be isolated and the logical relationships between variables can be identified. These underlying structural relationships give formal operational thought the characteristics of being hypothetical and deductive. Such reasoning is considered to be formal since the individual can reason not just about empirical realities but about propositional statements; it involves operations because the individual can act on or manipulate propositions in the solutions of problems. Whereas the younger concrete thinker can only organize (for example, classify or seriate) objects or events, the formal thinker can develop propositions and generate ways in which hypothetical propositions about data may be logically related. It is the ability to reason about propositions that allows the individual to subordinate what has been observed to what may be possible. In addition, the formal thinker can generate all possible combinations of propositions and thus consider all factors and combinations of factors related to a problem.

Inhelder and Piaget (1958) went beyond general descriptions of formal thought, however, to propose a highly technical description for combinatorial and propositional thinking and how they are logically interrelated or integrated. In the case of the combinatorial system, they proposed that sixteen binary operations involving the presence or absence of observations compose a lattice that allows individuals to generate all possible combinations of variables. These can then be interrelated via a set of logical operations known as the INRC group of transformations, which includes identity, negation, the reciprocal, and the correlative. According to Inhelder and Piaget, the lattice and group structures operate as a system or whole, which allows discrimination between all possible combinations and their integration in problem solving. For a review of research on formal reasoning in adulthood, see P. M. King (1986).

There has been considerable debate surrounding the meaning and interpretation of the construct of formal operations (Braine and Rumain, 1983; Neimark, 1982). While Inhelder and Piaget (1958) most often talked about the system as involving deductive inference, Kitchener and Kitchener (1981) have pointed out that formal operations also entail inductive inference since they include the nondeductive confirmation of hypotheses, depending upon whether certain experimental observations occurred. Thus, formal reasoning involves both cases in which reasoning leads to conclusions that are absolutely certain or necessary via deduction and cases in which reasoning leads to inferences that are only probable or likely.

The relevant question here is whether formal operations as a construct can explain the ability to solve ill-structured problems. Kitchener and Kitchener (1981) argue that it does not provide an adequate explanation. They point out that even in well-structured problems that involve causal relations between experimental variables and their empirical effects, the criterion for correctness is clear. However, in other kinds of problems (such as philosophical, ideological, or even some scientific problems), the direct empirical observation of the presence or absence of a particular outcome may not be an appropriate criterion. In these cases, it is the adequacy of the criteria themselves that is open to question. Neither deductive nor inductive logic will be adequate when it comes to the identification of the criteria for evaluation. Here, an individual's epistemological assumptions directly affect which criteria he or she will consider when evaluating two or more systems. For example, for the person who reasons that there is an ultimate authority who can provide the "true" or "real" answer to a problem, whole sets of data may be ignored or seen as irrelevant if they are not in agreement with the authority. Given the person's prior assumptions, empirical data may be an irrelevant criterion for solving a problem.

While deductive or inductive logic may be important once individuals decide on the relevant criteria, logic alone does not tell them how to identify those criteria. The important differences between their reasoning are ones that involve epistemological assumptions that lead them to use different criteria for evaluation. In other words, people's tacit theoretical assumptions color their perception of the problem involved, their evaluation of the evidence on that problem, and their solutions (Kitchener and Kitchener, 1981). As Neimark (1979, p. 61) suggests, the "narrow focus upon hypothetico-deductive reasoning overlooks all the richness and complexity of thought during early and middle adulthood which arises from dealing with attendant practical, social, and philosophical problems." These are the areas where epistemic cognition becomes critical.

The ability to use formal operations, that is, to reason about propositions and to generate all possible alternatives, allows individuals to reason in more valid ways about many issues. It is an important ability because it allows people to isolate and identify problematic variables. For example, we expect an automobile mechanic to be able to use these skills when diagnosing problems with car engines or for physicians to use these skills when identifying the cause of chest pain. However, formal operations alone do not provide people with the skills to select the criteria they can then apply when addressing ill-structured problems. When individuals are faced with relatively direct deductive or empirical problems (such as the physical experiments used in Inhelder and Piaget's work or calculating the solution to a calculus problem), formal operations may be sufficient. However, many problems of adult life are not of this nature; rather, they often throw fundamental assumptions into question. Although deductive and inductive reasoning may be necessary in these areas, they are not sufficient for mature rationality. While logical development and epistemological development are important for critical reasoning in adulthood, they nevertheless reflect different intellectual domains.

Only one study has investigated the empirical relationship between reflective judgment and formal operations. King (1977) administered the RJI and used the chemicals and pendulum tasks as measures of formal operational reasoning. Her sample included graduate students, college juniors, and high school juniors who were matched on scholastic aptitude. While there were significant differences between the three groups' RJI scores, there were no such differences between their formal operations scores. Despite the fact that 91 percent of the sample scored as fully formal on one or both of the tasks, their modal reflective judgment scores ranged from Stage 2 through Stage 7. The correlations between the formal operations measures and RJI scores were extremely low, providing further evidence that formal operations and reflective judgment are two different domains of intellectual development. Because the sample was so consistently formal operational, however, the necessary but not sufficient relationship between the two constructs could not be tested in this study.

Summary

Reflective judgment is a part of what we generally consider to be the intellectual domain. The empirical data on the relationship between the RJI and other measures of intellectual development support the contention that the RJI is measuring a construct that is different from the traditional constructs of critical thinking, verbal reasoning, and formal operations. The measures of these three constructs also differ from the RJI in terms of problem structure in that they typically assess problem solving about well-structured rather than ill-structured problems. In other words, the RJI does appear to be measuring a distinct aspect of intellectual development, one that has been either neglected or overlooked in the past.

To date, the studies reviewed here suggest that: (1) reflective judgment is more than the accumulation of logical reasoning skills; (2) the skills necessary for solving well-structured problems may be a necessary prerequisite for high levels of reflective judgment; and (3) differences in the skills necessary for addressing ill-structured problems cannot be accounted for by the logical skills necessary for solving well-structured problems.

These findings suggest that students need to focus their attention on both types of problem solving. Deficits in reasoning about ill-structured problems may result from inadequate epistemic assumptions, from poor inductive or deductive skills, or from both. "Good thinking" involves reasoning well about many types of problems, from correctly solving logical problems to offering plausible explanations about unresolved questions. Instructors concerned with reasoning about ill-structured problems need to listen to the epistemic assumptions their students are articulating, and they need to identify instructional methods that will provide the impetus for those assumptions to evolve (see Chapter Nine). They also need to ask whether their students have the inductive and deductive skills that appear to be necessary prerequisites for higher levels of reflective thinking.

Chapter Eight

Reflective Judgment
and Character Development

The goals of American higher education are often stated in terms of the development of students' character as well as of their intellect. In fact, Dewey (1897) argued that the development of character is the ultimate aim of all schooling. Almost a century later, Bok (1988, p. 50) asserted that "helping students understand how to lead ethical, reflective, fulfilling lives" is not only a goal but an obligation of higher education. Compared with other institutions that address moral issues (such as families or religious or civic groups), higher education has two distinct advantages in working toward this goal. First, as Bok (1988, p. 40) noted: "Almost every public servant, business executive, attorney, physician—indeed, virtually all leaders in every walk of life—enter our colleges and professional schools and remain there for several formative years." Second, college students are often enrolled in college during times of life transitions. Traditional-age students attend college at a time when they are actively experimenting with and consolidating a sense of identity: who they are, what they can do well, what is important to them, how they want others to see them, and so forth. Nontraditional-age students often enroll in educational programs to mediate other life transitions, such as needing to be economically independent after a divorce, having time to devote to one's own education after raising children, or wanting to understand the world better and to make a more lasting contribution. The desire for self-improvement and readiness for change are often accompanied by a higher motivation to learn and an openness to being challenged; these conditions provide fertile soil for growth in many areas, including intellectual, moral, and identity development.

What is the relationship between reflective thinking and character? Since moral problems are often ill structured, an individual's beliefs about the nature of problems may influence the approach she or he takes to a moral problem. Similarly, constructing one's identity may call for skills used in constructing solutions to ill-structured problems in other domains. It is reasonable to assume that epistemic assumptions and concepts of justification may influence a person's conceptions of morality and identity. Thus, what are commonly thought of as issues of intellectual development and issues of character development may well be interrelated.

The means of developing character, and even defining what is meant by the term, have often eluded educators and researchers alike. In the book *Character Development in College Students* (Whiteley and Associates, 1982), the authors argue that one of the difficulties in promoting character development has been that the specific values taken to constitute good character often change from generation to generation. Accordingly, they choose to define character not in terms of specific values but as a person's "understanding of what is the right, fair, or a good thing to do in a given circumstance" and the "ability to do those things (the courage to act in accordance with one's understanding of what is right, fair, and good)" (p. 14). In the pages that follow, we will define character in a similar way since this definition best corresponds to the ways that character has been measured in the studies reviewed here. Thus defined, character refers to the conceptions an individual has of what is right or fair, those personal attributes that influence an individual to act on those beliefs, as well as to other enduring personal traits that are central to the individual's identity, including wisdom.

Issues of character are in the limelight on college campuses whenever examples of misconduct are brought to the public's attention. Educators and the public alike express dismay over issues that include plagiarism, computer and software theft, preferential treatment for athletes, date rape, violence directed at ethnic minorities and homosexual students, and hazing pranks that result in humiliation, injury, or even death. Such events are at flagrant odds with a university's stated commitment to promote the development of character. Hills (1982) has even charged that some colleges actually serve as training grounds for white-collar crime.

What accounts for such incidents of misconduct in educational institutions that are ostensibly committed to the betterment of individuals and of society? Lickona (1980) has asked whether moral misconduct results from the separation of the development of the intellect from the development of moral values. Thus, it is important to raise the question of whether the development of character and that of the intellect follow different or similar courses. For example, does the development of the intellect deter or enhance the development of character? Conversely, does the development of character deter or enhance the development of the intellect?

In this chapter we first explore the relationship between the development of reflective thinking and the development of two aspects of character, moral reasoning and identity development. Specifically, we examine whether development in reflective judgment is related to the emergence of these aspects of character or whether they are indeed separate domains that need specific and different attention.

Moral Judgment and Reflective Judgment

When people are introduced to the concept of well- and ill-structured problems and are asked to generate examples of each, it is our experience that they often suggest examples that are of a moral nature. This response is not too surprising since moral problems are one type of ill-structured problems (Churchman, 1971; Wood, 1983).

For example, consider the moral problem of whether to continue to administer life-sustaining measures when a patient is in a coma. As with other ill-structured problems, there are arguments about many aspects of this question. Although there are people on both sides of the issue who argue that the problem has an absolute answer, the decision is very frequently an excruciatingly difficult one for the patient's family. As with problems in the intellectual domain, problems such as this one require a judgment that must be constructed by individual decision makers.

Questions requiring moral judgments, however, are different from questions requiring reflective judgments. For example, epistemological issues that would correspond to the moral question of whether to discontinue life supports include evaluating the prognosis for recovery and estimating the long-term financial and emotional effects on the family. Part of the ill-structured nature of moral problems derives from different values or conceptions of the good rather than from epistemological issues about the nature of knowledge. In this example, the epistemological issues include estimating the odds of recovery and whether the long-term consequences can really be known. The domain of moral judgment concerns itself with making decisions about social values, particularly with how humans ought to act in relationship to each other in order to further human welfare (Frankena, 1963; Kohlberg, 1981; Rest, 1979). The domain of reflective thinking focuses on issues of how we can know and how we can make the best possible decisions in light of intellectual uncertainty. Both address ill-structured problems, but in different domains and with different criteria for evaluation.

Nevertheless, there appears to be a structural similarity in the development of people's conceptions of moral rights and responsibility and conceptions of knowledge and justification (Kitchener, 1982); empirical research supports this observation (King, Kitchener, and Wood, 1985; King, Kitchener, Wood, and Davison, 1989). Comparable to the early levels of the developmental progression in the Reflective Judgment Model, initial concepts of morality are typically described as singular, absolute, and concrete; for example, "an act is either good or bad"

(Piaget, 1965; Kohlberg, 1981). Through the progression, the number of concepts, their differentiation, and their complexity all increase. More specifically, individuals can first use two concrete categories of moral reasoning and relate them. For example, "What is good for me is what I want; what is good for you is what you want." Later, concrete concepts become further differentiated and related. For example, "It is good for both of us to be considerate of each other." As with the development of reflective judgment, simple abstract conceptions of morality emerge as two or more complex, concrete concepts combine to form a higher-order concept. An example of an abstract concept in the moral domain is that of law, which serves to organize acceptable and unacceptable behavior for all members of a community; it also allows for the evaluation of one's own and others' behavior by a standard that is more encompassing than that allowed by individually oriented values. Even later, the ability to interrelate abstract concepts emerges. In the moral domain, this allows for the development and application of moral principles (such as nonmaleficence, justice, or the value of human life) to moral judgments. A description of the structural similarities between concepts of knowledge (based on the Reflective Judgment Model) and concepts of morality appears in Table 8.1.

Because reflective thinking and moral judgment represent different but related domains, several questions arise: Does the ability to make reflective judgments enable one to make better moral decisions? For example, is a person who accepts uncertainty in the intellectual domain more likely to accept uncertainty in the moral domain? Is a person who is aware that evidence about an issue is open to different perceptions and interpretations in the intellectual domain similarly aware when dealing with moral issues? The underlying question here is whether a person's ability to be reflective in the intellectual domain generalizes to comparable abilities in the moral domain. The structural similarities described above suggest that there may be mechanisms underlying development in both domains (as suggested by Fischer, 1980) that may affect how the individual operates on both sets of tasks. (Fischer's model and its relationship to reflective judgment are described in detail in Chapter Two.)

Table 8.1. Structural Similarities
Between Reflective Judgment and Moral Judgment.

Concepts of knowledge	*Concepts of morality*

Stage 1

Single concrete category for knowing. Certain knowledge is gained by direct personal observation and needs no justification.

Single concrete category for good and bad. Good gets rewarded; bad gets punished.

Stage 2

Two concrete categories of knowledge. A person can know with certainty through direct observation or indirectly through an authority.

Two concrete categories of morality. For me, good is what I want. For you, good is what you want. Bad is what is not wanted.

Stage 3

Several concrete categories of knowledge are interrelated. Knowledge is assumed to be either absolutely certain or temporarily uncertain. Justification is based on authorities' views or what "feels right."

Several concrete categories of morality are interrelated. Good is being considerate, nice, kind. Bad is being inconsiderate, mean, and unkind. This is true for self and others.

Stage 4

Knowledge is understood as a single abstraction. Knowledge is uncertain, and knowledge claims are assumed to be idiosyncratic to the individual.

Morality is understood as a single abstraction. Laws are understood as a mechanism for coordinating expectations about acceptable and unacceptable behavior within communities.

Stage 5

Two or more abstract concepts of knowledge can be related. Knowledge is seen as contextual and subjective. Beliefs are justified by using the rules of inquiry for the appropriate contexts.

Two or more abstract concepts of morality can be related. The moral framework from one context (such as a community's laws or standards of conduct) can be related to the moral framework in another context (those of another community).

Stage 6

Abstract concepts of knowledge can be related. Knowledge is actively constructed by comparing evidence and opinion on different sides of an issue; solutions are evaluated by personally endorsed criteria.

Abstract concepts of morality can be related. While the fairness of a given law may be interpreted differently, the well-being of people is a common consideration.

Table 8.1. Structural Similarities
Between Reflective Judgment and Moral Judgment, Cont'd.

Concepts of knowledge	Concepts of morality
Stage 7	
Abstract concepts of knowledge are understood as a system. The general principle is that knowledge is the outcome of the process of reasonable inquiry for constructing a well-informed understanding.	Abstract concepts of morality are understood as a system. Principles such as the value of human life, justice, serving others, and contributing to the common good unify diverse concepts of morality.

Source: Based on Kitchener, 1982, Table 1.

Because of the structural similarity between the development of reflective judgment (conceptions of knowledge) and the development of moral reasoning (conceptions of morality), we would expect a positive correlation between measures of these two concepts. However, it also seems reasonable to expect that different experiences promote the development of moral thinking and reflective thinking. For example, educational settings in which consideration is given to what individuals value and how they might decide between different conceptions of social cooperation should promote moral development. By contrast, educational settings in which consideration is given to what and how individuals can know should promote epistemological development. Thus, while the development of moral thinking and that of reflective thinking may follow similar developmental pathways (Rest, Bebeau, and Volker, 1986), the experiences that affect the progression along each pathway may differ.

The empirical relationship between the development of moral judgment and reflective judgment has been investigated in a series of longitudinal studies begun concurrently with our longitudinal study of the development of reflective judgment. The sample was the same as that described in the initial Kitchener and King (1981) research discussed in Chapter Six. Rest's (1979) Defining Issues Test (DIT) of moral judgment was used to measure moral reasoning.

As noted earlier, the sample for this study originally consisted of three groups of students who were first tested in 1977. The first group consisted of twenty sixteen-year-old college juniors, the second group consisted of forty twenty-year-old college juniors, and the third group consisted of twenty advanced doctoral students whose average age was twenty-eight. The three groups were retested in 1979, 1983, and 1987. As noted in Chapter Six, there were significant increases in RJI scores at each subsequent testing. There were also significant increases in moral judgment scores in 1979 (Kitchener and others, 1984) but not in 1983 (King, Kitchener, Wood, and Davison, 1989) or in 1987 (King, Kitchener, and Wood, 1991). The graduate students scored substantially higher on both measures than did the younger two groups at all testings. Additionally, both group and time differences in RJI scores remained significant when the effects of moral judgment scores were statistically removed. By contrast, neither group nor time effects remained significant on the DIT scores when RJI scores were statistically removed.

The RJI and DIT scores correlated moderately (between .46 and .58) at all four testings (King, Kitchener, Wood, and Davison, 1989; King, Kitchener, and Wood, 1991). The correlations between the measures remained positive but were lower when the effects of age and number of years of higher education were statistically controlled. Wood (1993a) evaluated the necessary but not sufficient relationship between the two measures on the six-year retest. This test supported the earlier findings: the development of reflective judgment is a necessary but not sufficient precursor of moral judgment, at least as it is measured by the DIT.

Josephson (1988) also evaluated the relationship between moral judgment and reflective judgment, using the RJI and Kohlberg's Moral Judgment Interview (MJI) (Colby, Kohlberg, Gibbs, and Lieberman, 1983). Using a sample of forty-three highly educated adult women, she obtained scores that were constricted, covering a narrow range of responses on both measures. She found no significant relationship between the two measures. This finding is puzzling in light of earlier data suggesting a consistent moderate relationship between reflective judgment and moral reasoning, especially since both measures use an interview format based on ill-structured problems. Because the formats of the MJI and RJI are more similar than those of the DIT and RJI and because the DIT and MJI measure related constructs, one would expect the relationship between the MJI and the RJI to be the stronger one. However, this lack of relationship may also be an artifact of the small, homogeneous sample and the restricted range of responses on both measures.

In these studies, Kohlberg's (1969, 1981) theory of moral development was used as the conceptual framework for defining and measuring moral development. Kohlberg's theory is sometimes characterized as a "justice orientation" to morality and contrasted with a "care orientation" (Gilligan, 1982; Noddings, 1984), typically in the context of gender differences. (For more extended discussions of gender issues in moral development, see Brabeck, 1989; Kerber and others, 1986; Nunner-Winkler, 1984; Thoma, 1986; and Walker, 1984.) Several of these authors note that it is conceptually confusing to attempt to draw this type of contrast since the underlying concepts between the two approaches have much in common and suggest that they are not accurately portrayed as falling on opposite ends of a continuum. Instead, we endorse Brabeck's (1983b) more integrative approach, which addresses the need for both perspectives in forming a more adequate conception of morality. Brabeck used Rest's (1979, 1984) four-component model of morality to analyze the two approaches. The first component in this model emphasizes moral sensitivity, which is an awareness of a moral dimension in a situation (that the welfare of others is affected by a course of action) and an appropriate affective response that shows empathy toward the affected person(s). The second component involves what type of moral standard (such as fairness) is applied in reasoning about moral issues; Rest places Kohlberg's theory here because different stages of moral development correspond to different definitions of fairness. Rest's third component involves weighing the moral and nonmoral factors that may affect moral decision making, and his fourth component involves implementing a moral plan of action. Brabeck concluded that the care orientation focuses on the first and third components, while Kohlberg's theory, by contrast, focuses on the second component. In other words, each approach emphasizes a critical aspect of morality, but neither offers a complete description. Since the studies reported here examined moral reasoning and not factors associated with the other components (including moral sensitivity), we cannot address the relationship between reflective thinking and other factors in the moral domain.

Earlier in this chapter, we cited Lickona's (1980) question of whether moral misconduct occurs, at least in part, from the separation of the development of moral values from the development of the intellect. While the above data do not provide a direct test of Lickona's hypothesis that it does and the data are limited to individuals with collegiate experiences, the longitudinal studies do suggest that reflective judgment and moral judgment are interrelated, as indicated by the positive correlations and the changes in scores over time. Further, the necessary but not sufficient analyses suggest that developing reflective judgment will not necessarily lead to but may be required for more principled moral thinking. In other words, promoting the development of reflective judgment may be one step in the process of developing higher levels of moral judgment. Educators who want to promote moral development might address this goal by helping students consider issues of how they can better reason about ill-structured problems in the intellectual domain as well as in the moral domain.

Identity Development and Reflective Judgment

Character consists of more than just a person's moral values and judgments. It also includes the outward manifestation of a person's identity and those attributes that affect whether one acts on or disregards the moral judgments one makes, those that lead one to follow what is considered to be customary and acceptable or to depart from such norms, those that effect one's conceptions of interpersonal relationships, and those attributes that reflect one's basic conceptions of oneself. These issues are usually considered to be the domain of ego development and psychosocial development. The relationship between these two aspects of character development and the development of reflective judgment will be considered in the next sections.

Ego Development

Kegan's (1982) model of the evolution of the self and Loevinger's (1976) theory of ego development have both suggested that conceptions of self and interpersonal relationships follow a developmental continuum. As with moral and reflective judgment, initial conceptions are simple, singular, and concrete; later conceptions reflect greater differentiation in perceptions of the self, the social world, and interpersonal relationships. Loevinger and Kegan further suggest that this developmental continuum can be divided into stages that chart the evolution of personal development within the framework of each perspective.

Although there is an increase in the underlying cognitive complexity associated with the later stages in both Kegan's (1982) and Loevinger's (1976) models, Loevinger makes a point of differentiating ego and intellectual development. This point has been supported by studies that have examined the relationship between ego development as measured by the Sentence Completion Test (SCT) (Loevinger and Wessler, 1970) and reflective judgment as measured by the RJI (King, Kitchener, and Wood, 1985; King, Kitchener, Wood, and Davison, 1989; Kitchener and others, 1984). Using the same sample that we used to initially test the Reflective Judgment Model and the relationship between moral judgment and reflective judgment (Kitchener and King, 1981), we evaluated the relationship between ego development and reflective judgment in 1977, 1979 and 1983 with the three groups of students. As with the RJI, SCT scores increased significantly over time. Unlike the RJI (and DIT) data, there were no significant differences between the scores of the three age groups, which raises serious questions about the usefulness of this measure to assess development with comparable samples of adults. The correlations and partial correlations (with the effects of age and educational level removed) between the two measures were generally very low at all three testings. These findings suggest that reflective judgment develops independently of ego development. Thus, we cannot assume that stimulating reflective thinking will lead to more complex thinking about self and others or that stimulating complex thinking about self and others will lead to more reflective judgments, at least when the SCT is used to measure identity.

In summary, the specific transition examined by Glatfelter (1982) involving the achievement of identity does involve solving ill-structured problems. In this case, the components of the problem involve various conceptions of the self. If individuals presume there is only one way to resolve the problem, they will probably remain in a foreclosed status. Constructing an identity may have similarities to constructing a solution to an ill-structured problem in other domains; for example, evidence about a specific aspect of the self needs to be integrated into the self-system as a whole.

Similarly, the purpose and relationships scales on the SDTI-2 reflect an ability to synthesize information about self into a plan about the future and an openness to different views and types of lifestyles, respectively. These psychosocial tasks have parallels in the reflective judgment stages that may account for the moderate correlations. Because the range of RJI and SDTI-2 scores in Polkosnik and Winston's (1989) sample was narrow and because their sample was small, these researchers could not evaluate the full extent of the relationship between the scales.

While it is not possible at this time to precisely describe the exact relationship between reflective judgment and psychosocial development, these data underscore the fact that college students and adults alike are struggling with ill-structured problems in many aspects of their lives. Educators might be more successful in promoting development in the intellectual domain if they acknowledged that similar struggles are occurring in students' personal lives and that these personal struggles may have a profound effect on the level of reflective thinking that students exhibit.

One parallel between ego development and the development of reflective judgment is noteworthy at this point. Over the six years of this study, the SCT and RJI scores of the youngest group (who were high school juniors at the first testing) increased the most, while the scores of the oldest group (advanced graduate students at the first testing) increased the least. This again testifies to the potential for growth among traditional-age college students and/or to the impact of education on the development of both intellect and character.

Psychosocial Development

Two studies have examined the relationship between reflective judgment and psychosocial development (Glatfelter, 1982; Polkosnik and Winston, 1989). Glatfelter examined the relationship between the development of identity and reflective judgment among a sample of eighty college women that included both traditional-age and adult first- and fourth-year students, as well as a group of adult nonstudents. She based her definition of identity on Marcia's (1965, 1967) conception of identity status. His model was derived from Erikson's (1963) theory, which describes eight psychosocial crises that the individual must confront and resolve in order to develop full ego maturity. Marcia expanded on Erikson's notion that for adolescents the crises involve issues of identity and role confusion and observed that there are several styles of coping with psychosocial demands for an individualized identity. These coping styles are determined by whether the adolescent accepts traditional roles and ideologies or experiences a crisis and begins to evaluate alternatives and, secondly, by whether the adolescent makes a commitment to an ideology or vocation or remains uncommitted. Based on this 2 x 2 model (that is, the presence or absence of commitment and crisis), Marcia identified four identity statuses: identity achieved, where the person has experienced a crisis and made a commitment; moratorium, where the person has had a crisis but has made no commitment; foreclosed identity, where the person has made a commitment but not had a crisis; and identity diffused, in which the person has neither made a commitment nor had a crisis. Glatfelter found that the RJI scores were ordered as she predicted, with those in the identity-achieved category scoring the highest and those in the moratorium, foreclosed, and diffused categories scoring successively lower on reflective judgment.

Since those in the achieved status are defined as having examined alternatives and made a commitment, it seems logical to expect that they would have higher RJI scores since examining alternatives is characteristic of the higher Reflective Judgment stages. Similarly, those in the diffused and foreclosed statuses would be expected to score lower on the RJI, since both of these presume that the individual has not gone through a crisis (as defined by Marcia) and has not therefore considered alternatives. The results suggest that development in reflective judgment is related to the examination of alternative vocational and ideological choices. (For a fuller discussion of this point, see Welfel, 1982a.)

Polkosnik and Winston (1989) also examined the relationship between reflective judgment and psychosocial tasks that are associated with the young adult years. Using the work of Chickering (1981) as a foundation for identifying critical psychosocial tasks for college students, they studied the relationship between reflective judgment and the three developmental task areas assessed by the Student Development Task Inventory (SDTI-2) (Winston and Miller, 1984), developing autonomy, developing purpose, and developing mature interpersonal relationships. Autonomy is defined as being self-sufficient and "realistically confident in one's abilities to meet life's challenges with appropriate dependence on others" (Polkosnik and Winston, 1989, p. 13). Purpose is defined as having "formulated clear, realistic educational goals and understand[ing] the relationship between academic study and other aspects of their lives" (Winston and Miller, 1984, p. 1). Mature interpersonal relationships are indicated by "relationships with peers and authority figures that may be described as open, respectful, honest and trusting" (Polkosnik and Winston, 1989, p. 13) rather than exploitative or characterized by stereotyping.

To examine these relationships, Polkosnik and Winston (1989) conducted a longitudinal study with a sample of twenty college students (Time 1) who were stratified by class; students completed the RJI and SDTI-2 and were interviewed about their life experiences (experiences that might be associated with developmental change) three times during one academic year; the sample size at Time 3 was fifteen. The researchers obtained a significant relationship between the autonomy scale and the RJI in the fall term ($r = .41$, $p < .01$), but this declined over the year to a low of .19 in the spring term. Although the relationship between the RJI and the purpose scale remained significant, it also declined over the year, from $r = .67$ ($p < .01$) to $r = .45$ ($p < .05$). The correlation with the relationship scale also declined over the year (from $r = .46$, $p < .05$, in the fall to .37 in the spring). In addition, Polkosnik and Winston discovered preliminary evidence that some life experiences may be related to changes in cognitive development. For example, they found that the RJI scores of two participants who were experiencing very stressful life events dropped at the midpoint testing but recovered and finished with higher RJI scores by the end of the year, after they had weathered the crises. Another two students showed significant increases in RJI scores after they entered therapy.

Taken together, the Glatfelter (1982) and Polkosnik and Winston (1989) studies suggest a moderate relationship between psychosocial development and the development of reflective judgment. Further, although their data are exploratory, they do suggest the possibility that certain life experiences may impede or facilitate the development of reflective thinking, a topic that merits further research.

In sum, the development of the ego (at least as measured by the SCT) does seem to occur independently of the development of reflective thinking (as measured by the RJI). And even though Loevinger (1976) sees the development of the ego as the core of character, it seems to develop independently of the ability to solve ill- or well-structured problems; thus, it may not call for skills that overlap with reflective judgment.

Wisdom: The Integration of Intellect and Character

Wisdom has often been cited as the culmination of adult development. Erikson (1982), for example, identifies wisdom versus despair as the last crisis of maturity, occurring when adults face

Note: This section is based on an article by Kitchener and Brenner, 1990.

the ultimate uncertainties of life as they come to terms with their impending death. The roots of the meaning of wisdom can be traced as far back as the beginning of the written word (Robinson, 1990). It is often characterized as including both a particularly deep or insightful way of knowing and a far-seeing or perceptive way of being with and understanding others. Both characteristics are called into play when a person is facing a thorny, socially relevant, important problem with pragmatic implications. While there are many definitions and descriptions of the psychological components of wise problem solving (see Sternberg, 1990), most involve an awareness of uncertainty and the ability to make sagacious judgments in the face of uncertainty. Thus, although there are many aspects of wisdom that are beyond the definition of reflective judgment, some of these aspects may be understood in light of the development of reflective thinking.

Three components of wisdom discussed in recent literature seem closely related to reflective judgment. First, many authors suggest that wisdom comes into play in the presence of the unavoidable, difficult problems that are inherent in the lives of adults. For example, Dixon and Baltes (1986) argue that wisdom is activated in the presence of difficult problems that do not have clear-cut solutions. Kekes (1983) similarly suggests that wisdom comes into play when people make good judgments about hard cases. These authors suggest that wisdom is not apparent unless individuals are faced with what we have discussed as ill-structured problems.

The second characteristic ascribed to wisdom is an understanding of the fallibility of knowledge (Kitchener, 1983; Meacham, 1990; Taranto, 1989). In other words, wisdom is more than an accumulation of knowledge or experience; it includes an awareness that even with increasing experience and information, uncertainty and doubt will remain about both what we know and what we can know (Meacham, 1990).

Kitchener and Brenner (1990) have noted that an awareness of the limits of human knowing is critical in understanding the kinds of problems that call for wise judgments. Taranto (1989, p. 10) further argues that such problems "appear to call for the kind of intelligence that can recognize not only the limits of one's own knowing in problem solving, but the limits of knowing strategies available for solving problems." These observations link wisdom with an awareness of limitations in knowing; they suggest that wise problem solving is also linked with epistemological assumptions that are consistent with the later reflective judgment stages.

A third characteristic frequently cited in the literature on wisdom is the ability to make astute decisions. This concept is common in biblical and other historical parables. For example, Solomon has been immortalized because of the perceived wisdom of his judgments. In addition, studies of contemporary laypeople suggest that exceptional judgment remains associated with conceptions of wisdom (Holliday and Chandler, 1986; Sternberg, 1985). It is therefore not surprising that many current researchers (Baltes and Smith, 1990; Dixon and Baltes, 1986) characterize wisdom as involving a willingness and ability to formulate sound judgments in the face of uncertainty.

The Reflective Judgment Model and its research base may illuminate at least these three aspects of wisdom. We have already shown in Chapter Six that individuals differ in their understanding of the limits of knowing and in the extent to which they recognize that some problems are ill structured. We have also shown that these characteristics develop with age and education. Furthermore, these data suggest that the ability to understand the fallibility of knowledge typically does not emerge until the early twenties and that the ability to make reasoned judgments in light of the awareness of the limits of knowing does not emerge until even later ages, if at all. If wisdom is dependent upon the awareness of the fallibility of knowledge and the ability to make reasonable judgments in light of these limits, then the development of wisdom may be dependent on the development of the epistemic assumptions that are characteristic of the later stages in the Reflective Judgment Model. Clearly, a person who reduces all problems to puzzles and who assumes that there is a single correct solution to all problems does not fit with our conventional understanding of a wise person. The Reflective Judgment Model suggests that the ability to recognize the uncertainty of knowing and the ability to find the shared meaning that allows a wise judgment is the outcome of a developmental sequence. This may in addition help explain why wisdom is associated with maturity.

Nevertheless, we do not want to suggest that reflective judgment accounts for all aspects of wisdom. Most authors who discuss wisdom relate it to socially relevant, pragmatic intelligence. The Reflective Judgment Interview has focused on socially relevant problems (such as deciding about the safety of food additives and whether to believe a news story). However, other authors have associated wisdom with good communication (Holliday and Chandler, 1986) and with a highly integrated personality that allows people to transcend their own egotistical motives and perspectives (Orwoll and Perlmutter, 1990). Although reflective judgment may be related to the emergence of identity, an integrated personality implies other attributes. Further, the development of reflective judgment has little to say about good communication. What this may suggest is that wisdom is a rare combination of attributes and that the development of reflective judgment as we have conceptualized it is a necessary prerequisite but is certainly not sufficient to account for the whole array of qualities associated with wisdom.

There is, however, one commonly recognized aspect of wisdom that may further our understanding of mature reflective thinking. Many have noted that wisdom assumes a comprehensive grasp of knowledge that is characterized by both breadth and depth (Clayton and Birren, 1980; Dixon and Baltes, 1986; Holliday and Chandler, 1986). These authors suggest that expertise or an expert knowledge base lies at the foundation of the wise person's exceptional understanding. Aristotle, for example, believed that education in philosophy and the classics is essential for the acquisition of wisdom. More recently, others (Clayton, 1982; Holliday and Chandler, 1986) have proposed that a wide range of life experiences and the learning that derives from these experiences are necessary for the emergence of wisdom.

Summary

What can we now say about the relationship between reflective judgment and the development of character? First, both reflective thinking and some aspects of character development are frequently identified as desired outcomes of education, often with the assertion that intellectual development is to be used in the service of helping others, improving society, being better citizens, or other prosocial ends. Research on moral development suggests that these relationships are probably complex and interrelated. For example, reflective thinking appears to be a necessary but not sufficient precursor of moral judgment. These findings suggest that before educators can help students learn to think more complexly about moral or identity problems, they may need to help students master the skills associated with complex thinking (or reflective thinking) itself so that they will have more complex thinking categories available to them. Additionally, while our current descriptions and understanding of wisdom show how much is yet to be learned, they do suggest that higher levels of reflective judgment may be necessary prerequisites for the emergence of wisdom.

In Chapter Seven and this chapter, we have discussed intellect and character as two distinct attributes, but it is important to remember that they are not distinct within the person, and it is unlikely that the intellect and identity develop independently. In fact, the same experience may contribute to growth in both domains. For example, in the context of higher education, Boyer (1987, p. 284) offers the following example of the relationship between these constructs: "When all is said and done, the college should encourage each student to develop the capacity to judge wisely in matters of life and conduct. Time must be taken for exploring ambiguities and reflecting on the imponderables of life—in the classrooms, in the rathskellers, and in bull sessions late at night. The goal is not to indoctrinate students, but to set them free in the world of ideas and provide a climate in which ethical and moral choices can be thoughtfully examined, and convictions formed."

The need for world citizens who can make informed choices and wise judgments is obviously great. If an educational investment in teaching students to think more reflectively also sets a foundation that enables them to make wise ethical and moral choices, that will have been a smart investment indeed.

Chapter Nine

Fostering Reflective Judgment in the College Years

Teaching students to engage in reflective thinking and to make reflective judgments about vexing problems is a central goal of higher education. The authors of *The Challenge of Connecting Learning* (Association of American Colleges, 1991, pp. 16–17) present this goal so lucidly that we believe the quotation with which we opened this book merits repeating: "In the final analysis, the challenge of college, for students and faculty members alike, is empowering individuals to know that the world is far more complex than it first appears, and that they must make interpretive arguments and decisions—judgments that entail real consequences for which they must take responsibility and from which they may not flee by disclaiming expertise."

Rising to this challenge so that students ask more complex questions and make more effective judgments is no small undertaking. As educators, we have the responsibility to teach students the "habits of mind" associated with making interpretative analyses and thoughtful, reasoned arguments. Attempting to teach students to think more reflectively is a complicated and often difficult task: as Bertrand Russell has reminded us, "Some people would rather die than think; in fact, they do" (cited in Flew, 1975, p. 5).

In previous chapters, we have focused on the systematic observation, description, and assessment of the development of reflective thinking. In this chapter, we discuss a variety of issues related to the question, How do students learn to think reflectively? In doing so, we move from an emphasis on the "science of research" to "the art of teaching." Here, we explore the implications of the research base on the Reflective Judgment Model for educational practice. Consistent with the focus and purpose of this book, we will not attempt to review the myriad of approaches that have been proposed to improve college teaching or to teach critical thinking. Rather, we will offer some observations and suggestions about the process of encouraging students to think reflectively, using the definitions and approaches presented in earlier chapters. We believe the Reflective Judgment Model provides a foundation that educators can use to assist students in responsibly questioning their assumptions about knowing and learning and in making better reasoned, more defensible judgments. It is our hope that those who work with students in a variety of settings will find this perspective on intellectual development useful for understanding students' thinking as well as for devising better approaches to deciding what and how they teach.

In this chapter, we use the words *teach* and *teaching* to refer to a wide variety of educationally purposive interactions with students. Such interactions occur between students and faculty but also between students and student affairs professionals in a variety of campus settings. This statement acknowledges that individuals in many roles foster reflective thinking in college students. Accordingly, the terms *teacher* and *educator* are used here inclusively and do not refer solely to those who serve in faculty roles. Although the focus of this chapter is on teaching at the college level, we believe that this chapter is also relevant for those who teach and work with high school students, as well as those who work with adults in noncollege settings.

No single model of intellectual development can capture and adequately describe all the complexities of human reasoning. Models, however, can provide heuristic tools that may be used to help understand some basic differences in the ways students reason and make judgments. They also can help educators learn how to take these differences into account in encouraging students to think more reflectively and to make more reasoned judgments. We offer the Reflective Judgment Model as one such heuristic tool.

Reflective Thinking Among College Students

First-year college students have typically scored just above 3.5 on the Reflective Judgment Interview (see Chapter Six); this means that they evidenced assumptions most consistent with Stages 3 and 4 of the Reflective Judgment Model. (The reader is reminded here that the RJI is a measure of functional rather than optimal level of development, as discussed in Chapter Five. Therefore, the scores summarized here reflect students' typical level of functioning assessed under relatively challenging conditions and probably underestimate the level of functioning they would evidence under more supportive conditions, such as those that could be created for given educational purposes.) Only one sample of academically talented college freshmen averaged a score of 4.0 or above (Kitchener, Lynch, Fischer, and Wood, 1993), and no sample of college freshmen averaged below 3.0. As discussed in earlier chapters, the prevalence of Stage 3 reasoning means that a sizable proportion of the freshmen tested expressed the beliefs that absolute truth is only temporarily inaccessible, that knowing is limited to one's personal impressions about the topic (uninformed by evidence), and that most if not all problems are well structured (defined with a high degree of certainty and completeness). When students such as these encounter more complex or ill-structured problems, they therefore have considerable difficulty in knowing what to believe or how to decide in the face of this uncertainty. Frequently, students who use these assumptions in their reasoning have difficulty relating evidence to their opinion and fall back on simply believing what they want to believe, at least until the truth is known.

The highest average mean score for the college student samples, 5.02, was found for the seniors. By contrast with the freshman samples, every senior sample had an RJI mean score of *over 3.5,* and half were over 4.0. The average score for seniors was 4.00, making the average freshman-senior difference about half a stage (see Table 6.6). Although this numerical difference is small, the development in reasoning it reflects is noteworthy: the Stage 4 reasoning prevalent among the senior samples is clearly more adequate than the reasoning it replaced. Recall that at Stage 4 comes the acknowledgment that uncertainty is not just a temporary condition of knowing, an acknowledgment that sometimes causes the developing student great consternation. As noted earlier, Kroll (1992b) has described this transition by noting that students are abandoning "ignorant certainty" in favor of "intelligent confusion." While confusion is not usually considered a desired educational outcome, it nevertheless indicates a move away from the absolutism of pre-reflective thinking and toward reflective thinking. It is also at Stage 4 that students begin to use evidence to support their judgments, an accomplishment of great educational relevance: skill at understanding the use of evidence provides a crucial foundation for learning how to make data-based interpretations.

These scores also tell us that many seniors are still at a loss when asked to defend their answers to ill-structured problems. A major characteristic of Stage 4 reasoning is the assumption that there are many possible answers to every question and no absolutely certain way to adjudicate between competing answers. Individuals with this assumption will therefore argue that knowledge claims are simply idiosyncratic to the individual. In other words, a solution to an ill-structured problem is seen as merely an opinion. Although individuals holding this assumption idiosyncratically refer to evidence in giving an argument, they do not understand that the interpretation of evidence may be influenced by one's point of view or perspective (a new development at Stage 5). Further, these individuals do not demonstrate the ability to defensibly critique their own judgments as being in some way better than or preferable to alternative judgments (Stage 7). Both of these attributes are hallmarks of reflective thinking. So while educators can take solace in the observation that upward movement is identifiable across educational levels, they may be discomfited by the fact that, as a group, college seniors show little evidence that their "habits of mind" are typically characterized by reflective thinking, at least as defined by the Reflective Judgment Model.

Assumptions About the Nature of the Development of Reflective Judgment

Because the Reflective Judgment Model is explicitly developmental and constructivist in its orientation, it carries with it assumptions about the nature of development that have special implications for educators concerned with fostering reflective thinking. The suggestions for promoting reflective thinking offered in the next section of this chapter are grounded in the following assumptions.

1. *Individuals actively interpret and attempt to make sense of what they experience.* People are not passive recipients of their experiences; rather, they act on their experiences every day as they attempt to understand the world and their role in it. For example, two students who have participated in the same discussion might give wildly different descriptions of the nature and quality of the individual contributions, of the climate of the room during the exercise, and of what they learned from the experience.

2. *How individuals interpret events is affected by their epistemic assumptions.* How individuals make meaning and decide what to believe about an experience, particularly an experience that involves problem solving, is consistent with (if not determined by) their epistemic assumptions (what can be known and with what certainty). When RJI transcripts are examined from the perspective of the individual who constructed the argument, an internal logic to the arguments is apparent, even within arguments that at first may seem to have little coherence. These arguments are consistent when seen from the perspective of the person's epistemic assumptions. When these assumptions are carried into the classroom, they color how students respond to assignments, interpret lectures, and participate in discussions. For example, a teacher of biology shared the following experi-

ence with us. He asked students to read an article that described the evidence for the theory of evolution and then presented a fundamentalist Christian critique of that evidence. The students were then asked to write a short essay in which they expressed an opinion about the issue, indicated whether they thought that their opinion could be "right or wrong," and explained why scientists might have different views on the issue. The students' responses to this assignment yielded rich information about their epistemic assumptions (and could have been taken directly from an RJI transcript). For example, one student argued that there was no solid evidence that proved evolution was a fact and that we would know the truth only when the "missing links between the facts" were found; such reasoning is characteristic of Stage 3, that certain knowledge is only temporarily inaccessible. The student also argued that there was no way to prove that one opinion was better than the other. While this view may have seemed illogical to the instructor, it was predictable in that it was consistent with the assumption stated above. Other students' papers clearly represented assumptions that were characteristic of Stages 4 and 5.

3. *People's ways of making meaning develop over time.* Earlier ways of making meaning mature over time, providing the foundation for later ways of making meaning. For example, the epistemic assumptions described in the reflective judgment stages evolve from simple, one-dimensional structures where truth is assumed to simply exist, received from a single source, to complex multidimensional structures that allow the individual to evaluate information from divergent sources in constructing an interpretation. (Research documenting the development of these thinking skills over time is presented in Chapter Six.)

4. *Individuals function within a "developmental range" of stages* (Fischer, 1980). Our assumption here is that when attempting to reason about an ill-structured problem, an individual has a repertoire of skills that she or he may use in constructing a response and that these may vary across stages. This assumption is consistent with what Rest (1979) has called a complex stage model and with Fischer's (1980) observation that individuals exhibit levels of skills corresponding to a range of stages.

Fischer contrasts a person's "optimal" level, the most advanced reasoning the person is able to use under supportive conditions, and the person's "functional" level, the reasoning that she or he uses under typical conditions. Which type of response an individual uses depends on such factors as the task demands and the context. (See Chapters Two and Four for further discussion of this point.) It also depends on pedagogical factors (the difficulty of the task, the amount of practice provided on the task, the clarity of feedback offered), environmental factors (noise, pressure to compete), and personal factors (emotional preoccupations, prior experiences of a similar nature, test anxiety, fatigue), among others. In other words, we do not make the assumption that individuals function in a single stage at a given point in time. This and other related assumptions of the simple-stage model of development (Rest, 1979) reflect an overly simplified description of the nature of development and of the process of education. Without a supportive learning environment, students will probably give responses that are close to their functional level of reasoning; however, under more supportive conditions, they may perform at a stage or more higher.

5. *Interactions with the environment strongly affect an individual's development.* As Dewey (1944, p. 19) noted: "We never educate directly, but indirectly by means of the environment. Whether we permit chance environments to do the work, or whether we design environments for the purpose makes a great difference." Teachers who design learning environments to foster reflective thinking attend to such factors as the types of intellectual challenges and supports offered, the clarity and quality of feedback, and opportunities for practice without fear of being penalized or failing. The quality of an individual's interactions with the learning environment (broadly defined) can have a dramatic influence on the quality, depth, and pace of development. That is, although the general pattern of development (the sequence of stages) is predictable, the depth and rate of change for any individual fluctuates, depending in part on the characteristics of the environment.

6. *Development is stimulated when an individual's experiences do not match his or her expectations.* Disjunctive experiences that en-

gage a person's attention may provoke him or her to reconsider, reinterpret, or reject prior assumptions or beliefs. Such provocative experiences prod the individual to review earlier assumptions and ways of thinking. Such reviews may lead the person to suspect or realize the drawbacks of prior (or even current) ways of thinking, which leads in turn to the creation of new assumptions and new ways of understanding. Consider the case of an individual who believes that disputes regarding news events ("what really happened") can be resolved by consulting an eyewitness. What does this person do to resolve the conflict created when the descriptions of two or three reputable eyewitnesses offer contradictory descriptions? Such an experience is disconcerting because it is incongruent with the person's assumptions and expectations. When events cannot be understood by using the existing cognitive categories, the individual who seeks to resolve this incongruity is then motivated to find more adequate ways to understand the experience. However, when the experience is so disconcerting that the individual can neither assimilate it nor accommodate to it, the developmental process may stop.

7. *Development in reflective thinking occurs within the context of the individual's background, previous educational experiences, and current life situation.* Development is a cumulative, integrative process. While this book is explicitly focused on only one aspect of an individual's development, the ability to think reflectively, development itself is not so clearly delineated and neither are the students we aspire to teach. College students, as well as other students at all educational levels, are experienced learners and developing individuals. Their characteristics reflect the sum of their prior learning as experienced in a wide variety of contexts from a variety of sources (families, schools, religious activities, peers, movies, television, and so on). Students bring with them the attributes, attitudes, and fears they associate with the part of themselves they identify as learner. These include characteristics associated with their gender, their racial or ethnic background, and/or their socioeconomic status. While some of these characteristics may seem particularly salient for understanding students' readiness (or reticence) to engage in reflective thinking, astute teachers recognize that the other characteristics are

there, too, and have the potential to affect students' success in
many areas. For example, students bring with them the predictable preoccupations and distractions that are associated with
their age or life stage (such as the striving for independence and
the testing of new identities among traditional-age students, or
the caring for children or aging parents among nontraditional-
age students). Unpredictable life events, from illness to family
emergencies to unexpected demands on the job, may also compete for a student's attention. In summary, development of any
aspect of a person occurs within the broader context of the individual's total life experience, and the individual draws from
these experiences in deciding how to make sense of and how
to respond to the educational opportunities presented on college campuses. In other words, the development of reflective
thinking—or any other aspect of the developing person—does
not occur in a vacuum.

Promoting Reflective Thinking:
Observations and Suggestions

Teaching students to think clearly and complexly, to argue co-
herently and persuasively, and to weigh competing claims fairly
and critically is obviously a complicated and difficult process.
Learning to think reflectively, as defined here, includes an ongoing evaluation of one's fundamental assumptions about knowledge itself and about the process of learning. The various steps
in this process are illustrated in the progression of stages in the
Reflective Judgment Model. How can college faculty and staff
members responsibly assist students in examining and reevalu-
ating their assumptions and making more reflective judgments?
More specifically, what kinds of strategies and learning environments can these educators create to encourage students to make
more reflective judgments? That is the topic to which we now
turn our attention.

It is our assumption here that teaching students to think
reflectively is an institutional goal that is best met when it is
built into the whole curriculum—and cocurriculum—of the college, not when it is seen as the sole purview of one group, such

as faculty who teach English composition or even those who teach critical thinking courses. Accordingly, we have drawn from a wide variety of sources in compiling the following suggestions. These are based on numerous discussions with faculty colleagues, research associates, student affairs staff members, students, and our own insights and experiences in teaching and working with students, both in the classroom and in nonclassroom settings. Some of these suggestions relate directly to course assignments and activities; others relate to attitudes and behaviors expressed in other campus settings. All are designed to help those who work with students to become more effective in promoting reflective thinking. (Earlier versions of some of these ideas may be found in Davison, King, and Kitchener, 1990; King, 1992a, 1992b; and Kitchener and King, 1990b.)

In compiling these observations and suggestions, we recognize that teaching is a complex and intensely personal process, that teaching styles and other ways of interacting with students vary dramatically between individuals, and that different approaches are attractive to and effective with different types of students. Therefore, it is not our intent to suggest that there is a single best method for teaching reflective thinking but rather to share our observations and suggestions about this complex process that are derived from our understanding of the development of reflective judgment.

Show respect for students as people regardless of the developmental level(s) they may be exhibiting. The characteristics of the early stages set out in the Reflective Judgment Model are not consistent with true reflective thinking (or with the attributes most colleges are seeking to develop in students). Nevertheless, they are reflections of the sincerely held assumptions about knowledge that some students use to solve controversial problems and are steps in a developmental progression. Therefore, it is important that respect and emotional acceptance be shown to all students, even when their reasoning is not very reflective. A student who feels this acceptance may be more receptive when the insufficiencies of earlier (or current) ways of reasoning are pointed out; the student may also be more willing to take the kinds of intellectual risks that are associated with abandoning comfortable ways of thinking. Educators may find it helpful to recognize the strong internal logic that exists in the patterns of reasoning at each stage (including the early stages, which often appear illogical) and how these assumptions provide building blocks for subsequent, more adequate ways of understanding and resolving problems.

Understand that students differ in regard to their epistemic assumptions (assumptions about knowledge). This understanding allows an educator to respond to these differences on an individual basis. Good teachers are known for their creativity and innovation in adapting their feedback to the nature of the student's response. For example, when Kroll (1992b) tries to foster what he calls reflective inquiry, he attends to the epistemic assumptions that are apparent in student responses and uses these to guide his feedback to students:"When their responses are dogmatic, I foster all their doubts; when they seem mired in skepticism or paralyzed by complexity, I push them to make judgments; when their tactics are not fully reflective, I encourage their best efforts to use critical, evaluative thinking" (p. 13).*

When encouraging reflective thinking with individual students, faculty should recognize that different instructional goals and strategies may be appropriate for students with different epistemic assumptions and that these strategies may need to be changed throughout the course. The choice of goal and strategy, including the skills required or addressed by different activities, as well as the types of feedback offered, depends on the degree to which a student is demonstrating reflective thinking skills, what types of supports she or he needs to master the skills being practiced, and what types of supports the instructor is able (or willing) to offer. In this way, faculty can design assignments and feedback to complement learner characteristics in order to help students think more reflectively.

Student affairs staff, too, can foster reflective thinking by adapting their responses to students' assumptions about knowl-

---

*This brief summary of how Kroll attempts to foster reflective inquiry oversimplifies the insights and the significance of his educational proposals. For an engaging and lucid description of his model of reflective inquiry (connected inquiry, literary inquiry, critical inquiry and ethical inquiry), see Kroll, 1992b.

edge. For example, a yearly event on many campuses occurs when student groups make formal requests to the Student Activities General Fee Allocation Board for financial support of the group's activities. Suppose that an adviser from one of these groups is helping his group prepare its request and overhears several group members complaining about their task. Specifically, he hears that preparing a rationale is a waste of time; why should they have to explain how they want to spend their money? According to the adviser, these students assume that the merit of their request is self-evident; they do not differentiate opinions and beliefs from supporting information. He could encourage them to brainstorm a list of reasons why their request should be funded, as well as possible reasons why the request might be denied. He could write down the supporting reasons in resolution form ("Whereas . . . /therefore . . . "). Another group of students might be having trouble constructing a convincing rationale because they are using supporting reasons and unsubstantiated conclusions interchangeably, assuming that all possible reasons in support of their request are equally valid and that opinions are just as convincing as facts. The adviser could encourage these students not only to participate in the brainstorming but to present the reasons in order of their relevance to the case and their importance. He would not only be helping both sets of group members prepare a better proposal, but he would also be helping them learn and practice the skills associated with reflective thinking. For other examples from student affairs contexts of how students' assumptions about knowledge can be used to help select an educational strategy, see Table 9.1. This table shows how student affairs staff members can assist students in achieving selected educational goals by considering strategies that would be challenging if the students held the epistemic assumptions that are associated with the specified Reflective Judgment stages.

Familiarize students with ill-structured problems within your own discipline or areas of expertise. Do this even early in their educational experience. Such problems should not be viewed as the exclusive domain of seniors, senior seminars, or graduate courses. Students are usually attracted to a discipline because

Table 9.1. Student Affairs Strategies for Promoting Reflective Thinking.

Student affairs area and purpose	Student reflective judgment stage assumption	Educational strategies
Student activities Help students prepare requests for funding to the University Activities General Fee Allocation Board in support of their organization's activities.	Students do not differentiate opinions and beliefs from factual evidence, assuming that the merit of their request is self-evident and that preparing a rationale is a waste of time (Stage 3).	Have students brainstorm a list of reasons why the request should be funded, as well as possible reasons why the request might be denied. Write the supporting reasons in the form of a resolution.
Same as above.	Students assume that all possible reasons in support of the request are equally valid and that opinions are just as convincing as facts (Stage 4).	Have students brainstorm a list of reasons why the request should be funded, as well as possible reasons it might be denied, then present the reasons in order of their importance.
Career development office Help students understand the career selection process and formulate a plan for exploring career possibilities.	Students believe that since career choice is a mysterious process, one should simply choose a career that "seems to fit" (Stage 3).	Administer career inventories, and encourage students to identify specific reasons why some fields might be more comfortable than others.

Residence halls		
RAs help students select a group of sophomores and juniors to participate in a peer advising program.	Students understand the arguments in favor of the different candidates but have difficulty choosing which to hire (Stage 5).	Have students list the specific attributes of each candidate and evaluate how these relate to specific job responsibilities and special staff needs.
Advising student groups		
Help students appreciate that differences in points of view sometimes occur for legitimate reasons (for example, because different people may understand the issue differently).	Group members believe that differences in points of view exist because people deliberately bias information (Stage 4).	Encourage members to explicitly share the reasons for their points of view. When they are considering a controversial decision, have them generate reasons for and against various alternatives.
Academic advising		
Help students understand the rationale for distribution requirements and choose suitable courses in light of this understanding.	Students see no need for general education courses; they believe that disciplines differ only in content and therefore that other disciplines are not relevant to one's major (Stage 4).	Encourage students to take courses from two different disciplines that address the same topic (for example, biology and political science on pollution problems).

Note: This table was first presented by Patricia M. King at the Annual Convention of the American College Personnel Association, March 1991.

it promises a way of better understanding contemporary problems in a particular field, yet they are often asked to "cover the basics" for three or four years before they are permitted to wrestle with the compelling, unresolved issues of the day. Ill-structured problems should be viewed as essential aspects of undergraduate education. When the aim is to help students develop a more complex epistemological framework, opportunities to help students examine the evolution of knowledge itself are especially relevant.

Ill-structured problems exist in most, if not all, disciplines and are not beyond the understanding of most college students. For example, when teaching general chemistry, Finster (1992) illustrates the evolution of knowledge by using historical examples of beliefs about chemistry that were once considered "facts" but are currently seen as errors. In addition, he asks students to consider contemporary scientific problems, such as whether rain is becoming increasingly acidic and causing environmental damage. In addressing such problems, students must struggle with issues involving the reliability and validity of measurement and, more fundamentally, how and what one knows in science. Similarly, an accounting professor composed an ill-structured problem for her college sophomore students that focused on whether to capitalize or expense the costs of a major advertising campaign (Joyce Frakes, personal communication with Karen Kitchener, 1992). Students were asked to evaluate each perspective and judge which was the better approach under the given circumstances.

As noted in Chapter Three, the assumptions students hold about knowledge, about how beliefs can and should be justified, and about the certainty with which knowledge claims can be made affect their assumptions about the learning process and reflect their skill in addressing ill-structured problems. On the basis of this observation, faculty members should insist that the problems students tackle include ill-structured ones, and when students press for easy answers to complicated questions, they should find ways to retain the problematic elements of the questions. As suggested by the authors of *The Challenge of Connecting Learning:* "The role of faculty members is to provide structures and languages . . . that enhance and challenge students' capacities to frame issues, to test hypotheses and arguments against evidence, and to address disputed claims" (Association of American Colleges, 1991, pp. 4–5).

We recognize, of course, that encouraging students to wrestle with ill-structured problems may be easier said than done. Consider the following comment from an instructor of environmental science who is attempting to teach students to evaluate competing hypotheses in ecology: "Major conceptual ideas in ecology are still debated regularly, with no end to the debate in sight. So I try to present both sides, even in introductory ecology. However, no matter how hard I try, this baffles the students. I recently got a memorable comment on a teacher evaluation form: "Don't tell us what the controversies are. Tell us LIKE IT IS!!" (Palmer, personal communication to P. M. King, 1992).

Create multiple opportunities for students to examine different points of view on a topic reflectively. In creating such opportunities, educators should recognize that some students will need more encouragement than others to suspend judgment while becoming informed about a variety of perspectives. Students should be given many opportunities and incentives to *practice* looking at issues from a variety of perspectives, paying particular attention to the evidence used and emphasized by each. For example, students could be encouraged to evaluate contrasting perspectives such as the following: pre-Civil War slavery laws from the perspectives of the abolitionists and states' rights activists; U.S. involvement in Vietnam from the perspectives of the Vietnamese, the French, the U.S. military, and American peace activists; food-labeling proposals from the perspectives of food manufacturers and nutritionists. Examinations that emphasize only factual recall or that do not require students to compare perspectives will not serve this purpose.

Educators in all settings should encourage students to develop and practice strategies for presenting information and ideas from a variety of perspectives so that different views are accurately represented. For example, before offering their own interpretation of a historical event, students should be encouraged to read widely on the topic, including essays that present alternative points of view. (Textbooks that smooth out such differences and synthesize conclusions for the students will probably not be effective for this purpose.) For students who hold early-stage assumptions, reading the essays of others reveals the fact that different perspectives exist on the issue, even among "authorities" in the field, thereby challenging an authority-based view of knowledge. For those who hold the assumptions of the middle stages, such reading can help demonstrate various types of evidence and how each is used and show how evidence can be used to draw conclusions about ill-structured problems. In both cases, reading directed toward breadth and depth should assist students in the process of achieving a more complex understanding of the topic.

Multiple opportunities for practice in understanding and appreciating different points of view exist in both formal and informal settings, using both oral and written approaches. While reading and writing serve as crucial media for understanding different perspectives, faculty and staff should also be aware of the power of the spoken word in modeling reflective thinking and in exposing problems associated with unreflective thinking.

Students have multiple opportunities to watch and listen to others both in the classroom and on television, in newspapers, in the workplace, in the residence halls, and in other places on campus. For example, students who are involved in campus decision making (as members of a residence hall council) or as student representatives on a departmental or campus committee) have a wealth of opportunities to observe and practice reflective thinking and to make judgments about "real world" problems. Hall directors, organization advisers, and other student affairs staff members who work with students in these settings should encourage them to develop their own thinking skills by teaching them how to critique more actively and adequately the reasoning they see and hear so that they can begin to understand the issues they face from a more informed position.

Create opportunities and provide encouragement for students to make judgments and to explain what they believe. In learning to make reflective judgments, students need to practice making and evaluating their own judgments about controversial issues. Students who are introverted or unaccustomed to expressing their own point of view may feel more secure practicing these skills in small groups rather than in front of the entire class. Both small and large campus decision-making bodies offer students rich opportunities to practice arriving at judgments based on more than prior belief or peer pressure. Where such opportunities are not in place, they should be created, not just for the many benefits associated with involvement in the life of the campus (Astin, 1985; Kuh, Schuh, Whitt, and Associates, 1991) but because they provide opportunities to practice making judgments about issues that are relevant to students (Strange, 1992). As Woodrow Wilson once remarked, "the real intellectual life of a body of undergraduates, if there be any, manifests itself not in the classroom, but in what they do and talk of and set before themselves as their favorite objects between classes and lectures" (cited in Bowen, 1977, p. 33). Activities in which students are given the responsibility to make and defend their decisions can be simulated in many arenas, such as in class assignments or activities where they vote in mock elections or hold referenda on current issues or where they are asked to "be the judge," arrive at a verdict about an important case, and then explain the rationale for their judgment. Whether these activities foster thinking and judgments that are truly reflective will depend on the encouragement and support students receive to make an informed judgment and to base their decision on the evidence. It will also depend on whether students see such activities as consistent with and as a valued part of their education. Classes in which students are expected to receive information passively rather than to participate actively will probably not be effective in encouraging students to think reflectively. Similarly, tests and assignments that emphasize only others' definitions of the issues or others' conclusions will not help students learn to define and conclude for themselves.

Student affairs staff members have varied points of contact with students and thus varied opportunities to create environments that encourage and enable students to make reasoned judgments. For example, students who participate as regular voting members on bona fide decision-making committees (not just advisory committees) not only gain the opportunity to practice and refine the skills associated with reflective thinking but to see firsthand the implications of their own judgments and the importance of making good judgments. Involving students in substantive roles on campus judicial boards, staff selection committees, programming committees, fee allocation committees, and even on the board of trustees helps students take better advantage of the educational resources of the college and is consistent with the definition of colleges as intentionally educating communities.

We believe that students will be more likely to learn to think reflectively when this institutional goal is communicated in many institutional contexts, with multiple opportunities in both curricular and cocurricular settings to learn and practice thinking skills involved. As Nevins (1992, p. 27) has noted, "Institutionally, the common language, common mission, and collaborative spirit are critical elements that foster community and commitment to student development."

Informally assess students' assumptions about knowledge and how beliefs should be justified. Reflective journals, response papers, and other assignments and exercises can provide faculty members with a window through which they can view students' epistemic assumptions. For example, a professor could draw a continuum on the chalkboard, with the word *fact* at one end and the word *theory* at the other end. Students could be given a variety of concepts from the field being studied and asked to place them along this continuum. The teacher could ask such questions as, How do you know that something is a fact? What makes something a fact? Can you know for sure that a fact is true? Finster (1992, p. 16) poses questions such as these: "How do we come to know what we claim to know in science? What are scientific facts? Is the scientific method objective? Which questions in science are well-defined and which are ill-defined?"

Kroll (1990a, 1990b) uses a more focused version of this approach in an attempt to stimulate what he calls the skills of critical inquiry. For example, he instructed students to read two reports of the Battle of Ap Bac that took place during the Vietnam War. Then he asked them questions such as, When historical accounts of the same event differ, can you believe one of the accounts more than another? and Is either of these accounts more likely to be true? Having students wrestle with such issues through reflective journals prior to submitting formal papers yielded a wealth of information not only about what students were drawing upon as the basis for their beliefs but what questions, personal issues, or emotional responses were keeping them from making a fully reasoned judgment about the battle.

Other teachers ask students to respond to an ill-structured problem by means of a guided essay format. For example, Wood asked students enrolled in a graduate statistics course whether an obtained correlation coefficient of .5 ($p<.01$) between two measures — problem-solving ability and depression — demonstrated a relationship between the two constructs (Phillip K. Wood, personal communication with Patricia King, 1992). Next, he asked the students to respond in writing to a series of questions similar to those on the RJI, such as the following: "Do you know for sure that your opinion is correct? If so, explain this in terms of statistical significance. If not, why not? What would you have to know (or what would have to be done in the study) in order to know for sure if your opinion is correct?" "Consider for a moment your opinion about experts in this area. Could experts disagree about whether this study showed that problem solving was related to depression? If yes, how could it happen that experts could disagree? What are the implications for your interpretation of the results of this study when it happens that experts disagree about the meaning of the study? If experts could not disagree about whether the constructs were related or not, how could it happen that controversy about the relationship of problem solving to depression might still exist?" Wood has found that such questions help students get beyond an authority-based, right-wrong orientation to learning statistics and make more qualified, thoughtful judgments about statistical questions.

Information gleaned from assignments and exercises such as these is not strictly comparable to that obtained from the RJI. Nevertheless, such assignments can provide teachers with insights about the conceptual orientations their students are using to understand the information they are learning in their courses.

In college counseling centers, counselors often informally assess clients during initial interviews, both for pathology and for developmental functioning. Adding questions that tap students' levels of reflective judgment may give a counselor important insights into the ways they approach and solve the problems in their lives. For example, in the career area, a counselor might ask how students think people ought to go about making career decisions, whether they believe that a single career is "right" for them, and what kind of evidence might convince them that a particular career was a good choice. Clarifying clients' assumptions about problem solving at the outset may help a counselor understand clients' "blocks" to engaging in problem solving or decision making and also help him or her avoid labeling developmentally appropriate assumptions as resistance.

Acknowledge that students work within a developmental range of stages, and target expectations and goals accordingly. Students display different levels of reasoning when addressing ill-structured problems, depending on the context of the assessment, including the amount of "conceptual support" (Fischer, 1980) that is available. These levels of reasoning range from an individual's typical or *functional level* to her or his *optimal level,* the highest level of performance that the individual is capable of producing under supportive conditions. (More recently, Bidel and Fischer [1992, p. 25] have proposed an extension beyond optimal level, the *scaffolded level,* which requires that a third person with a higher level of skill coach the child or assist with the task.) Kitchener, Lynch, Fischer, and Wood (1993) have found that, on average, students' optimal level is about one stage higher than their functional level of reflective judgment.

In contrast to simple-stage models of development, where a person is assumed to be "in" one stage of development at a time, the Reflective Judgment Model assumes that individuals function within a range of stages; this suggests a different set of educational implications. The first of these is derived from our conviction that any determination of a student's developmental "level" is affected by the context of the assessment, including such factors as fatigue, noise, and other distractions, as well as the types of problems posed and whether and how the necessary skills needed to resolve these problems have been taught. In light of this predictable degree of variability, faculty and student affairs staff should at minimum rely on multiple forms of assessment rather than a single measure or even a series of measures that use a single format.

Second, we suggest that educators provide multiple examples in which higher-level reasoning skills are used so that they can offer students clear feedback on the skills they are using and can find many means to encourage students to practice higher-level skills. This suggestion is based on Fischer's (1980) claim that a person's optimal level of development is elicited when two basic "contextual supports" are in place: when the individual has received instruction or feedback ("contextual cues") regarding the nature of high level performance and when he or she has practiced the skill. Finding out what skills a student can use under optimal conditions requires sustained contact with the student, and probably a trusting relationship as well. Those who are privileged to enjoy sustained contact with students through courses, committees, residential arrangements, or other means have a distinct advantage in creating or capitalizing on opportunities to assist students in refining their higher-level skills rather than relying solely on their prior skills, even though these are more familiar and more comfortable.

Third, we encourage faculty and student affairs staff to aim their educational efforts at a student's functional *and* optimal levels of reasoning. As Kroll (1992a, p. 13) has proposed, educators should "work at the leading edge of development rather than its center." In doing so, they should recognize that a student may lack some of the skills necessary to operate fully at her or his optimal level without substantial opportunities to develop and practice these new skills. Since a student's developmental range appears to span two or at most three stages, educators need to be prepared to target their educational strategies across a range of stages. (It is unlikely that any given group of college students would evidence reasoning at all seven Reflective Judgment stages.)

Unfortunately, there is no precise formula that will quickly and easily tell teachers what skills each individual student has mastered and which she or he is missing. What is necessary is that teachers ascertain the epistemic issues with which students are struggling (using exercises such as those proposed in the preceding section), model higher-level reasoning themselves, and provide opportunities for students to consider issues and practice skills that will help them resolve that struggle.

Provide both challenges and supports in interactions with students. This suggestion is grounded in the work of Nevitt Sanford (1966), who claimed that the environmental forces that challenge students to grow and develop must be balanced by environmental forces that provide personal support. Challenges involve those activities that are explicitly designed to engage students in new ways of thinking. For students who are using pre-reflective assumptions, this may involve introducing them to several alternative views of an issue. For those who are using quasi-reflective assumptions, the goal may be to help them use evidence to argue persuasively. Many professors use debates on controversial issues to help students develop this skill, requiring participants to present specific sets of reasons for their conclusions, with other class members or invited guests voting on the most persuasive rationale or offering other evaluative assessments. Student affairs staff members also use debates on campus issues to help students better understand issues that affect them and become more productively involved in their resolution. In these examples, the strategies not only help students gain a fuller understanding of both (or several) sides of an issue, but they involve students in the process of examining the basis for holding different beliefs and the relationship between evidence and conclusions. These skills are essential for reflective thinking.

One implication of this model for educators who wish to offer highly challenging activities is that they must also lay a supportive foundation so that students will risk using those higher-level reasoning skills that feel unfamiliar or that introduce doubt and perplexity. Laying such a foundation involves making the topics interesting and engaging, ensuring that students have the necessary background and skills to engage in the challenging task, and legitimizing students' discomfort with the challenges posed. The support can come from the clarity of rules governing the debate, the support of peers who are also involved, and the engaging atmosphere that is created to stimulate interest in the event.

Another favorite strategy is to analyze examples from familiar advertisements so that students will recognize the fallacious reasoning behind some claims. For example, an instructor of marketing wanted students to evaluate arguments for targeting alcohol advertisements to a particular racial group. One focus of this assignment was on the ethical implications of this strategy; the other was on evaluating the evidence on both sides of the issue and making a judgment about the potential effectiveness of the campaign. Providing support for the assignment involved ensuring that the students had the necessary background information to evaluate the arguments, providing some earlier experience in evaluating arguments concerning a less volatile issue, and providing verbal reassurance that this was both a difficult and an important task for the students to undertake.

In attempting to provide appropriate supports and challenges, educators should be aware that what students perceive as challenges and supports differs by developmental level, an insightful observation made by Widick, Knefelkamp, and Parker (1975). For example, students who believe that viewpoints should be grounded in evidence would find it especially challenging to defend orally a point of view they did not personally hold. Educators could provide support for these students by affirming their assumptions that arguments need to be based on convincing evidence (the focus on argument-building skills inherent in the exercise) and by assuring them that other class members were "in the same boat" and faced with the same constraints. However, for students who believe that points of view are selected arbitrarily (Stage 3 reasoning), the supports and challenges would be reversed; these students would find it relatively easy to state a point of view they did not endorse because the criteria for endorsement are not clear. For them, the challenge would lie in building an argument based on evidence. They, too, would probably feel supported because their peers would be facing the same constraints on the undertaking.

In teaching reflective thinking, it is crucial to recognize that students' epistemic assumptions affect their perceptions of challenging and supportive interactions. This essential insight explains why a favorite strategy works quite effectively with some students, yet fails to elicit reflective thinking with others. It also illustrates the complexity of teaching reflective thinking.

Recognize that challenges and supports can be grounded emotionally as well as cognitively. In most of the foregoing examples, the "supports" were cognitive supports. However, the quality of teachers' emotional supports (an encouraging comment, a vote of confidence, an acknowledgment that this is a difficult assignment) may also affect a student's willingness to tackle or persevere on a difficult problem. Similarly, "challenges" can also entail affective dimensions: when certain topics or educational strategies are emotionally challenging for particular students, this situation should be acknowledged. For example, learning about atrocities conducted in a war in which a student's own relatives fought might make her wonder whether her grandfather had been involved in such reprehensible conduct; studying about campus violence has made some men wonder if they have committed a rape; studying evolution in a biology course or biblical passages in a literature course may cause students to reexamine the basis for their own religious beliefs. To expect students to write detached, objective analyses of situations for which they have unresolved or emerging personal issues is to deny that students are multifaceted individuals, not just "talking heads," and that emotionally powerful questions may serve as barriers to reflective thinking on particular issues.

In his book on the evolution of knowing, Kegan (1982) notes that affect is inherently involved in the development of new ways of making meaning of the world. From his perspective, affect is "the felt experience of a motion (hence, e-motion)" (p. 81). Thus, when educators actively engage students in a developmental process, they are involving them in activities that are intrinsically emotional as well as cognitive. Student affairs staff members are typically very attuned to students' emotional needs and have a wealth of firsthand experience in helping students gain the self-confidence, personal stability, self-discipline, assertiveness, or other personal attributes that can dramatically affect their adjustment to college and how well they take advantage of their collegiate opportunities. As a group, these staff members are very adept at anticipating and providing emotional supports for students.

In working with faculty members interested in reflective thinking, we have found that as a group, these individuals are very adept, experienced, and articulate when asked to identify the intellectual challenges of concepts or assignments from their classes; they are less facile and articulate in identifying the intellectual supports. But in our experience, they have the most difficulty identifying the emotional challenges and supports; this seems to be very unfamiliar territory to many faculty members. For some, the notion that their effectiveness in assisting students to think reflectively may require that they attend to the emotional side of learning adds a genuinely new dimension to their role. Providing emotional support or challenge is quite foreign and not a little uncomfortable for these professors because this goes beyond their conception of what it means to foster good thinking. (For an eloquent defense of the importance of paying attention to students' emotional reactions to course material and classroom process, see Kroll, 1992b.) However, educators need to acknowledge that the revolutions in thinking that are associated with development in reflective thinking may be disturbing, frustrating, and even frightening to students. At minimum, their frustrations need be acknowledged. Additional support may be offered in a variety of ways, such as showing confidence in students' ability to master the task, publicly recognizing their effort, suggesting additional examples or resources when they are floundering, being available for consultation, encouraging them to take intellectual risks, and providing environments that allow them to practice the targeted skills and correct their own mistakes without penalty. Here, too, faculty and staff need to be aware that the behaviors they perceive as supportive (holding more office hours, showing personal interest in students) may be seen as threatening by a student overwhelmed at the possibility of a one-to-one conversation or a personal relationship with a member of the professional staff of the college. This is yet one more example of the need to build trusting relationships with students.

Be cognizant of which skills are required for selected activities or assignments. Recognize that students with different reasoning skills and varying assumptions about knowledge and learning will not perceive those tasks in the same ways: they will find different activities to be threatening or engaging, and they will find different characteristics of the learning environment to be challenging or supportive. We also encourage all educators to recognize the interrelationships between educational goals, learner characteristics (especially as these change over time and tasks), and specific educational activities.

It is noteworthy that almost all of our preceding points presume that students are actively engaged in the learning process. (The importance of this is addressed by Chickering and Gamson, 1991.) As we discussed earlier in this chapter, people are not passive recipients of experience, and development is inexorably tied to active processing. This implies that faculty need to use strategies such as discussions, simulations, and writing assignments that involve students in actively assimilating new information and ideas. It is only by such activity that underlying conceptual structures will change. This is not to say that lectures do not play a role in the classroom: they can be used to efficiently provide students with information. It is more often the case, however, that lectures treat students as vessels to be filled with information, and students may or may not actively engage in considering the information supplied. One of the greatest drawbacks of the lecture format is that a student's independent analysis of the information provided is usually optional. Teaching strategies that require students to process new concepts will probably be more effective in changing underlying epistemic assumptions. Giving students individual feedback on their progress toward specified thinking skills is not only important but time-consuming. In their summary of the research on class size and teaching effectiveness, Pascarella and Terenzini (1991, p. 87) note that while factual knowledge can be effectively conveyed in large classes, "smaller classes are somewhat more effective than larger ones when the goals of instruction

are motivational, attitudinal, or higher-level cognitive processes."
Smaller contexts allow educators to match more intentionally
the skills required for a selected activity to specified student characteristics and to give developmentally appropriate feedback in
order to foster reflective thinking. We encourage faculty to take
advantage of these smaller contexts where they already exist and
to create them where necessary for this purpose.

To be more explicit about the relationships between course
activities and student characteristics (in particular, their epistemic assumptions), we developed a series of resource exhibits.
These exhibits grew out of extended discussions about the educational implications of the reasoning that is characteristic of various Reflective Judgment stages.* Each exhibit contains five sections: (a) a brief summary of the characteristic assumptions of
a given stage of reasoning, (b) sample instructional goals for
students who hold such assumptions, (c) a sampling of difficult
tasks from the perspective of someone holding this set of stage-
related assumptions, (d) sample assignments designed to stimulate development (challenges), and (e) types of supportive activities that would complement the challenges in the service of
the instructional goals. These are presented in Exhibits 9.1
through 9.5. We offer these exhibits in the hope that they will
stimulate educators to consider carefully the individual elements
presented here (students' assumptions about knowledge, instructional goals, skills required for various assignments), as well as
their interrelationships, and to engage in the thoughtful exchange
of ideas with colleagues as well as students about the process
of learning to think reflectively.

Several other resources are available for readers interested
in applications based on the Reflective Judgment Model. One
is a special issue of *Liberal Education* (King, 1992c) that describes
a series of five sets of strategies teachers have used to stimulate

*These examples, as well as many of the other suggestions presented in this chapter
were developed in part through the support of a grant from the Fund for the Improvement of Postsecondary Education, Application No. P116B00926, "Assessing
Reflective Thinking in Curricular Contexts." The authors would like to acknowledge the contributions of Jonathan Dings, Tammy Gocial, and Cindy Lynch,
our former graduate students, to earlier drafts of these exhibits.

reflective thinking. The articles in this issue range from the teaching of English to the study of chemistry (Kroll, 1992a; Finster, 1992); they include using learner characteristics as the focus of a faculty development program (Nevins, 1992); they consider teaching honors students (Haas, 1992); and they address issues of teaching reflective thinking outside formal classroom settings (Strange, 1992). Other articles that have appeared elsewhere

Exhibit 9.1. Promoting Reflective Thinking — Stage 2 Reasoning.

Characteristic assumptions of Stage 2 reasoning

1. Knowledge is certain, but some people do not have access to it.
2. Authorities such as scientists, teachers, and religious leaders know the truth.
3. When the truth is uncertain, accept the view of an authority.
4. Evidence is not a criterion for establishing truthfulness.

Instructional goals for students

1. Accept that there may be several opinions about a controversial issue, none of which is known to be absolutely correct.
2. Recognize that authorities sometimes disagree with each other.
3. Give reasons for beliefs beyond relying on the word of an authority.

Difficult tasks from a Stage 2 perspective

1. Recognizing that there are legitimate differences of opinion about some issues.
2. Giving reasons for a belief beyond reference to an authority's view.
3. Accepting that even authorities do not have right or wrong answers for some issues.

Sample developmental assignments

1. Consider two interpretations of a poem, historical event, scientific study, and so forth.
2. Provide arguments on two sides of an issue, giving reasons for the arguments.
3. Identify the evidence for different views on the same issue.
4. Consider the views of different experts on a particular event.

Developmental support for instructional goals

1. Acknowledge that decisions are harder when there are no right or wrong answers.
2. Attempt to legitimize students' feelings of anxiety when confronted with multiple perspectives on an issue.
3. Provide clear, unambiguous directions (including details and deadlines) for assignments.
4. Point out noted authorities who hold alternative points of view.

Exhibit 9.2. Promoting Reflective Thinking—Stage 3 Reasoning.

Characteristic assumptions of Stage 3 reasoning

1. Knowledge is absolutely certain in some areas and temporarily uncertain in other areas.
2. Beliefs are justified according to the word of an authority in areas of certainty and according to what "feels right" in areas of uncertainty.
3. Evidence can neither be evaluated nor used to reason to conclusions.
4. Opinions and beliefs cannot be distinguished from factual evidence.

Instructional goals for students

1. Learn to use evidence in reasoning to a point of view.
2. Learn to view their own experiences as one potential source of information but not as the only valid source.

Difficult tasks from a Stage 3 perspective

1. Recognizing legitimate sources of authority as better qualified than themselves in making a judgment about a controversial issue.
2. Understanding the difference between interpretation and opinion.
3. Using evidence to justify a point of view.
4. Appreciating multiple evidence-based perspectives on a single issue.

Sample developmental assignments

1. Evaluate an inadequate argument [one that uses Stage 2 reasoning] in terms of its use of evidence, dependence upon authority, and understanding of the other side of the argument.
2. Here is one point of view on an issue. What are other possible perspectives on this issue? Cite evidence for each perspective.
3. Critique a specified point of view, paying particular attention to the use of evidence.
4. Defend a specified point of view, giving the best evidence you can find in support of it.
5. Give the best evidence you can find for a specific point of view, bearing in mind issues of what counts as evidence and what makes one source of evidence more credible than another.

Developmental support for instructional goals

1. Attempt to legitimize students' struggle with feelings of being confused and overwhelmed by the issue of what counts as evidence.
2. Model good use of evidence by explicitly presenting justification for both sides of an argument, distinguishing inapplicable evidence from relevant evidence, and explaining the rationale behind one's choice of appropriate authorities.
3. Provide detailed assignments and clear expectations whenever possible.

Exhibit 9.3. Promoting Reflective Thinking—Stage 4 Reasoning.

Characteristic assumptions of Stage 4 reasoning

1. Knowledge is uncertain because of limitations of the knower.
2. Beliefs are justified by idiosyncratic uses of evidence and opinion.
3. Differences in points of view exist because of people's upbringing or because they deliberately distort information.
4. Evidence is used in support of a point of view along with unsubstantiated opinion.

Instructional goals for students

1. Learn that interpretation is inherent in all understanding and that the uncertainty of knowledge is a consequence of the inability to know directly.
2. Learn that some arguments can be evaluated as better within a domain on the basis of the adequacy of the evidence.

Difficult tasks from a Stage 4 perspective

1. Understanding that the nature of knowing itself leads to the uncertainty of knowledge.
2. Understanding that all points of view are not equally valid.
3. Understanding that opinions should be based on evidence.
4. Understanding that different perspectives may lead to different legitimate interpretations of evidence but that this is not the same as bias.
5. Understanding the difference between facts and interpretations.

Sample developmental assignments

1. Explicitly consider the extent to which knowledge is certain within a specific discipline and across disciplines by comparing and contrasting the reasons for uncertainty in difficult cases.
2. Compare good and bad arguments on one side of an issue; evaluate the adequacy of these arguments by looking at the evidence and how it is interpreted and noting what makes a stronger argument.
3. Here are two conflicting points of view on an issue. Explain how the author of each arrived at his or her conclusions. Pay careful attention to the academic discipline or perspective from which the issue was approached.
4. Distinguish between evaluating the adequacy of arguments and making judgments about people.

Developmental support for instructional goals

1. Model evaluating arguments without being intolerant.
2. Model and explain how different interpretations may legitimately arise.
3. Legitimize students' discomfort with evaluation.

Exhibit 9.4. Promoting Reflective Thinking—Stage 5 Reasoning.

Characteristic assumptions of Stage 5 reasoning

1. Interpretation is inherent in all understanding; therefore, no knowledge is certain.
2. Beliefs may be justified only within a given context or from a given perspective.
3. Evidence can be evaluated qualitatively: within a perspective, some evidence is stronger or more relevant than other evidence.

Instructional goals for students

1. Learn to relate alternative perspectives on an issue to each other by comparing and contrasting them and evaluating their strengths and weaknesses.
2. Learn to determine whether it is possible to arrive at an appropriate integration of the competing alternatives.

Difficult tasks from a Stage 5 perspective

1. Choosing among competing evidence-based interpretations.
2. Explaining relationships between alternative perspectives on an issue.
3. Recognizing that choosing one alternative does not deny the legitimacy of other alternatives.

Sample developmental assignments

1. Compare and contrast two competing (and unequal) points of view, citing and evaluating evidence and arguments used by proponents of each. Determine which proponent makes the better interpretation of the given evidence and which conclusion is stronger.
2. Here are two conflicting points of view on the same issue. Explain how each author arrived at his or her conclusions. Identify the evidence and arguments for each point of view, suggesting which has stronger support. Explain which view you would endorse and why you would do so.
3. Select and analyze one controversial issue from among those discussed in class or in the course readings. Your analysis should consist of (a) a summary of the issue, including an explanation of its significance to this discipline; (b) a description of at least two points of view from which this issue has been addressed by scholars; and (c) some indication of which point of view you believe to be the most appropriate of those selected and the grounds upon which you base this decision.

Developmental support for instructional goals

1. Model and explain appropriate scholarly inquiry, explicitly approaching issues from several inter- or intradisciplinary perspectives.
2. Give relevant interpretations of evidence from each perspective chosen, and explain the reasoning behind choosing one interpretation over another.
3. Legitimize students' struggle to adjudicate between competing interpretations and perspectives, both cognitively and affectively.

Exhibit 9.5. Promoting Reflective Thinking — Stage 6 Reasoning.

Characteristic assumptions of Stage 6 reasoning

1. Knowledge is uncertain and must be understood in relationship to context and evidence.
2. Some points of view may be tentatively judged as better than others.
3. Evidence on different points of view can be compared and evaluated as a basis for justification.

Instructional goals for students

1. Learn to construct one's own point of view and to see that point of view as open to reevaluation and revision in light of new evidence.
2. Learn that even though knowledge must be constructed, strong conclusions are epistemologically justifiable.

Difficult tasks from a Stage 6 perspective

1. Understanding that even though knowledge may change at some future point, some principles or procedures are currently generalizable beyond the immediate situation.
2. Constructing one's own point of view and defending it on the basis of evidence or argument as being better (for example, having greater truth value) than other points of view.

Sample developmental assignments

1. Develop and defend firm arguments for a particular point of view, perhaps in conjunction with your own research.
2. Provide your own organization of a given field of study (for example, concept mapping of a course or a discipline), with explicit reference to the interrelationships between elements.

Developmental support for instructional goals

1. Model holding and defending firm points of view without exhibiting intolerance for other points of view.
2. Provide examples of increasingly better points of view (for example, more comprehensive, more coherent) developed over time as more and better evidence, arguments, and techniques become available.
3. Emphasize the importance of developing and defending arguments about complex ill-structured problems, as well as the difficulty in doing so.

---

apply the Reflective Judgment Model to the teaching of writing (Davison, King and Kitchener, 1990), adult education (Kitchener and King, 1990b), counseling theory (Brabeck and Welfel, 1985) and career counseling (Welfel, 1982a).

Kronholm (1993) has also developed a model of teaching called the Reflective Judgment — Developmental Instruction

Model. This seven-phase model details a sequence of activities designed to actively engage students in the process of arriving at and defending points of view about controversial issues. While Kronholm's examples focus on an undergraduate class in environmental education, this model is appropriate for use in a variety of disciplines.

Foster a climate that promotes thoughtful analysis of issues throughout the campus. This suggestion recognizes that learning to think reflectively occurs within the context of a student's intellectual community, from the immediate environment of his or her living group or specific class to the broader community of the college and its environs. Fostering such a climate can be done by encouraging the exchange of a broad variety of ideas in many campus forums, from classes to campuswide lecture series to theater productions. In a college committed to thoughtful discourse, educators are encouraged to foster an atmosphere of thoughtful reasoning, whether they are in the classroom or involved in student activities. Faculty who interact with students in classrooms or laboratories, advisers who work with student government or other student organizations, and student affairs staff members who work in residence halls, counseling centers, or other campus offices all have special opportunities and the collective responsibility for teaching students to think reflectively. Together, they can model reflective thinking and support reasoned discourse on the campus, thereby exemplifying the educational values of the institution. Those values include both the importance of educational activities that elicit a reflective, reasoned response from students and the importance of understanding individual differences in point of view and appreciating diverse views for the perspectives they contribute. This need to understand and appreciate perspectives is as necessary at the national and international levels as it is at the personal and community levels.

Why are such values so important? As Boyer (1987, p. 280) states so succinctly, they are important because "where human survival is at stake, ignorance is not an acceptable alternative." He goes on to say: "We need concerned people who are participants in inquiry, who know how to ask the right questions, who understand the process by which public policy is shaped, and are prepared to make informed, discriminating judgments on questions that affect the future. Obviously, no one institution in society can single-handedly provide the leadership we require. But we are convinced that the undergraduate college, perhaps more than any other institution, is obliged to provide the enlightened leadership our nation urgently requires if government by the people is to endure" (p. 280). To meet this goal, colleges must teach students to make reflective judgments.

Summary

Many educational activities can be designed to give students opportunities to engage in higher-order reasoning and to gain skill in making reflective judgments. Educators in a variety of collegiate settings already encourage such skills as recognizing and understanding divergent perspectives, making data-based interpretations, reasoning to conclusions in light of uncertainty, and making connections between course materials and contemporary issues. But teaching strategies address only one element of a complex equation. Many other factors influence the process of learning to make reflective judgments, including a student's established reasoning skills, his or her emotional readiness to defend a point of view in front of peers, the cognitive and emotional supports that are available in the specific learning environment (whether a classroom or residence hall), the educational values that are emphasized in the student's college, and the broader societal norms and expectations for reasoned discourse about current events.

Research on the Reflective Judgment Model suggests that college students are wrestling with issues of certainty and uncertainty, and that they are struggling to find methods for resolving perplexity when they must make and defend judgments. Students need to learn the skills that allow them to make judgments in light of that uncertainty: how to think about the relationship between evidence and a point of view, how to evaluate evidence on different sides of issues, how to conceive of objectivity or impartiality, and how to construct judgments in the face of complexity and uncertainty. Moreover, students need to understand the relevance and importance of these skills for their own lives — as effective citizens, consumers, or parents. While it may be unrealistic to assume that all college students will become advanced reflective thinkers in four or five years, it is a laudable goal nevertheless. At minimum, we believe that as members of educating communities, we should strive to foster intellectual development, doing all that we can to encourage reflective thinking in college students.

The Reflective Judgment Interview

This resource includes four sections: (1) a list of the standard RJI problems; (2) examples of discipline-based problems from psychology, business, and chemistry; (3) procedures for conducting the RJI; and (4) procedures for scoring RJI transcripts. The first four problems are taken from King (1977) and Kitchener (1977–78). The fifth problem was developed for the ten-year longitudinal study reported in this book and in King, Kitchener, and Wood (1990, 1991). The standard RJI probe questions are given in Table 5.1.

Standard Problems

1. Most historians claim that the pyramids were built as tombs for kings by the ancient Egyptians, using human labor, and aided by ropes, pulleys, and rollers. Others have suggested that the Egyptians could not have built such huge structures by themselves, for they had neither the mathematical knowledge, the necessary tools, nor an adequate source of power.

2. Some people believe that news stories represent unbiased, objective reporting of news events. Others say that there is no such thing as un-

biased, objective reporting, and that even in reporting the facts, the news reporters project their own interpretations into what they write.

3. Many religions of the world have creation stories. These stories suggest that a divine being created the earth and its people. Scientists claim, however, that people evolved from lower animal forms (some of which were similar to apes) into the human forms known today.

4. There have been frequent reports about the relationship between chemicals that are added to foods and the safety of these foods. Some studies indicate that such chemicals can cause cancer, making these foods unsafe to eat. Other studies, however, show that chemical additives are not harmful, and actually make the foods containing them more safe to eat.

5. The safety of nuclear energy is currently being debated by scientists in many fields. Some scientists believe that nuclear energy is safe and that nuclear energy can substantially alleviate our dependence on non-renewable resources. Others argue that nuclear energy is inherently unsafe and that nuclear energy plants will lead to widespread and long-term environmental pollution.*

Examples of Discipline-Based Problems

The following two psychology problems were developed by Phillip Wood and Kurt DeBord, University of Missouri, Columbia. The following business problems were developed by Karen Kitchener and Cindy Lynch, University of Denver. The chemistry problems were developed by Patricia King, Bowling Green State University, with the assistance of David Finster, Wittenberg University.

*This problem was developed in 1987.

Psychology Problems

Some researchers contend that alcoholism is due, at least in part, to genetic factors. They often refer to results from a number of family studies to support this contention. Other researchers, however, do not think that alcoholism is in any way inherited. They claim that alcoholism is psychologically determined. They also claim that the reason that several members of the same family often suffer from alcoholism is due to the fact that they share common family experiences, socioeconomic status, or employment.

Some counselors conduct therapy with depressed clients who desire medication as a part of their therapy. These counselors believe medication is a positive, powerful force in therapy. They conduct therapy sessions with such clients and also refer them to physicians who prescribe the appropriate medications. Other counselors do not believe medications are appropriate for depressed clients. These counselors argue that counseling alone is the best way to overcome depression. They believe that the benefits of medication never outweigh the physical disadvantages or the psychological disadvantages of "using drugs to solve your problems."

Business Problems

Selecting and hiring the best employee is a difficult decision for employers. Some people believe that the most important criterion is how highly qualified the applicant is in relation to the written job description. Others believe it is more important that a new employee fit in with the personalities of the other members of the work team, assuming the applicant's qualifications are adequate.

The 1980s was a decade of relative prosperity in the United States. Some people suggest this prosperity was due to lower tax rates. Others dispute the benefits of lower tax rates, claiming that this decade of prosperity was primarily due to other economic factors, such as low inflation or stable growth in the money supply.

Chemistry Problems

Determining the mass of an electron is an experiment that chemists have been conducting for decades. Some say that we can now know this mass with certainty because we can determine it with such a high degree of precision. Others say that because all measurements involve uncertainty, we can never know the true mass of an electron.

Some scientists believe that explanations of chemical phenomena, such as atomic theory, are accurate and true descriptions of atomic structure. Other scientists say that we cannot know whether or not these theories are accurate and true, but that scientists can only use such theories as working models to explain what is observed.

Conducting the Reflective Judgment Interview

The interviewer first reads the following introductory statement, in which the purpose of the interview is explained.

> During this hour we will be talking about several issues which are of general concern and about which most people are at least vaguely familiar. I am not concerned with *how much information* you have about any issue, but *how you think* about them. In order to standardize what we talk about, I will be asking the same series of questions for each issue; I am not repeating the questions because I am looking for a particular answer. For each issue, I will read a statement out loud while you follow along on a card. After I finish reading the statement, I'll give you a minute or so to think about the issue and then we will talk about it. Are there any questions before we begin?

The interviewee is also informed of the fact that the interview will be tape-recorded.

The interviewer next reads the first problem aloud while the participant follows along on a typed card. (This makes it possible to use the interview with those for whom reading is difficult.) Participants are then asked to state and justify their own point of view about this issue and to respond, in order, to the six follow-up questions (listed in Table 5.1). These questions are asked for each of the problems used in the interview, which are presented in random or counterbalanced order. The complete interview takes about forty-five to sixty minutes when four problems are used.

As noted in Table 5.1, the first question asks participants for their point of view on the problem. Occasionally, a person will not take a point of view on the issue. In this case, six parallel probe questions are used to elicit the individual's rationale for not taking a point of view and how this is related to his or her assumptions about knowing.

If the response to a given probe question is incomplete, ambiguous, or contradictory to earlier statements, interviewers are instructed to ask for clarification or elaboration, asking such questions as: "What do you mean by 'the most reasonable' explanation?" or "What's the difference between 'knowing for sure' and 'being fairly certain'?" "And how did that experience change your thinking about [news reporting, chemical additives in foods, and so on]?"

Occasionally, the response to the probe is such that the respondent "dismisses" the controversy before it has been fully explored with the interviewer. In this case, the interviewer is instructed to reframe the controversy in order to retain it. For example, a person might reply that two experts disagree about the creation of the universe because one believes in God and the other is an atheist. The interviewer would then ask, "What if they both believed in God [or were both atheists] and still held different views about whether or not evolution occurred?" Or a respondent might reply that experts disagree because they had access to different information. The interviewer would then ask, "What if they both had access to the *same* information?" Such probing is designed to focus the interview on questions that are likely to yield information about people's epistemic assumptions, to encourage the participants to take the interview seriously, to explain the meaning they ascribe to their own experiences in dealing with ill-structured problems, and ultimately to yield clearer, more easily ratable data by clarifying participants' understandings and assumptions.

The interviews are usually conducted in person, but they have been successfully conducted over the telephone by experienced interviewers. The disadvantage of telephone interviews is that it is more difficult to pick up nonverbal cues. For example, an interviewee could be silent because she or he was thinking, puzzled by the question, fatigued, or distracted, each of which might lead the interviewer to proceed somewhat differently (give the person more time to think quietly or regain the person's attention).

Scoring Reflective Judgment Interview Transcripts

In preparation for scoring, the participant responses to each problem are transcribed as separate units, and different participant code numbers are assigned to each problem. (Using this procedure, raters are "blind" to the same person's scores on the other problems.)

Each problem is then independently rated by two certified raters, according to the Reflective Judgment Scoring Rules (Kitchener & King, 1985). For each of the seven stages, these scoring rules are divided into two major sections, each of which is subsequently divided into three subsections: (1) nature of knowledge (view of knowledge, "right versus wrong" knowledge, legitimacy of differences in viewpoints) and (2) nature of justification (concept of justification, use of evidence, role of authority in making judgments). Responses to each of the follow-up questions are rated by referring to one of the subsections in the scoring rules. For example, information about the respondent's *view of knowledge* is gleaned from the questions regarding whether or not she or he *knows for sure* about the issue. The response is given a stage score based on its fit with that section of the scoring rules.

If responses to all of the standard questions are ratable, the rater assigns seven scores per problem. In some cases, however, responses to questions are unratable; in these cases, no score is given for those questions. Scores for each transcript are then summarized into a three-digit code. If only one stage is used in rating the responses to a problem, all three digits assigned are the same. If two stages are used in the ratings, the one that occurs most frequently is noted twice in the overall rating. For example, if five out of seven ratings were at Stage 3 and two were at Stage 4, the rating would be 3-3-4. On the rare occasion (in less than 1 percent of the cases) that three different stages are used to rate the responses to a single problem, each is represented in the overall score, for example, 5-6-4. This procedure is based on the assumption that no single stage score best represents the person's response to that problem; further, it allows for subject variability seen in the transcript to be reflected in the overall rating of that transcript.

The scores first submitted by the raters are called the Round 1 ratings. Next, any transcripts on which raters' mean scores are discrepant by one stage or more are returned to the raters, along with at least one transcript on which the ratings were *not* discrepant. (This procedure is designed to encourage the raters to reevaluate their scores with an open mind and not to assume that their scores need to be changed solely because they are discrepant.) These transcripts are then blindly rerated: the second set of scores is referred to as Round 2 ratings. Any remaining discrepancies are discussed by the raters, who then agree on a consensus rating (Round 3 ratings). A mean score for each participant is derived by averaging the scores from both raters (when these are less than one stage discrepant) over all four problems. These could be Round 1, Round 2, or Round 3 scores, depending on the degree of agreement between the raters' scores for each round. Mean scores are used for group comparison purposes. For examination of individual scores, frequency distributions of all scores assigned by both raters may be constructed. (See Kitchener and others, 1984, for an example.) Interrater reliability and agreement are typically calculated on the Round 1 ratings, which give the most conservative estimate.

Resource B

Statistical Tables

Table B5.1. RJI Interrater Reliability and Agreement by Study.

Study and sample characteristics	Interrater reliability	Interrater agreement[a]
1. Bowen (1989) n = 43 college freshmen and seniors	NR	NR
2. Brabeck (1983a) n = 119 high school, college, and master's students	.77	76% (76%)
3. Brabeck and Wood (1990) n = 25: follow-up of high school sample from Brabeck (1983a)	NR	77%
4. Evans (1988) n = 38 college freshmen and seniors	NR	93%
5. Glatfelter (1982) n = 80 traditional and adult students and nonstudents	.63[b]	89% (85%)[b]
6. Glenn and Eklund (1991)[c,d] n = 40 elderly adults, with and without college degrees	.75	53
7. Hayes (1981)[e] n = 60 teacher education students (college juniors and seniors)	.46	80%
8. Josephson (1988) n = 43 educated adult females	NR	NR
9. Kelton and Griffith (1986) n = 118 college freshmen and seniors, traditional-age and adult learners	NR	NR
10. King, J. W. (1986)[c] n = 39 nursing students and nurses	.92[b]	98%[b]
11. King and others (1983) n = 59; 2-year follow-up of Kitchener and King (1981) sample	.97	72% (62%)
12. King, Kitchener, and Wood (1990) n = 54: 10-year follow-up of Kitchener and King (1981) sample	.69	72%
13. King, Taylor, and Ottinger (1993) n = 146 African-American college students (all class levels)	.34	99%
14. King, Wood, and Mines (1990) n = 80 college seniors and graduate students	.97	90%
15. Kitchener and King (1981) n = 80 high school, college, and doctoral students	.96	77% (70%)

Table B5.1. RJI Interrater Reliability and Agreement by Study, Cont'd.

Study and sample characteristics	Interrater reliability	Interrater agreement[a]
16. Kitchener, King, Wood, and Davison (1989) n = 48: 6-year follow-up of Kitchener and King (1981) sample (also reported in King, Kitchener, and Wood, 1985)	.81	75%
17. Kitchener, Lynch, Fischer, and Wood (1993) n = 156 students 14 to 28 years old	.78	78%
18. Kitchener and Wood (1987)[g] n = 48 German university and doctoral students	.83	79–100%[h] (60–100%)
19. Lawson (1980) n = 80 doctoral students and nonstudent adults	.75[d]	69%[d]
20. Lynch (1989)[f] n = 104 students 14 to 24 years old	.78	77%
21. McKinney (1985) n = 56 high school freshmen and seniors	.64, .71, .71, .74[h]	96% (95%)
22. Millard (1992) n = 29 college freshmen	NR	90%[d] (pretest) 77%[d] (posttest)
23. Mines, King, Hood, and Wood (1990) n = 100 college seniors and graduate students	.97	90%
24. Nickerson (1991)[e] n = 26 senior nursing students	.90	88%
25. Polkosnik and Winston (1989)[e] n = 20 college students	NR	90%, 87%[i]
26. Sakalys (1984)[e] n = 50 senior nursing students	.69–.89[h]	75%
27. Schmidt (1985) n = 98 college freshmen and juniors	.29[j]	89% (52%)
28. Shoff (1979)[k] n = 56 college freshmen and seniors, traditional-age and adult learners	.51	74%
29. Strange and King (1981)[k] n = 64 college freshmen and seniors, traditional-age and adult learners	.53, .53, .65[l,m]	64%, 70%, 76%[l,m] (52%, 60%, 68%)
30. Van Tine (1990) n = 42 high school freshmen and juniors	.59, .60, .62, .64[h]	76%

Table B5.1. RJI Interrater Reliability and Agreement by Study, Cont'd.

Study and sample characteristics	Interrater reliability	Interrater agreement[a]
31. Welfel (1982b) $n = 64$ college freshmen and seniors	.84, .88[l]	80% (73%)
32. Welfel and Davison (1986) $n = 25$: 4-year follow-up of Welfel (1982b) sample	.89	68%

Note: In all studies listed, certified interviewers and raters used the four standard RJI problems except where noted otherwise. The studies also reported reliability data across all raters, problems, and subgroups except as noted otherwise. Interrater reliability and agreement coefficients are based on first-round ratings only (see Resource A for scoring procedures). Where specific data are not reported, the designation NR is used.

[a]Numbers in parentheses indicate agreement level corrected for chance.

[b]Consistency coefficients are based on one-third of the transcripts.

[c]This study used three of the four standard RJI problems.

[d]Consistency coefficients are based on a 25 percent random sample of transcripts.

[e]This study used two standard and two new problems developed by Hayes.

[f]This study used two of the four standard RJI problems.

[g]This study used a German translation of the RJI.

[h]No overall interrater consistency is reported, only the scores for each dilemma or the range across dilemmas.

[i]Thirty percent of the transcripts were scored by a certified rater; the remainder were scored by a rater who was trained but not certified. Reported agreement levels were calculated on two sets of transcripts, the first twenty rated and an additional fifteen transcripts rated later.

[j]These data are reported in Schmidt's dissertation study (1983), on which the cited article is based. The reliability results are based on a 10 percent random sample of transcripts. Schmidt notes that these are not strictly comparable to other reliability coefficients because they are based on a single dilemma rather than on the total RJI score. She estimated the reliability of the RJI total score (that is, the score based on four RJI problems) using a Spearman Brown coefficient and the estimated reliability of a single dilemma score; this procedure yielded an estimate of the total score reliability for these data of .62.

[k]This study was completed before the rater certification program was begun.

[l]These calculations are based on the scores of three raters working in pairs.

[m]These data are reported in Strange's dissertation study (1978), on which the cited article is based.

Table B5.2. RJI Internal Consistency Reliability by Study.

Study and sample characteristics	Alpha	Interproblem correlations						Problem-total correlations[a]			
		1/2	1/3	1/4	2/3	2/4	3/4	1	2	3	4
1. Bowen (1989) n = 43 college freshmen and seniors	NR	NR						NR			
2. Brabeck (1983a)[b] n = 119 high school, college, and master's students	.75	.44	.43	.50	.45	.41	.39	.58	.55	.53	.55
3. Brabeck and Wood (1990) n = 25: follow-up of high school sample from Brabeck (1983a)	.77	NR						NR			
4. Evans (1988) n = 38 college freshmen and seniors	NR	NR						.69	.65	.69	.73
5. Glatfelter (1982) n = 80 traditional-age and adult students and nonstudents	.47, .64, .77, .86[c]	.52	.53	.61	.45	.32	.42	.62	.42	.46	.52
6. Glenn and Eklund (1991) n = 40 elderly adults with and without college degrees	.99[d]	NR						NR			
7. Hayes (1981) n = 60 teacher education students (college juniors and seniors)	.72[e]	—	.50	—	—	—	—	.61	—	.48	—
8. Josephson (1988) n = 43 educated adult females	NR	NR						NR			
9. Kelton and Griffith (1986) n = 118 college freshmen, seniors, and adults	NR	NR						NR			
10. King, J. W. (1986) n = 39 nursing students and nurses	NR	—	.31	.45	—	—	.61	.43	—	.66	.56
11. King and others (1983) n = 59: 2-year follow-up of Kitchener and King (1981) sample	.96	NR						NR			

Table B5.2. RJI Internal Consistency Reliability by Study, Cont'd.

Study and sample characteristics	Alpha	Interproblem correlations						Problem-total correlations[a]			
		1/2	1/3	1/4	2/3	2/4	3/4	1	2	3	4
12. King, Kitchener, and Wood (1990) n = 54: 10-year follow-up of Kitchener and King (1981) sample	.87			.52–.73[f]						.65–.78[g]	
13. King, Taylor, and Ottinger (1993) n = 146 African-American college students (all class levels)	.50				NR					.65–.74[g]	
14. King, Wood, and Mines (1990) n = 80 college seniors and graduate students	.85				NR					NR	
15. Kitchener and King (1981)[h] n = 80 high school, college, and doctoral students	.96	.84	.86	.86	.85	.87	.88	.90	.89	.91	.92
16. Kitchener, King, Wood, and Davison (1989) n = 48: 6-year follow-up of Kitchener and King (1981) sample; also reported in King, Kitchener, and Wood (1985)	.91			.68–.76[f]						.79–.81[g]	
17. Kitchener, Lynch, Fischer, and Wood (1993) n = 156 students 14 to 28 years old	NR				NR					NR	
18. Kitchener and Wood (1987)[i] n = 48 German university and doctoral students	.75				NR					NR	
19. Lawson (1980) n = 80 doctoral students and nonstudent adults	.79				NR					NR	
20. Lynch (1989) n = 104 students 14 to 24 years old	NR				NR					NR	

Study											
21. McKinney (1985) n = 56 high school freshmen and seniors	NR	.42	.20	.18	.18	.14	.23		NR		
22. Millard (1992) n = 29 college freshmen	NR				NR				NR		
23. Mines, King, Hood, and Wood (1990)[j] n = 100 college seniors and graduate students	.89	.62	.68	.62	.71	.66	.72	.71	.75	.81	.75
24. Nickerson (1991)[d] n = 26 senior nursing students	NR	—	.62	.64	—	—	.82	.82	—	.91	.94
25. Polkosnik and Winston (1989)[d,k] n = 20 college students	.89				.71–.81[f]				NR		
26. Sakalys (1984) n = 50 senior nursing students	.66[l]				NR				NR		
27. Schmidt (1985)[m] n = 98 college freshmen and juniors	.74 (Time 1) .54 (Time 2)	.40	.44	.48	.29	.45	.59	.52	.45	.51	.66
28. Shoff (1979)[n] n = 56 college freshmen and seniors, traditional-age and adult learners	NR	.11	.48	.38	.44	.72	.46	.61	.83	.74	.84
29. Strange and King (1981)[n,o] n = 64 college freshmen and seniors, traditional-age and adult learners	.63–.85[c]	.50	.55	.64	.48	.38	.50	.45–.67	.48–.66	.38–.62	.42–.78[p]
30. Van Tine (1990) n = 42 high school freshmen and juniors	.87	.57	.55	.49	.45	.45	.44		NR		
31. Welfel (1982b)[q] n = 64 college freshmen and seniors	.62	.38	.17	.22	.31	.38	.29	.35	.52	.35	.41
32. Welfel and Davison (1986) n = 25: 4-year follow-up of Welfel (1982b) sample	NR				NR				NR		

Table B5.2. RJI Internal Consistency Reliability by Study, Cont'd.

Note: All studies listed used the four standard RJI problems with certified interviewers and raters except where noted otherwise. Internal consistency coefficients are based on final ratings. (See Resource A for scoring procedures.) Where data are not reported, the designation *NR* is used.

Problem 1 = how the Egyptian pyramids were built, 2 = the objectivity of news reporting, 3 = creation/evolution, 4 = the safety of chemical additives in foods.

[a] A problem-total correlation is the correlation between the RJI score for each problem and the average of the RJI scores on the other three problems.

[b] Specific correlations are from Brabeck's 1980 dissertation study, on which this article is based. Interproblem correlations reported in Brabeck (1983a) appear to be based on first-round ratings rather than resolved ratings.

[c] Alphas are based on combinations of the four RJI problems, taken three at a time. Overall alpha is not reported.

[d] This study used three of the four standard RJI problems.

[e] The alpha reported here appears to be based on all four problems used, two standard RJI problems and two problems related to teacher education.

[f] Correlations for specific problem combinations are not reported.

[g] Correlations for specific problems are not reported.

[h] Correlations are reported in King (1977) and Kitchener (1977–78), the dissertations on which this article is based.

[i] This study used a German translation of the RJI.

[j] Correlations are from Mines (1980) and Wood (1980), on which this study is based.

[k] About one-third of the transcripts were scored by a certified rater; the remainder were scored by a rater who was trained but not certified.

[l] A KR-20 was used to calculate internal consistency.

[m] Data are reported in Schmidt's 1983 dissertation study, on which the cited article is based.

[n] This study was completed before the rater certification program was begun.

[o] Correlations are reported in Strange's 1978 dissertation study, on which the cited article is based.

[p] These correlations are based on combinations of the four problems, taken three at a time.

[q] Correlations are reported in Welfel's 1979 dissertation study, on which the cited article is based.

Table B5.3. Summary of RJI Interproblem
and Problem-Total Correlations.

Problem	Number of studies reporting this correlation	Range	Median
Interproblem correlations			
Pyramids/News reporting	10	.11–.84	.44, .50
Pyramids/Creation-evolution	13	.17–.86	.50
Pyramids/Chemicals in foods	12	.18–.86	.49, .50
News/Creation-evolution	10	.18–.85	.45
News/Chemicals in foods	10	.14–.87	.41–.45
Creation-evolution/Chemicals in foods	12	.23–.88	.46, .50
Problem-total correlations			
Egyptian pyramids	11	.35–.90	.61
News reporting	8	.42–.89	.55, .65
Creation-evolution	11	.35–.91	.66
Chemicals in foods	10	.41–.94	.66, .73

Table B6.1. Ten-Year Study: RJI Scores by Group and Time.

| | Educational level in 1977 | | | | | | | | |
| | High school juniors (n = 10) | | | College juniors (n = 17) | | | Doctoral students (n = 11) | | |
Time	M	sd	Range	M	sd	Range	M	sd	Range
1977	2.92	.56	2.21–4.04	3.79	.73	2.46–5.58	6.20	.57	5.25–6.91
1979	3.70	.49	2.83–4.50	4.10	.87	3.33–6.38	6.31	.42	5.62–6.92
1983	5.24	.62	3.92–6.17	4.85	.50	4.21–6.33	6.35	.34	5.67–6.92
1987	5.51	.70	4.12–6.59	5.15	.66	3.97–6.44	6.42	.35	5.94–6.94
Change, 1977–1987	+2.49			+1.36			+.20		

Note: Scores are based on only those tested all four times (1977, 1979, 1983, and 1987). The results of a three-way (time × group × gender) repeated-measures ANOVA were as follows:

Time main effect: $F(3,96) = 119.79$, $p < .001$

Group main effect: $F(2,32) = 58.04$, $p < .001$

Gender main effect: $F(1,32) = 3.05$, $p < .10$

Time × group interaction: $F(6,96) = 29.21$, $p < .001$

Time × gender interaction: $F(3,96) = 1.79$, ns

Group × gender interaction: $F(2,32) = 1.46$, ns

Time × group × gender interaction: $F(6,96) = 2.41$, $p < .05$

Table B6.2. Individual RJI Scores:
1977, 1979, 1983, and 1987.

	1977		1979		1983		1987	
ID	Mean	Mode[a]	Mean	Mode	Mean	Mode	Mean	Mode
High school juniors in 1977								
101	2.92	3(2)	4.08	4(5)	5.42	5(6)	—	—
102	3.00	3(4/2)	4.25	4(5)	5.00	5(6/4)	5.54	6(5)
103	3.17	3(4)	3.63	4(3)	5.96	6(5)	5.27	5(6)
104	2.67	3(2)	3.33	3(4)	5.75	6(5)	5.96	6(5)
105	3.17	3(4)	3.96	4(3)	5.67	6(5)	6.59	7(6)
106	2.21	2(3)	—	—	—	—	4.19	4(5)
107	3.50	4(3)	3.96	4(3)	4.96	5(4)	5.94	6(5)
108	2.42	2(3)	3.42	3(4)	—	—	—	—
109	2.38	2(3)	2.83	3(2)	4.04	4(5)	4.12	4(5/3)
111	3.21	3(4)	3.88	4(3)	—	—	—	—
112	2.17	2(3)	3.17	3(4)	—	—	4.53	4(5)
113	4.04	4(5)	4.50	4(6)	5.46	6(5)	5.61	6(5)
114	2.46	2(3)	3.42	3(4)	5.54	6(5)	5.59	6(5)
115	2.67	3(2)	3.75	4(3)	5.42	6(5)	5.84	6(5)
116	2.25	2(3)	2.92	3(2)	3.46	4(3)	—	—
117	2.75	3(2)	3.58	4(3)	4.38	4(5)	—	—
118	2.21	2(3)	3.33	4(3)	4.50	4(5)	4.68	5(4)
119	3.04	3(4)	—	—	4.71	5(4)	4.96	5(4)
120	2.42	2(3)	3.33	3(4)	3.63	4(3)	—	—
College juniors in 1977 (College of Liberal Arts)								
203	3.33	3(4)	3.96	4(3)	4.25	4(5)	5.26	5(6)
204	3.63	4(3)	—	—	4.71	4(6)	4.38	4(5)
205	3.42	4(3)	4.08	4(5)	—	—	—	—
207	4.75	4(7)	—	—	6.17	6(7)	—	—
208	4.42	4(5)	3.96	4(3)	5.38	6(5)	5.65	6(5)
209	3.38	3(4)	3.58	4(3)	4.63	5(4)	3.97	4(3)
210	3.00	3(4/2)	3.63	4(3)	5.21	6(5)	4.94	5(4)
211	4.63	4(5)	4.42	4(5)	4.88	5(4)	5.19	5(6)
212	4.33	4(5)	4.54	5(6)	5.04	5(4)	—	—
213	3.33	3(4)	—	—	4.67	5(4)	—	—
214	2.96	3(2)	3.21	3(4)	—	—	—	—
215	5.58	6(5)	6.38	7(6)	6.13	6(7)	6.44	6(7)
216	4.00	4(5/3)	—	—	5.25	5(6)	5.43	5(6)
217	3.21	3(4)	3.71	4(3)	4.04	4(5)	4.16	4(5)
218	2.46	2(3)	3.38	3(4)	4.88	5(4)	5.14	5(6)
219	4.23	4(5)	4.54	4(5)	5.71	6(5)	5.64	6(5)
220	3.04	3(4)	4.29	4(3)	5.13	5(6)	—	—
College juniors in 1977 (College of Agriculture)								
401	3.29	3(4)	—	—	—	—	4.25	4(5)
402	3.33	4(3)	3.33	3(4)	4.96	5(4)	4.58	4(5)

Table B6.2. Individual RJI Scores:
1977, 1979, 1983, and 1987, Cont'd.

ID	1977 Mean	1977 Mode[a]	1979 Mean	1979 Mode	1983 Mean	1983 Mode	1987 Mean	1987 Mode
405	4.04	4(5)	5.21	5(6)	—	—	5.30	6(5)
406	5.04	5(4)	6.04	6(7)	—	—	4.95	5(4)
407	4.17	4(5)	—	—	4.29	4(5)	4.30	4(5)
408	3.71	4(3)	3.75	4(3)	4.33	4(5)	4.36	4(5)
409	3.75	4(3)	3.92	4(3)	4.63	5(4)	5.24	6(5)
410	3.54	3(4)	3.83	4(3)	4.54	4(5)	5.00	5(4)
411	3.96	4(3)	—	—	—	—	4.98	5(4)
412	4.00	4(5/3)	3.54	4(3)	5.17	5(6)	—	—
413	3.33	3(4)	3.92	4(3)	4.83	5(4)	5.19	5(4)
414	2.67	3(2)	3.67	4(3)	4.46	5(4)	—	—
415	4.42	4(5)	5.71	6(7)	5.00	5(6/4)	5.53	5(6)
416	3.83	4(3)	4.08	4(5/3)	—	—	5.29	6(5)
417	3.92	4(3)	3.63	4(3)	4.54	4(5)	4.96	5(6/4)
418	4.25	4(5)	4.08	4(5)	4.67	5(4)	6.23	6(7)
419	4.25	4(5)	—	—	—	—	4.99	6(5)
420	3.38	3(4)	4.42	4(5)	5.42	5(6)	—	—

Doctoral students in 1977

ID	1977 Mean	1977 Mode[a]	1979 Mean	1979 Mode	1983 Mean	1983 Mode	1987 Mean	1987 Mode
301	6.83	7(6)	6.50	7(6)	6.71	7(6)	6.62	7(6)
302	5.58	6(5)	6.29	6(7)	5.96	6(5)	—	—
303	6.13	6(7)	6.08	6(7)	6.21	6(7)	6.50	7(6)
304	6.92	7(6)	6.67	7(6)	6.50	7(6)	6.08	6(5)
305	6.13	6(7)	6.71	7(6)	6.13	6(7)	6.68	7(6)
306	6.38	7(6)	6.63	7(6)	6.46	7(6)	6.76	7(6)
307	4.75	4(6)	4.97	5(4)	—	—	5.17	5(4)
308	6.50	7(6)	6.96	7	6.46	6(7)	6.73	7(6)
309	4.38	4(5)	—	—	5.21	5(6)	5.06	4(6)
310	5.29	5(6)	5.63	6(5)	5.71	6(5)	6.02	6(7/5)
311	5.25	6(4)	5.75	6(5)	6.38	7(6)	6.18	6(7)
312	5.83	6(7)	—	—	—	—	6.08	6(7)
313	6.00	6(7)	6.25	6(7)	6.33	6(7)	6.19	7(6)
314	5.67	5(6)	6.29	6(7)	—	—	—	—
316	6.00	6(7)	6.00	6(7)	6.04	6(7)	5.94	6(5)
317	6.29	7(6)	6.54	7(6)	—	—	—	—
319	6.79	7(6)	6.25	6(7)	6.88	7(6)	6.94	7

Note: This listing includes the scores of all those who participated at least twice.

[a]First digit indicates the stage score most frequently assigned across all raters and all problems. Digits in parentheses indicate the second most frequently assigned stage score (minimum of 2); where there was a tie, both stage scores are listed.

Table B6.3. Mean Reflective Judgment Scores
by Educational Level for High School Students.

RJI mean	Grade 9			Grade 10			Grade 11			Grade 12		
	M	SD	n	M	SD	n	M	SD	n	M	SD	n
3.8[a]										3.83(c)[b]	.69	9
3.7							3.66(c)	.30	13			
3.6												
3.5												
3.4	3.38(e)	.29	21	3.46(c)	.35	15				3.41(a)	.42	30
3.3	3.29(c)	.22	8									
3.2												
3.1												
3.0	2.98(d2)	.21	14							2.92(d1)	.22	14
										2.96(d2)	.33	14
2.9												
2.8							2.77(b)	.49	20			
2.7												
2.6	2.60(d1)	.31	14									
2.5												
Overall	3.08	.41	57	3.46	.35	15	3.12	.61	33	3.27	.51	67

Note: Data are for five studies, eleven samples, 172 individuals.

[a]A mean score of 3.0 includes the range 2.96–3.05; 3.1 includes 3.06–3.15; and so on.

[b]Letters in parentheses correspond to the following studies:

(a) Brabeck (1983a), all females, enrolled in a Catholic school in New England.

(b) Kitchener and King (1981), matched to a sample of graduate students on MSAT scores. Students enrolled in communities in or near the Minneapolis metropolitan area.

(c) Kitchener, Lynch, Fischer, and Wood (1993), academically talented students with SAT scores of over 1000 or ACT scores of over 22 in the Denver metropolitan area. Scores based on two of the standard RJI dilemmas; specific scores reported in Kitchener (1992) and Wood (1993a).

(d) McKinney (1985), students enrolled in semirural school district in southern Colorado: 1 = low-achieving students; 2 = high-achieving students.

(e) Van Tine (1990), students enrolled in semirural school district in southern Colorado; group matched to McKinney's (1985) freshman subjects on a measure of achievement.

Table B6.4. Mean Reflective Judgment Scores by Educational Level for Traditional-Age College Students.

RJI mean[a]	Freshman			Sophomore			Junior			Senior		
	M	SD	n	M	SD	n	M	SD	n	M	SD	n
5.0 ///										5.02(f)[b]	1.30	26
4.5							4.50(l)	.67	18			
4.4												
4.3										4.34(l)	.71	13
										4.27(s)	.29	16
4.2	4.16(l)	.73	10	4.24(l)	.41	10				4.18(c)	.34	19
										4.17(n1)	.52	13
4.1										4.14(j1)	.44	20
4.0										4.08(m)	.56	40
										4.05(t2)	.58	16
										4.01(j2)	.67	20
										4.00(a)	.43	31
										3.97(e)	.43	30
										3.97(n2)	.39	13
3.9	3.95(a)	.54	12				3.93(h)	.58	20	3.94(t1)	.56	16
	3.87(c)	.34	19									
3.8	3.81(f)	.75	92							3.78(r)	.46	14
3.7	3.74(s)	.16	16				3.73(e)	.43	30	3.70(b)	.42	30
	3.72(t1)	.32	16							3.69(o)	.62	5
										3.68(p1)	.58	25
										3.68(i)	.19	21
3.6				3.63(i)	.17	32	3.65(k)	.81	20	3.59(p2)	.52	25
										3.56(d)	.54	16
3.5	3.54(i)	.11	67	3.50(g)	.39	13	3.55(i)	.14	26			
	3.52(t2)	.33	16				3.54(q)	.44	40			
3.4	3.36(q)	.26	40	3.38(b)	.42	30						
3.3	3.31(m)	.37	20									
	3.31(o)	.44	5									
3.2	3.23(d)	.34	16	3.17(o)	.47	4	3.20(o)	.42	5			
Overall	3.63	.53	329	3.57	.43	89	3.74	.59	159	3.99	.67	369[c]

Note: Data are for twenty studies, forty-four samples, 966 individuals.

[a] A mean score of 4.0 includes the range 3.96–4.05; 4.1 includes 4.06–4.15; and so on.

[b] Letters in parentheses correspond to the following studies:

[c] This column sums to 369 rather than 409 since studies (j) and (m) are based on the same sample of college students.

(a) Bowen (1989), students enrolled at East Texas State University. Almost half the seniors (n = 14) were over twenty-six years of age.

(b) Brabeck (1983a), all females, enrolled in a Catholic college in New England.

(c) Evans (1988), students enrolled at a Seventh Day Adventist liberal arts college in the South. Seniors matched to freshmen on gender, high school, ACT score, and GPA.

Table B6.4. Mean Reflective Judgment Scores by
Educational Level for Traditional-Age College Students, Cont'd.

(d) Glatfelter (1982), all females, enrolled at Utah State University.
(e) Hayes (1981), all females, teacher education students enrolled at the University of Utah. Two standard RJI dilemmas used (pyramids and chemicals), along with two new dilemmas focusing on teacher education issues. Means based on all four dilemmas. Students did not score significantly higher on the education dilemmas, as hypothesized; rather, they scored significantly lower on the pyramids dilemma.
(f) Kelton and Griffith (1986), students enrolled at Davidson College, North Carolina.
(g) King, J. W. (1986): Female students enrolled in associate degree nursing programs at five community colleges and a state university in the lower Midwest. Scores based on three of the standard RJI problems (news reporting problem omitted).
(h) King and Parker (1978), College of Agriculture majors at the University of Minnesota; matched to Kitchener and King's (1981) juniors on MSAT scores, gender, and size of hometown when in high school.
(i) King, Taylor, and Ottinger (1993), all African-American students at Bowling Green State University, Ohio.
(j) King, Wood, and Mines (1990): 1 = mathematical science majors, 2 = social science majors at the University of Iowa. Same seniors reported in sample (m).
(k) Kitchener and King (1981): College of Liberal Arts majors at the University of Minnesota.
(l) Kitchener, Lynch, Fischer, and Wood (1993), students enrolled at the University of Denver with SATs over 1000 or ACTs over 22. Scores based on two of the standard RJI dilemmas.
(m) Mines, King, Hood, and Wood (1990), students enrolled at the University of Iowa. Same seniors as in sample (j).
(n) Nickerson (1991), female BA nursing students enrolled in nursing programs in the eastern United States; 1 = building design curriculum, 2 = progressive design curriculum; no significant difference between groups; three dilemmas used (evolution dilemma omitted).
(o) Polkosnik and Winston (1989), students enrolled at the University of Georgia. Means by class level calculated on basis of information provided in Polkosnik (1985). Means reported are first-testing scores. One certified rater and one trained rater used.
(p) Sakalys (1984), female nursing students enrolled at the University of Colorado: 1 = enrolled in a research course, 2 = control group. Means reported are first-testing scores.
(q) Schmidt (1985), students enrolled at the University of Minnesota in either the College of Liberal Arts or the Institute of Technology. SDs by class level calculated with information provided by author. Means reported are first-testing scores.
(r) Shoff (1979), students enrolled at the University of Utah.
(s) Strange and King (1981), students enrolled at the University of Iowa.
(t) Welfel (1982b), students enrolled at the University of Minnesota; 1 = engineering majors, 2 = humanities/social science majors.

Table B6.5. Mean Reflective Judgment Scores by
Educational Level for Nontraditional-Age College Students.

RJI mean[a]	Freshman			Sophomore			Senior		
	M	SD	n	M	SD	n	M	SD	n
4.4							4.41(e)[b]	.91	16
4.3				4.30(b)	.59	13			
4.2									
4.1									
4.0									
3.9									
3.8	3.79(e)	.26	16						
	3.77(a1)	.45	16						
							3.76(d3)	.61	14
3.7							3.74(a2)	.41	16
3.6									
3.5	3.53(d2)	.38	14						
	3.47(c)	.39	18						
3.4									
3.3	3.26(d1)	.43	14						
Overall	3.57	.42	78	4.30	.59	13	3.98	.74	46

Note: Data are for five studies, nine samples, 137 individuals.
    [a]A mean score of 4.0 includes the range 3.96 to 4.05; 4.1 includes 4.06
to 4.15; and so on.
    [b]Letters in parentheses correspond to the following studies:
(a) Glatfelter (1982), students enrolled at Utah State University; 1 = first-year
    reentry women (age twenty-six-plus years), 2 = fourth-year reentry women
    (age twenty-six-plus years). First-year students classified as freshmen and
    fourth-year students classified as seniors.
(b) King, J. W. (1986), female second-year students enrolled in associate degree
    nursing programs at five community colleges and a state university in the
    lower Midwest (twenty-eight to thirty-six years, Md = 30 years). Scores based
    on three of the standard RJI problems (news reporting problem omitted).
(c) Schmidt (1985), nontraditional-age freshmen (about age twenty-one) at the
    University of Minnesota.
(d) Shoff (1979), students enrolled in continuing education (CE) programs at
    the University of Utah; 1 = younger students, twenty-two to twenty-four years
    (M = 23) with no prior college education; 2 = older CE students, thirty-plus
    years (M = 37 years), humanities majors; 3 = older seniors. Younger CE stu-
    dents classified as freshmen since they had no prior college experience.
(e) Strange and King (1981), nontraditional-age freshmen (age twenty-two) and
    nontraditional-age seniors (age twenty-six) at the University of Iowa.

Table B6.6. Mean Reflective Judgment Scores by
Educational Level for Graduate Students.

RJI mean[a]	Graduate students					
	Master's/Early doctoral			Advanced doctoral (at least third year)		
	M	SD	n	M	SD	n
6.0						
5.9				5.86(d3)[b]	.27	3
5.8						
5.7				5.67(c)	.92	20
5.6						
5.5						
5.4						
5.3				5.32(e)	.85	16
5.2	5.18(b2)	.73	20			
5.1						
5.0	4.97(d1)	.79	37	4.94(f2)	.81	20
4.9				4.93(d2)	.86	11
4.8	4.76(g)	.78	40			
4.7						
4.6	4.60(f1)	.71	20			
4.5						
4.4	4.36(b1)	.61	20			
4.3						
4.2						
4.1						
4.0	4.00(a)	.57	29			
Overall	4.62	.81	126[c]	5.27	.89	70

Note: Data are for eight studies, twelve samples, 196 individuals.
[a]A mean score of 4.0 includes the range 3.96 to 4.05; 4.1 includes 4.06 to 4.15; and so on.
[b]Letters in parentheses correspond to the following studies:
[c]This column sums to 126 instead of 146 since studies (b) and (g) are based on the same sample of doctoral students.
(a) Brabeck (1983a), female master's degree students at a Catholic college in New England.
(b) King, Wood, and Mines (1990), two groups of second-year doctoral students at the University of Iowa: 1 = mathematical science majors; 2 = social science majors. (Based on same sample as Mines, King, Hood, and Wood [1990] study.)
(c) Kitchener and King (1981), third-year doctoral students in liberal arts at the University of Minnesota.
(d) Kitchener, Lynch, Fischer, and Wood (1993), students enrolled at the University of Denver; 1 = 0 to 45 hours graduate credit; 2 = 46 to 90 hours graduate credit; 3 = over 135 hours graduate credit. Scores based on two of the standard

Table B6.6. Mean Reflective Judgment Scores
by Educational Level for Graduate Students, Cont'd.

RJI dilemmas. (Source for subgroup means: personal communication from K. S. Kitchener.)

(e) Kitchener and Wood (1987), doctoral students enrolled at the University of Tübingen (Germany); mean age = 29.5 years. Problem on safety of nuclear power substituted for the creation/evolution problem.

(f) Lawson (1980), students enrolled at the University of Minnesota: 1 = first-year doctoral students; 2 = third-year doctoral students.

(g) Mines, King, Hood, and Wood (1990), second-year doctoral students at the University of Iowa. (Based on same sample as King, Wood, and Mines [1990] study.)

Table B6.7. Mean Reflective Judgment Scores by
Degree Attainment for Nonstudent Adults.

RJI mean[a]	Without college degrees			With college degrees		
	M	SD	n	M	SD	n
5.2				5.20(b1)[b]	.98	20
///						
4.3				4.29(c)	.51	43
4.2				4.25(f2)	.51	20
				4.20(e)	.53	13
4.1						
4.0				4.03(d)	.66	39
				4.02(f1)	.67	20
3.9						
3.8						
3.7	3.67(b2)	.96	20			
3.6						
3.5	3.52(a)	.40	16			
Overall	3.60	.76	36	4.29	.74	155

Note: Data are for six studies, seven samples, 191 individuals.

[a]A mean score of 3.0 includes the range 2.96 to 3.05; 3.1 includes 3.06 to 3.15; and so on.

[b]Letters in parentheses correspond to the following studies:

(a) Glatfelter (1982), dropouts from Utah State University; all twenty-six years or older; all female.

(b) Glenn and Eklund (1991), elderly (at least sixty-five years old); 1 = retired college professors with doctorates (ten males and ten females); 2 = adults with up to a high school education (ten males and ten females).

(c) Josephson (1988), professional women (about half from human services professions) with graduate training, most at the master's level; of these, two had J.D. degrees and four had Ph.D.s. Separate means not reported by educational level.

(d) Kelton and Griffith (1986), female adults; age and other demographic characteristics not reported; length or type of collegiate experience not reported.

(e) King, J. W. (1986), female employed nurses twenty-six to twenty-eight years old.

(f) Lawson (1980), two groups, matched by age to first- and third-year doctoral students; all college-educated; 1 = "younger" group, twenty-two to thirty years old, M = twenty-five years; 2 = "older" group, twenty-six to thirty-four years old, M = thirty years.

Table B7.1. Correlations Between Reflective Judgment Scores and Intelligence and Aptitude Measures.

Study	Sample[a]	Measure	Correlation
Glatfelter (1982)	80 Utah State U. women	CMT	.37
	16 traditional first-year students	CMT	.55
	16 reentry first-year students	CMT	.16
	16 traditional first-year students	CMT	.16
	16 reentry fourth-year students	CMT	.17
	16 nonstudent women (U. dropouts)	CMT	.53
Kitchener and King (1981)	60 students	CMT	.79
	20 high school juniors	CMT	.63
	20 U. of Minn. juniors	CMT	.30
	20 U. of Minn. graduate students	CMT	.79
King and others (1983)	57 18- to 30-year-olds; 2-year follow-up of Kitchener and King (1981) study	CMT	.61
King, Kitchener, Wood, and Davison (1989)	57 22- to 34-year-olds; 6-year follow-up of Kitchener and King (1981) study	CMT	.55
King, Kitchener, and Wood (1991)	41 26- to 38-year-olds; 10-year follow-up of Kitchener and King (1981) study	CMT	.49
Lawson (1980)	80 Minnesota adults	CMT	.44
	20 advanced graduate students	CMT	.29
	20 first-year graduate students	CMT	.22
	20 older nonstudents	CMT	.13
	20 younger nonstudents	CMT	.37

Study	Sample	Measure	r
Welfel (1982b)	64 U. of Minn. freshmen and seniors	CMT	.14
Glenn and Eklund (1991)	40 adults over age 65	WAIS-R Verbal	.55
Kitchener, Lynch, Fischer, and Wood (1993)	56 14- to 28-year-old Denver high school students and U. of Denver undergraduate and graduate students	WISC-R/WAIS-R vocabulary scaled score	.37
McKinney (1985)	28 Colorado ninth graders 28 Colorado twelfth graders	WISC-R Verbal[c] WAIS-R Verbal[c]	.49 .44
Van Tine (1990)	42 Colorado ninth and twelfth graders	WISC-R Verbal[c]	.45
Hayes (1981)[b]	46 U. of Utah junior and senior education students	ACT composite	.26
King, Taylor, and Ottinger (1993)	112 Bowling Green State U. African-American students (freshmen through seniors)	ACT composite	.07
Sakalys (1982)	50 U. of Colorado B.A. nursing students	Verbal SAT/ACT	–.17
Strange and King (1981)[b]	64 U. of Iowa, traditional and adult freshmen and seniors	ACT composite	.19
Evans (1988)	38 conservative, private college, traditional age freshmen and seniors	ACT composite	.12

[a]For more detailed sample descriptions, see Chapter Six.
[b]This study was conducted before the RJI certification program was established.
[c]Four verbal subtests with highest loadings on verbal comprehension.

References

Amthauer, R. *I-S-T-Eignungsuntersuchung.* (2nd ed.) Göttingen, Germany: Hogrete, 1955.

Anastasi, A. "Evolving Trait Concepts." *American Psychologist,* 1983, *38*(2), 175–184.

Apps, J. W. *The Adult Learner on Campus.* Chicago: Follett, 1991.

Association of American Colleges. *Integrity in the College Curriculum: A Report to the Academic Community.* Washington, D.C.: Association of American Colleges, 1985.

Association of American Colleges. *The Challenge of Connecting Learning.* Project on Liberal Learning, Study-in-Depth, and the Arts and Sciences Major. Washington, D.C.: Association of American Colleges, 1991.

Astin, A. *Achieving Educational Excellence.* San Francisco: Jossey-Bass, 1985.

Baltes, P. B., and Smith, J. "Toward a Psychology of Wisdom and Its Ontogenesis." In R. Sternberg (ed.), *Wisdom: Its Nature, Origins and Development.* Cambridge, England: Cambridge University Press, 1990.

Baron, J. "Reflective Thinking as a Goal of Education." *Intelligence,* 1981, *5*(4), 291–309.

Baron, J. *Rationality and Intelligence.* Cambridge, England: Cambridge University Press, 1985.

Baron, J. *Thinking and Deciding.* Cambridge, England: Cambridge University Press, 1988.

Barone, R. "The Progressive Growth of Relativistic Reasoning in the Development of Psychotherapists." Unpublished doctoral dissertation, Department of Educational Psychology, Southern Illinois University, 1989.

Basseches, M. "Dialectical Schemata: A Framework for the Empirical Study of the Development of Dialectical Thinking." *Human Development,* 1980, *23,* 400–421.

Basseches, M. *Dialectical Thinking and Adult Development.* Norwood, N.J.: Ablex, 1984a.

Basseches, M. "Dialectical Thinking as a Metasystematic Form of Cognitive Organization." In M. L. Commons, F. A. Richards, and C. Armon (eds.), *Beyond Formal Operations: Late Adolescent and Adult Cognitive Development.* New York: Praeger, 1984b.

Basseches, M. "Dialectical Thinking and Young Adult Cognitive Development." In R. A. Mines and K. S. Kitchener (eds.), *Adult Cognitive Development,* New York: Praeger, 1986.

Baxter Magolda, M. "A Comparison of Open-Ended and Standardized Instrument Measures of Intellectual Development on the Perry Scheme." *Journal of College Student Personnel,* 1987, *28,* 443–448.

Baxter Magolda, M. "Measuring Gender Differences in Intellectual Development: A Comparison of Assessment Methods." *Journal of College Student Development,* 1988, *29,* 528–537.

Baxter Magolda, M. B. *Knowing and Reasoning in College: Gender-Related Patterns in Students' Intellectual Development.* San Francisco: Jossey-Bass, 1992.

Baxter Magolda, M. B., and Porterfield, W. D. "A New Approach to Assessing Intellectual Development on the Perry Scheme." *Journal of College Student Personnel,* 1985, *26,* 343–351.

Baxter Magolda, M. B., and Porterfield, W. D. *Assessing Intellectual Development: The Link Between Theory and Practice.* Alexandria, Va.: American College Personnel Association, 1988.

Belenky, M. F., Clinchy, B. M., Goldberger, N. R., and Tarule, J. M. *Women's Ways of Knowing.* New York: Basic Books, 1986.

Benack, S. "Postformal Epistemologies and the Growth of Empathy." In M. L. Commons, F. A. Richards, and C. Armon (eds.), *Beyond Formal Operations: Late Adolescent and Adult Development.* New York: Praeger, 1984.

Benack, S., and Basseches, M. A. "Dialectical Thinking and Relativistic Epistemology: Their Relation in Adult Development." In M. L. Commons, J. D. Sinnott, F. A. Richards, and C. Armon (eds.), *Adult Development,* Vol. 1: *Comparisons and Applications of Developmental Models.* New York: Praeger, 1989.

Benderson, A. "Critical Thinking: Critical Issues." *Focus.* Princeton, N.J.: Education Testing Service, 1990.

Berger, A. "Review of the Watson-Glaser Critical Thinking Appraisal." In J. W. Mitchell, Jr. (ed.), *The Ninth Mental Measurement Yearbook.* Lincoln: Buros Institute of Mental Measurements, University of Nebraska, Lincoln, 1985.

Bernstein, R. J. *Praxis and Action.* Philadelphia: University of Pennsylvania Press, 1971.

Bidel, T. R., and Fischer, K. W. "Beyond the Stage Debate: Action, Structure, and Variability in Piagetian Theory and Research." In R. Sternberg and C. Berg (eds.), *Intellectual Development.* New York: Cambridge University Press, 1992.

Bok, D. "Ethics, the University, and Society." *Harvard Magazine,* May–June, 1988, pp. 39–50.

Bowen, H. R. *Investment in Learning: The Individual and Social Value of American Higher Education.* San Francisco: Jossey-Bass, 1977.

Bowen, J. L. "The Combined Predictive Effect of Creativity Level and Personality Type on College Students' Reflective Judgment." *Dissertation Abstracts International,* 1989, *51,* 110.

Boyer, E. *College: The Undergraduate Experience in America.* New York: Harper & Row, 1987.

Brabeck, M. "Critical Thinking Skills and Reflective Judgment Development: Redefining the Aims of Higher Education." *Journal of Applied Developmental Psychology,* 1983a, *4*(1), 23–34.

Brabeck, M. "Moral Judgment: Theory and Research on Differences Between Males and Females." *Developmental Review,* 1983b, *3,* 274–291.

Brabeck, M. "Longitudinal Studies of Intellectual Development During Adulthood: Theoretical and Research Models." *Journal of Research and Development in Education,* 1984, *17*(3), 12–27.

Brabeck, M. Editorial. *Journal of Moral Education,* 1987, *16*(3), 163–166.

Brabeck, M. *Who Cares? Theory, Research and Educational Implications of the Ethic of Care.* New York: Praeger, 1989.

Brabeck, M., and Welfel, E. R. "Counseling Theory: Understanding the Trend Toward Eclecticism from a Developmental Perspective." *Journal of Counseling and Development,* 1985, *63*(6), 343–348.

Brabeck, M., and Wood, P. "Cross-Sectional and Longitudinal Evidence for Differences Between Well-Structured and Ill-Structured Problem Solving Abilities." In M. L. Commons, C. Armon, L. Kohlberg, F. A. Richards, T. A. Grotzer, and J. D. Sinnott (eds.), *Adult Development 2: Models and Methods in the Study of Adolescent and Adult Thought.* New York: Praeger, 1990.

Brainard, C. J. "The Stage Question in Cognitive Development." *Behavioral and Brain Sciences,* 1978, *2,* 173–213.

Braine, M.D.S., and Rumain, B. "Logical Reasoning." In J. H. Flavell and E. M. Markman (eds.), *Handbook of Child Psychology,* Vol. 3: *Cognitive Development.* New York: Wiley, 1983.

Brookfield, S. D. *Developing Critical Thinkers: Challenging Adults to Explore Alternative Ways of Thinking and Acting.* San Francisco: Jossey-Bass, 1987.

Broughton, J. M. "The Development of Natural Epistemology in Years 11 to 16." Unpublished doctoral dissertation, Graduate School of Education, Harvard University, 1975.

Broughton, J. M. "Development of Concepts of Self, Mind, Reality, and Knowledge." In W. Damon (ed.), *Social Cognition.* New Directions for Child Development, no. 1. San Francisco: Jossey-Bass, 1978.

Case, R. *Intellectual Development: Birth to Adulthood.* New York: Academic Press, 1985.

Chickering, A. *Education and Identity.* San Francisco: Jossey-Bass, 1969.

Chickering, A. W. "Conclusion." In Chickering and Associates, *The Modern American College: Responding to the New Realities of Diverse Students and a Changing Society.* San Francisco: Jossey-Bass, 1981.

Chickering, A. W., and Gamson, Z. F. (eds.). *Applying the Seven Principles for Good Practice in Undergraduate Education.* New Directions for Teaching and Learning, no. 47. San Francisco: Jossey-Bass, 1991.

Churchman, C. W. *The Design of Inquiring Systems: Basic Concepts of Systems and Organizations.* New York: Basic Books, 1971.

Clayton, V. "Wisdom and Intelligence: The Nature and Function of Knowledge in the Later Years." *International Journal of Aging and Human Development,* 1982, *15,* 315–321.

Clayton, V., and Birren, J. E. "The Development of Wisdom Across the Life Span." In P. Baltes and O. G. Brim (eds.), *Life Span Development and Behavior.* Vol. 3. New York: Academic Press, 1980.

Clinchy, B., and Zimmerman, C. "Epistemology and Agency in the Development of Undergraduate Women." In P. Perun (ed.), *The Undergraduate Woman: Issues in Educational Equity.* Lexington, Mass.: Heath, 1982.

Colby, A., Kohlberg, L., Gibbs, J., and Lieberman, M. "A Longitudinal Study of Moral Judgment." *Monographs of the Society for Research in Child Development,* 1983, *48,* 1–124.

Commons, M. L., and Richards, F. A. "A General Stage Model of Stage Theory." In M. L. Commons, F. A. Richards, and C. Armon (eds.), *Beyond Formal Operations,* Vol. 1: *Late Adolescent and Adult Cognitive Development.* New York: Praeger, 1984.

Commons, M. L., Richards, F. A., and Armon, C. (eds.) *Beyond Formal Operations: Late Adolescent and Adult Cognitive Development.* New York: Praeger, 1984.

Commons, M. L., Richards, F. A., and Kuhn, D. "Systematic and Metasystematic Reasoning: A Case for a Level of Reasoning Beyond Piaget's Formal Operations." *Child Development,* 1982, *53*(4), 1058–1069.

Commons, M. L., Sinnott, J. D., Richards, F. A., and Armon, C. (eds.) *Adult Development,* vol. 1: *Comparisons and Applications of Developmental Models.* New York: Praeger, 1989.

Commons, M. L., Stein, S. A., and Richards, F. A. "A General

Model of Stage Theory: Stage of a Task." Paper presented at the annual meeting of the Society for Research in Child Development, Apr. 1987.

Commons, M. L., and others (eds.). *Adult Development,* Vol. 2: *Models and Methods in the Study of Adolescent and Adult Thought.* New York: Praeger, 1990.

Currier, S. "Levels of Reflective Judgment Among Educated and Working Class Women." Unpublished doctoral dissertation, Department of Educational Psychology, Southern Illinois University, 1989.

Darlington, R. B. *Regression and Linear Models.* New York: McGraw-Hill, 1990.

Davison, M. L. "Testing a Metric Unidimensional, Qualitative, Unfolding Model for Attitudinal or Developmental Data." *Psychometrika,* 1979, *44*(2), 179–194.

Davison, M. L., King, P. M., and Kitchener, K. S. "Developing Reflective Thinking and Writing." In R. Beach and S. Hynds (eds.), *Developing Discourse Practices in Adolescence and Adulthood.* Norwood, N.J.: Ablex, 1990.

Davison, M. L., King, P. M., Kitchener, K. S., and Parker, C.A. "The Stage Sequence Concept in Cognitive Social Development." *Developmental Psychology,* 1980, *16,* 121–131.

Demetriou, A., and Efklides, A. "Structure and Sequence of Formal and Post Formal Thought: General Patterns and Individual Differences." *Child Development,* 1985, *56*(4), 1062–1091.

Dewey, J. *Ethical Principles Underlying Education.* Third Yearbook of the National Herbart Society. Chicago: National Herbart Society, 1897.

Dewey, J. "The Logic of Judgments of Practice." *Journal of Philosophy,* 1916, *12*(19), 505–523.

Dewey, J. *How We Think: A Restatement of the Relation of Reflective Thinking to the Educative Process.* Lexington, Mass.: Heath, 1933.

Dewey, J. *Logic: The Theory of Inquiry.* Troy, Mo.: Holt, Rinehart & Winston, 1938.

Dewey, J. *Democracy and Education: An Introduction to the Philosophy of Education.* New York: Free Press, 1944.

Dings, J. D. "Faculty Members' Assumptions About College

Students' Reasoning Using the Reflective Judgment Model." Unpublished master's thesis, Department of College Student Personnel, Bowling Green State University, 1989.

Dixon, R. A., and Baltes, P. B. "Toward Life Span Research on the Functions and Pragmatics of Intelligence." In R. J. Sternberg and R. K. Wagner (eds.), *Practical Intelligence.* New York: Cambridge University Press, 1986.

Dove, W. R. "The Identification of Ill-Structured Problems by Young Adults." *Dissertation Abstracts International,* 1990, *51/06 B,* 3156.

Ennis, R. H. "A Concept of Critical Thinking." *Harvard Educational Review,* 1962, *32*(1), 81–111.

Ennis, R. H. "Critical Thinking and the Curriculum." *National Forum,* 1985a, *65*(1), 28–31.

Ennis, R. H. "A Logical Basis for Measuring Critical Thinking Skills." *Educational Leadership,* 1985b, *43,* 44–48.

Ennis, R. H. "A Taxonomy of Critical Thinking Dispositions and Abilities." In J. B. Baron and R. J. Sternberg (eds.), *Teaching Thinking Skills: Theory and Practice.* New York: Freeman, 1987, pp. 9–26.

Ennis, R. H., and Millman, J. *Cornell Critical Thinking Test Manual.* Urbana: Critical Thinking Project, University of Illinois, 1971.

Ennis, R. H., and Norris, S. P. "Critical Thinking Assessment: Status, Issues, Needs." In S. Legg and J. Algina (eds.), *Cognitive Assessment of Language and Math Outcomes.* Norwood, N.J.: Ablex, 1990.

Erikson, E. H. *Childhood and Society.* (rev. ed.) New York: Norton, 1963.

Erikson, E. H. *Identity: Youth and Crisis.* New York: Norton, 1968.

Erikson, E. H. *The Life Cycle Completed.* New York: Norton, 1982.

Erwin, T. D. "The Scale of Intellectual Development: Measuring Perry's Scheme." *Journal of College Student Development,* 1983, *1,* 6–11.

Evans, D. J. "Effects of a Religious-Oriented, Conservative, Homogeneous College Education on Reflective Judgment." *Dissertation Abstracts International,* 1988, *49,* 3306.

Facione, P. A. *Critical Thinking: A Statement of Expert Consensus for Purposes of Educational Assessment and Instruction.* Research findings and recommendations prepared for the Committee on Pre-College Philosophy, American Philosophical Association, 1990.

Finster, D. C. "New Pathways for Teaching Chemistry: Reflective Judgment in Science." *Liberal Education,* 1992, *78*(1), 14–19.

Fischer, K. W. "A Theory of Cognitive Development: The Control and Construction of Hierarchies of Skills." *Psychological Review,* 1980, *87*(6), 477–531.

Fischer, K. W. "Illuminating the Processes of Moral Development." *Monographs of the Society for Research in Child Development,* 1983, *48* (1–2, Serial No. 200).

Fischer, K. W., and Bullock, D. "Patterns of Data: Sequence, Synchrony, and Constraint in Cognitive Development." In K. W. Fischer (ed.), *Cognitive Development.* New Directions for Child Development, no. 12. San Francisco: Jossey-Bass, 1981.

Fischer, K. W., and Canfield, R. L. "The Ambiguity of Stage and Structure in Behavior: Person and Environment in the Development of Psychological Structures." In I. Levine (ed.), *Stage and Structure.* New York: Plenum, 1986.

Fischer, K. W., and Farrar, M. J. "Generalizations About Generalization: How a Theory of Skill Development Explains Both Generality and Specificity." *International Journal of Psychology,* 1987, *22*(5/6), 643–677.

Fischer, K. W., Hand, H. H., and Russell, S. "The Development of Abstractions in Adolescence and Adulthood." In M. L. Commons, F. A. Richards, and C. Armon (eds.), *Beyond Formal Operations.* New York: Praeger, 1984.

Fischer, K. W., and Kenny, S. L. "Environmental Conditions for Discontinuities in the Development of Abstractions." In R. A. Mines and K. S. Kitchener (eds.), *Adult Cognitive Development.* New York: Praeger, 1986.

Fischer, K. W., and Pipp, S. L. "Processes of Cognitive Development: Optimal Level and Skill Acquisition." In R. J. Sternberg (ed.), *Mechanisms of Cognitive Development.* New York: Freeman, 1984.

Fischer, K. W., Pipp, S. L., and Bullock, D. "Detecting Developmental Discontinuities: Methods and Measurements." In R. Emde and R. Harmon (eds.), *Continuities and Discontinuities in Development*. New York: Plenum, 1984.

Fischer, K. W., and Silvern, L. "Stages and Individual Differences in Cognitive Development." *Annual Review of Psychology*, 1985, *36*, 613–647.

Flavell, J. *The Developmental Psychology of Jean Piaget*. New York: Van Nostrand Reinhold, 1963.

Flavell, J. "Stage Related Properties of Cognitive Development." *Cognitive Psychology*, 1971, *2*(4), 421–453.

Flavell, J. *Cognitive Development*. Englewood Cliffs, N.J.: Prentice-Hall, 1977.

Flavell, J. "On Cognitive Development." *Child Development*, 1982a, *53*(1), 1–10.

Flavell, J. "Structures, Stages and Sequences in Cognitive Development." In W. A. Collins (ed.), *Minnesota Symposium on Child Development*, Vol. 15: *The Concept of Development*. Hillsdale, N.J.: Erlbaum, 1982b.

Flew, A. *Thinking About Thinking: (Or, Do I Sincerely Want to Be Right?)*. Glasgow, Scotland: William Collins Sons, 1975.

Frankena, W. K. *Ethics*. Englewood Cliffs, N.J.: Prentice-Hall, 1963.

Gilligan, C. *In a Different Voice: Psychological Theory and Women's Development*. Cambridge, Mass.: Harvard University Press, 1982.

Ginsberg, H., and Opper, S. *Piaget's Theory of Intellectual Development: An Introduction*. Englewood Cliffs, N.J.: Prentice-Hall, 1969.

Glaser, E. M. "Critical Thinking: Educating for Responsible Citizenship in a Democracy." *National Forum*, 1985, *65*(1), 24–27.

Glatfelter, M. "Identity Development, Intellectual Development, and Their Relationship in Reentry Women Students." *Dissertation Abstracts International*, 1982, *43*, 3543A.

Glenn, D. D., and Eklund, S. S. "The Relationship of Graduate Education and Reflective Judgment in Older Adults." Paper presented at the annual meeting of the American Education Research Association, Bloomington, Ind., Apr. 1991.

Guthrie, V. L. "Hate Speech and Intellectual Development: An Exploration of the Relationship Between Racial Harassment Policies and the Development of Reflective Judgment." Unpublished paper, Bowling Green State University, 1991.

Haas, P. F. "Honors Programs: Applying the Reflective Judgment Model." *Liberal Education,* 1992, *78*(1), 20–23.

Harvey, L. J., Hunt, D. E., and Schroder, H. M. *Conceptual Systems and Personality Organization.* New York: Wiley, 1961.

Hayes, A. B. "An Investigation of the Effect of Dilemma Content on Level of Reasoning in the Reflective Judgment Interview." *Dissertation Abstracts International,* 1981, *40,* 2564B.

Helmstadter, G. C. "Review of the Watson-Glaser Critical Thinking Appraisal." In J. W. Mitchell, Jr. (ed.), *The Ninth Mental Measurement Yearbook.* Lincoln: Buros Institute of Mental Measurements, University of Nebraska, Lincoln, 1985.

Hills, S. L. "Crime and Deviance on the College Campus: The Privilege of Class." *Humanity and Society,* 1982, *6,* 257–266.

Holliday, S. G., and Chandler, M. J. *Wisdom: Explorations in Adult Competence.* Basel, Switzerland: Karger, 1986.

Horn, J. L. "The Aging of Human Abilities." In B. B. Wolman (ed.), *Handbook of Developmental Psychology.* Englewood Cliffs, N.J.: Prentice-Hall, 1982.

Horn, J. L., and Cattell, R. B. "Refinement and Test of the Theory of Fluid and Crystallized Intelligence." *Journal of Educational Psychology,* 1966, *57*(5), 253–270.

Horn, J. L., and Donaldson, G. "Cognitive Development II: Adulthood Development of Human Abilities." In O. G. Brim and J. Kagan (eds.), *Constancy and Change in Human Development: A Volume of Review Essays.* Cambridge, Mass.: Harvard University Press, 1980.

Inhelder, B., and Piaget, J. *The Growth of Logical Thinking from Childhood to Adolescence.* New York: Basic Books, 1958.

Irwin, R. R., and Sheese, R. L. "Problems in the Proposal for a 'Stage' of Dialectical Thinking." In M. L. Commons, J. D. Sinnott, F. A. Richards, and C. Armon (eds.), *Adult Development,* Vol. 1: *Comparisons and Applications of Developmental Models.* New York: Praeger, 1989.

Jacoby, M., Astin, A., and Ayala, F., Jr. *College Student Outcomes Assessment: A Talent Development Perspective.* ASHE-ERIC Higher Education Report No. 7. Washington, D.C.: Association for the Study of Higher Education, 1987.

Josephson, J. S. "Feminine Orientation as a Mediator of Moral Judgment." *Dissertation Abstracts International,* 1988, *50,* 751.

Kegan, R. *The Evolving Self.* Cambridge, Mass.: Harvard University Press, 1982.

Kekes, J. "Wisdom." *American Philosophical Quarterly,* 1983, *20*(3), 277–296.

Kelton, J., and Griffith, J. "Learning Context Questionnaire for Assessing Intellectual Development." Unpublished report, Davidson College, 1986.

Kerber, L. K., and others. "On *In a Different Voice:* An Interdisciplinary Forum." *Signs: Journal of Women in Culture and Society,* 1986, *11*(2), 304–333.

King, J. W. "The Relationship of Age to Reflective Judgment Levels of Traditionally and Nontraditionally Aged Associate Degree Nursing Students and Employed Registered Nurses." *Dissertation Abstracts International,* 1986, *48,* 1126.

King, P. M. "The Development of Reflective Judgment and Formal Operational Thinking in Adolescents and Young Adults." *Dissertation Abstracts International,* 1977, *38,* 7233A.

King, P. M. "William Perry's Theory of Intellectual and Ethical Development." In L. Knefelkamp, C. Widick, and C. Parker (eds.), *Applying New Developmental Findings.* New Directions for Student Services, no. 4. San Francisco: Jossey-Bass, 1978.

King, P. M. "Choice-Making in Young Adulthood: A Developmental Double-Bind." *Counseling and Human Development,* 1985, *18*(3), 1–12.

King, P. M. "Formal Reasoning in Adults: A Review and Critique." In R. Mines and K. Kitchener (eds.), *Adult Cognitive Development.* New York: Praeger, 1986.

King, P. M. "Assessing Development from a Cognitive Developmental Perspective." In D. Creamer and Associates (eds.), *College Student Development: Theory and Practice for the 1990s.* Alexandria, Va.: ACPA Media, 1990.

King, P. M. "Reflective Judgment in a Pluralistic Society: The Mixed Results." Paper presented at the annual meeting of the Association of American Colleges, Washington, D.C., Jan. 1991.

King, P. M. "Creating Environments for Moral Development." *Proceedings of the 1992 Florida State University Institute on College Student Values.* Tallahassee, Fla.: Florida State University, 1992a.

King, P. M. "How Do We Know? Why Do We Believe? Learning to Make Reflective Judgments." *Liberal Education,* 1992b, *78*(1), 2–9.

King, P. M. (ed.). Special Issue on Reflective Judgment. *Liberal Education,* 1992c, *78*(1).

King, P. M., and Bauer, B. A. "Leadership Issues for Nontraditional-Aged Women Students." In M.A.D. Sagaria (ed.), *Empowering Women: Leadership Development Strategies on Campus.* New Directions for Student Services, no. 44. San Francisco: Jossey-Bass, 1988.

King, P. M., and Kitchener, K. S. "The Development of Reflective Thinking in the College Years: The Mixed Results." In C. G. Schneider and W. S. Green (eds.), *Not an End in Itself: Reforming the Liberal Arts Major.* New Directions for Higher Education, no. 84. San Francisco: Jossey-Bass, 1993.

King, P. M., Kitchener, K. S., and Wood, P. K. "The Development of Intellect and Character: A Longitudinal Study of Intellectual and Moral Development in Young Adults." *Moral Education Forum,* 1985, *10*(1), 1–13.

King, P. M., Kitchener, K. S., and Wood, P. K. "Changes in Students' Reasoning over Time: A Ten-Year Longitudinal Study of the Development of Reflective Judgment." Paper presented at the annual meeting of the American Association for the Study of Higher Education, Portland, Ore., Nov. 1990.

King, P. M., Kitchener, K. S., and Wood, P. K. "Moral and Intellectual Development Beyond the College Years: A Ten-Year Study." Paper presented at the annual meeting of the Association for Moral Education, Athens, Ga., Nov. 1991.

King, P. M., Kitchener, K. S., Wood, P. K., and Davison,

M. L. "Relationships Across Developmental Domains: A Longitudinal Study of Intellectual, Moral and Ego Development." In M. L. Commons, J. D. Sinnott, F. A. Richards, and C. Armon (eds.), *Adult Development,* Vol. 1: *Comparisons and Applications of Developmental Models.* New York: Praeger, 1989.

King, P. M., and Parker, C. A. "Assessing Intellectual Development in the College Years: A Report of the Instructional Improvement Project, 1976–1977." Unpublished manuscript, University of Minnesota, 1978.

King, P. M., Taylor, J. A., and Ottinger, D. C. "Intellectual Development of Black College Students on a Predominantly White Campus." Paper presented at the annual meeting of the Association for the Study of Higher Education, Atlanta, Ga., Nov. 1993.

King, P. M., Taylor, J. A., and Ottinger, D. C. "Intellectual Development, Institutional Integration, and Persistence Among African-American Students on a Predominantly White Campus." Unpublished paper, 1993.

King, P. M., Wood, P. K., Kitchener, K. S., and Lynch, C. L. "The Development of the Reflective Thinking Appraisal." Unpublished paper, 1994.

King, P. M., Wood, P. K., and Mines, R. A. "Critical Thinking Among College and Graduate Students." *Review of Higher Education,* 1990, *13*(3), 167–186.

King, P. M., and others. "The Justification of Beliefs in Young Adults: A Longitudinal Study." *Human Development,* 1983, *26*(2), 106–116.

Kitchener, K. S. "Intellectual Development in Late Adolescents and Young Adults: Reflective Judgment and Verbal Reasoning." *Dissertation Abstracts International,* 1977–78, *39,* 956B.

Kitchener, K. S. "Human Development and the College Campus: Sequences and Tasks." In G. R. Hanson (ed.), *Measuring Student Development.* New Directions for Student Services, no. 20. San Francisco: Jossey-Bass, 1982.

Kitchener, K. S. "Cognition, Metacognition and Epistemic Cognition: A Three-Level Model of Cognitive Processing." *Human Development,* 1983, *4,* 222–232.

Kitchener, K. S. "The Reflective Judgment Model: Character-
istics, Evidence, and Measurement." In R. A. Mines and K.
S. Kitchener (eds.), *Cognitive Development in Young Adults.* New
York: Praeger, 1986.

Kitchener, K. S. "The Development of Critical Reason: Does
a College Education Make a Difference?" Lecture given at
the University of Denver, 1992.

Kitchener, K. S., and Brenner, H. G. "Wisdom and Reflec-
tive Judgment: Knowing in the Face of Uncertainty." In R.
Sternberg (ed.), *Wisdom: Its Nature, Origins and Development.*
Cambridge, England: Cambridge University Press, 1990.

Kitchener, K. S., and Fischer, K. W. "A Skill Approach to the
Development of Reflective Thinking." In D. Kuhn (ed.), *Contributions to Human Development: Developmental Perspectives on
Teaching and Learning.* Vol. 21. Basel, Switzerland: Karger,
1990.

Kitchener, K. S., and King, P. M. "Reflective Judgment: Concepts of Justification and Their Relationship to Age and Education." *Journal of Applied Developmental Psychology,* 1981, *2*(2),
89–116.

Kitchener, K. S., and King, P. M. "Reflective Judgment Scoring
Manual." 1985. (Available from K. S. Kitchener, School of
Education, University of Denver, Denver, Colo. 80208 or
P. M. King, Department of Higher Education and Student
Affairs, Bowling Green State University, Bowling Green,
Ohio 43403.

Kitchener, K. S., and King, P. M. "The Reflective Judgment
Model: Ten Years of Research." In M. L. Commons and
others (eds.), *Adult Development,* Vol. 2: *Models and Methods in
the Study of Adolescent and Adult Thought.* New York: Praeger,
1990a.

Kitchener, K. S., and King, P. M. "The Reflective Judgment
Model: Transforming Assumptions About Knowing." In J.
Mezirow and Associates (eds.), *Fostering Critical Reflection in
Adulthood: A Guide to Transformative and Emancipatory Learning.*
San Francisco: Jossey-Bass, 1990b.

Kitchener, K. S., King, P. M., Wood, P. K., and Davison,
M. L. "Consistency and Sequentiality in the Development

of Reflective Judgment: A Six Year Longitudinal Study." *Journal of Applied Developmental Psychology*, 1989, *10*, 73–95.

Kitchener, K. S., King, P. M., Wood, P. K., and Lynch, C. L. "Assessing Reflective Thinking in Curricular Contexts." Technical Report of the Reflective Thinking Appraisal, Fund for the Improvement of Postsecondary Education, Application No. P116B00926, 1994.

Kitchener, K. S., and Kitchener, R. F. "The Development of Natural Rationality: Can Formal Operations Account for It?" In J. Meacham and M. R. Santilli (eds.), *Contributions to Human Development: Social Development in Youth: Structure and Content.* Vol. 5. Basel, Switzerland: Karger, 1981.

Kitchener, K. S., Lynch, C. L., Fischer, K. W., and Wood, P. K. "Developmental Range of Reflective Judgment: The Effect of Contextual Support and Practice on Developmental Stage." *Developmental Psychology*, 1993, *29*(5), 893–906.

Kitchener, K. S., and Wood, P. K. "Development of Concepts of Justification in German University Students." *International Journal of Behavioral Development*, 1987, *10*(2), 171–185.

Kitchener, K. S., and others. "A Longitudinal Study of Moral and Ego Development in Young Adults." *Journal of Youth and Adolescence*, 1984, *13*(3), 197–211.

Kitchener, R. F. *Piaget's Theory of Knowledge.* New Haven, Conn.: Yale University Press, 1986.

Knefelkamp, L. L. "Developmental Instruction: Fostering Intellectual and Personal Growth of College Students." Unpublished doctoral dissertation, Department of Counseling and College Student Personnel Psychology, University of Minnesota, 1974.

Knowles, M. *The Adult Learner: A Neglected Species* (3rd ed.) Houston, Tex.: Gulf, 1984.

Kohlberg, L. "Stage and Sequence: The Cognitive-Developmental Approach to Socialization." In D. A. Goslin (ed.), *Handbook of Socialization Theory and Research.* Skokie, Ill.: Rand McNally, 1969.

Kohlberg, L. *Essays on Moral Development*, Vol. 1: *The Philosophy of Moral Development.* San Francisco: Harper & Row, 1981.

Kohlberg, L. *The Psychology of Moral Development: The Nature and Validation of Moral Stages.* San Francisco: Harper & Row, 1984.

Kramer, D. A. "Post-Formal Operations? A Need for Further Conceptualization." *Human Development,* 1983, *26*(2), 91–105.

Kramer, D. A. "A Life-Span View of Social Cognition." *Educational Gerontology,* 1986, *12,* 227–289.

Kramer, D. A. "The Development of an Awareness of Contradiction Across the Life Span and the Question of Postformal Operations." In M. L. Commons, J. D. Sinnott, F. A. Richards, and C. Armon (eds.), *Adult Development,* Vol. 1: *Comparisons and Applications of Developmental Models.* New York: Praeger, 1989.

Kroll, B. M. "Reflective Inquiry in a College English Class." *Liberal Education,* 1992a, *78*(1), 10–13.

Kroll, B. M. *Teaching Hearts and Minds: College Students Reflect on the Vietnam War in Literature.* Carbondale: Southern Illinois University Press, 1992b.

Kronholm, M. "The Impact of a Developmental Instruction Approach to Environmental Education at the Undergraduate Level on Development of Reflective Judgment." Unpublished doctoral dissertation, Southern Illinois University, 1993.

Kuh, G. D., Schuh, J. H., Whitt, E. J., and Associates. *Involving Colleges: Successful Approaches to Fostering Student Learning and Development Outside the Classroom.* San Francisco: Jossey-Bass, 1991.

Kuhn, D. "Children and Adults as Intuitive Scientists." *Psychological Review,* 1989, *96,* 674–689.

Kuhn, D. "The Skills of Argument." Paper presented at the meeting of the Jean Piaget Society, Philadelphia, June 1990.

Kurfiss, J. G. "Critical Thinking: Theory, Research, Practice and Possibilities." ASHE-ERIC Higher Education Report No. 2. Washington, D.C.: Association for the Study of Higher Education, 1988.

Labouvie-Vief, G. "Dynamic Development and Mature Autonomy: A Theoretical Prologue." *Human Development,* 1982, *25*(3), 161–191.

Lakatos, I. "Falsification and the Methodology of Scientific Research Programs." In I. Lakatos and A. Musgrave (eds.),

Criticism and the Growth of Knowledge. Cambridge, England: Cambridge University Press, 1970.

Lamborn, S. D., and Fischer, K. W. "Optimal and Functional Levels in Cognitive Development: The Individual's Developmental Range." *Newsletter of the International Society for the Study of Behavioral Development,* no. 2 (serial no. 14), 1988.

Lawson, J. M. "The Relationship Between Graduate Education and the Development of Reflective Judgment: A Function of Age or Educational Experience." *Dissertation Abstracts International,* 1980, *47,* 402B.

Leadbeater, B. "The Resolution of Relativism in Adult Thinking: Subjective, Objective or Conceptual?" *Human Development,* 1986, *29*(5), 291–300.

Levinson, D. *Seasons of a Man's Life.* New York: Ballantine, 1978.

Liberto, J., Kelly, F. J., Shapiro, C., and Currier, S. "Levels of Reflective Judgment Among Noncollege Trained Adults." *Psychological Reports,* 1990, *66,* 1091–1100.

Lickona, T. "Preparing Teachers to Be Moral Educators: A Neglected Duty." In M. L. McBee (ed.), *Rethinking College Responsibilities for Values.* New Directions for Higher Education, no. 31. San Francisco: Jossey-Bass, 1980.

Lindemann, J. E., and Matarazzo, J. D. "Intellectual Assessment of Adults." In G. Goldstein and M. Hersen (eds.), *Handbook of Psychological Assessment.* Elmsford, N.Y.: Pergamon Press, 1984.

Lipman, M. "Philosophy for Children." *National Forum,* 1985, *65*(1), 18–21.

Lipman, M. "Critical Thinking: What Can It Be?" *Educational Leadership,* 1988, *46*(1), 38–43.

Loevinger, J. *Ego Development: Conceptions and Theories.* San Francisco: Jossey-Bass, 1976.

Loevinger, J., and Wessler, R. *Measuring Ego Development,* Vol. 1: *Construction and Use of a Sentence Completion Test.* San Francisco: Jossey-Bass, 1970.

Lynch, C. "The Impact of a High Support Condition on the Exhibition of Reflective Judgment." *Dissertation Abstracts International,* 1989, *50,* 4246.

McCall, R. B. "Nature-Nurture and the Two Realms of Development: A Proposed Integration with Respect to Mental Development." *Child Development,* 1981, *52,* 1–12.

McKinney, M. "Reflective Judgment: An Aspect of Adolescent Cognitive Development." *Dissertation Abstracts International,* 1985, *47,* 402B.

McMillan, J. H. "Enhancing College Students' Critical Thinking: A Review of Studies." *Research in Higher Education,* 1987, *26*(1), 3–29.

McMillan, L. "Many Professors Now Start at the Beginning by Teaching Students How to Think." *Chronicle of Higher Education,* March 1986, pp. 23, 25.

McPeck, J. E. *Critical Thinking and Education.* New York: St. Martin's Press, 1981.

Marcia, J. E. "Determination and Construct Validity of Ego Identity Status." *Dissertation Abstracts International,* 1965, *25,* 6763. (University Microfilms No. 65-5606)

Marcia, J. E. "Ego Identity Status: Relationship to Self-Esteem, 'General Maladjustment,' and Authoritarianism." *Journal of Personality,* 1967, *35,* 119–133.

Meacham, J. A. "The Loss of Wisdom." In R. Sternberg (ed.), *Wisdom: Its Nature, Origins and Development.* Cambridge, England: Cambridge University Press, 1990.

Mednick, M. T. "On the Politics of Psychological Constructs: Stop the Bandwagon, I Want to Get Off." *American Psychologist,* 1989, *44*(8), 1118–1123.

Mentkowski, M., Moeser, M., and Strait, M. J. *Using the Perry Scheme of Intellectual and Ethical Development as a College Outcomes Measure: A Process and Criteria for Judging Student Performance.* Vol. 1. Milwaukee, Wis.: Alverno College Productions, 1983.

Mezirow, J., and Associates. *Fostering Critical Reflection in Adulthood: A Guide to Transformative and Emancipatory Learning.* San Francisco: Jossey-Bass, 1990.

Millard, M. K. "The Dialectic Transformation: Process and Product." Unpublished doctoral dissertation, Department of Education, Rutgers University, 1992.

Milman, L. F. "The Effect of Specific Knowledge Content in the Reasoning Judgment of Ill-Defined Issues." Unpublished doctoral dissertation, Department of Educational Psychology, Southern Illinois University, 1988.

Mines, R. A., King, P. M., Hood, A. B., and Wood, P. K. "Stages of Intellectual Development and Associated Critical Thinking Skills in College Students." *Journal of College Student Development,* 1990, *31,* 537–547.

Mines, R. A., and Kitchener, K. S. (eds.). *Adult Cognitive Development.* New York: Praeger, 1986.

Modjeski, R. B., and Michael, W. B. "An Evaluation by a Panel of Psychologists of the Reliability and Validity of Two Tests of Critical Thinking." *Educational and Psychological Measurement,* 1983, *43,* 1187–1197.

Montecinos, C. "A Cross-Sectional Study of the Development of Reflective Judgment Among Medical Students." Unpublished doctoral dissertation, Department of Educational Psychology, Southern Illinois University, 1989.

Moore, W. "The Measure of Intellectual Development: A Brief Review." Unpublished paper, Center for Applications of Developmental Instruction, University of Maryland, College Park, 1982.

Moore, W. "The Learning Environment Preferences: Exploring the Construct Validity of an Objective Measure of the Perry Scheme of Intellectual Development." *Journal of College Student Development,* 1989, *30,* 504–519.

Moshman, D., and Lukin, L. E. "The Creative Construction of Rationality." In J. A. Glover, R. R. Ronning, and C. R. Reynolds (eds.), *Handbook of Creativity.* New York: Plenum, 1989.

National Commission on Excellence in Education. *A Nation at Risk: The Imperative for Educational Reform.* Washington, D.C.: U.S. Government Printing Office, 1983.

Neimark, E. D. "Current Status of Formal Operations Research." *Journal of Human Development,* 1979, *22*(1), 60–67.

Neimark, E. D. "Adolescent Thought: Transition to Formal Operations." In B. B. Wolman (ed.), *Handbook of Developmental Psychology.* Englewood Cliffs, N.J.: Prentice-Hall, 1982.

Nevins, K. J. "Understanding Students as Learners Using Student Development Models." *Liberal Education,* 1992, *78*(1), 24–27.

Nickerson, C. "Curricular Design and Levels of Reflective Judgment." *Dissertation Abstracts International,* 1991, *52,* 2040.

Noddings, N. (1984). *Caring: A Feminine Approach to Ethics and Moral Education.* Berkeley and Los Angeles: University of California Press.

Nunner-Winkler, G. "Two Moralities: A Critical Discussion of an Ethic of Care and Responsibility Versus an Ethic of Rights and Justice." In W. M. Kurtines and J. L. Gewirtz (eds.), *Morality, Moral Behavior, and Moral Development,* New York: Wiley, 1984.

Orwoll, L., and Perlmutter, M. "The Study of Wise Persons: Integrating a Personality Perspective." In R. Sternberg (ed.), *Wisdom: Its Nature, Origins and Development.* Cambridge, England: Cambridge University Press, 1990.

Pape, S. L., and Kelly, F. J. "Reflective Judgment: A Cross-Sectional Study of Undergraduate Education Majors." *Psychological Reports,* 1991, *68,* 387–395.

Pascarella, E. T., and Terenzini, P. T. *How College Affects Students: Findings and Insights from Twenty Years of Research.* San Francisco: Jossey-Bass, 1991.

Paul, R. W. "The Critical-Thinking Movement: A Historical Perspective." *National Forum,* 1985, *65,* 2–3.

Paul, R. W. *Critical Thinking: What Every Person Needs to Survive in a Rapidly Changing World.* Rohnert Park, Calif.: Center for Critical Thinking and Moral Critique, Sonoma State University, 1990.

Perkins, A., Allen, R., and Hafner, J. "Difficulties in Everyday Reasonings." *Proceedings of the Conference on Thinking, 1982, University of the South Pacific, Suva, Fiji.* Philadelphia: Franklin Institute Press, 1983.

Perkins, D. N. "Postprimary Education Has Little Impact on Informal Reasoning." *Journal of Educational Psychology,* 1985, *77,* 562–571.

Perkins, D. N., Farady, M., and Bushey, B. "Everyday Reasoning and the Roots of Intelligence." In J. F. Voss, D. N. Perkins, and J. W. Segal (eds.), *Informal Reasoning and Education.* Hillsdale, N.J.: Erlbaum, 1991.

Perry, W. G., Jr. *Patterns of Development in Thought and Values of Students in a Liberal Arts College: A Validation of a Scheme.* Washington, D.C.: U.S. Department of Health, Education, and Welfare, 1968. (Final Report, Project No. 5-0825, Contract No. SAE-8973)

Perry, W. G., Jr. *Forms of Intellectual and Ethical Development in the College Years: A Scheme.* Troy, Mo.: Holt, Rinehart & Winston, 1970.

Perry, W. G., Jr. "Cognitive and Ethical Growth: The Making of Meaning." In A. W. Chickering and Associates, *The Modern American College: Responding to the New Realities of Diverse Students and a Changing Society.* San Francisco: Jossey-Bass, 1981.

Piaget, J. "The General Problems of the Psychobiological Development of the Child." In J. M. Tanner and B. Inhelder (eds.), *Discussions on Child Development: Proceedings of the Fourth Meeting of the World Health Organization Study Group on the Psychobiological Development of the Child.* Vol. 4. London: Tavistock, 1960.

Piaget, J. *The Moral Judgment of the Child.* New York: Free Press, 1965.

Piaget, J. "Piaget's Theory." In P. H. Mussen (ed.), *Carmichael's Manual of Child Psychology.* Vol. 1. New York: Wiley, 1970.

Piaget, J. "Stages of Intellectual Development in the Child and Adolescent." In J. Piaget, *The Child and Reality,* (A. Rosin, trans.). New York: Viking, 1974. (Originally published 1956.)

Piaget, J., and Inhelder, B. *The Psychology of the Child.* New York: Basic Books, 1969.

Polkosnik, M. C. "A Multiple Case-Study Investigation of the Rates of Maturation of Cognitive and Psychosocial Development in College Students," *Dissertation Abstracts International,* 1985, *46,* 10A.

Polkosnik, M. C., and Winston, R. B., Jr. "Relationships Between Students' Intellectual and Psychological Development: An Exploratory Investigation." *Journal of College Student Development,* 1989, *30,* 10–19.

Popper, K. R. *Conjectures and Refutations.* New York: Harper & Row, 1969.

Rest, J. *Development in Judging Moral Issues.* Minneapolis: University of Minnesota Press, 1979.

Rest, J. "The Major Components of Morality." In W. M. Kurtines and J. L. Gerwitz (eds.), *Morality, Moral Behavior, and Moral Development,* pp. 24–38. New York: Wiley, 1984.

Rest, J. *Moral Development: Advances in Research and Theory.* New York: Praeger, 1986.

Rest, J. *Guide to the Defining Issues Test.* Minneapolis: Center for the Study of Ethical Development, University of Minnesota, 1987.

Rest, J., Bebeau, M., and Volker, J. "An Overview of the Psychology of Morality." In J. Rest (ed.), *Moral Development: Advances in Research and Theory,* pp. 1–27. New York: Praeger, 1986.

Rest, J., and others. "Life Experiences and Developmental Pathways." In J. Rest, *Moral Development: Advances in Research and Theory.* New York: Praeger, 1986.

Richards, F. A. "Detecting Metasystematic, Systematic and Lower-Stage Relations: An Empirical Investigation of Postformal Stages." In M. L. Commons, and others (eds.), *Adult Development,* Vol. 2: *Models and Methods in the Study of Adolescent and Adult Thought.* New York: Praeger, 1990.

Richards, F. A., and Commons, M. L. "Systematic, Metasystematic, and Cross-Paradigmatic Reasoning: A Case for Stages of Reasoning Beyond Formal Operations." In M. L. Commons, F. A. Richards, and C. Armon (eds.), *Beyond Formal Operations,* Vol. 1: *Late Adolescent and Adult Development.* New York: Praeger, 1984.

Robinson, D. N. "Wisdom Through the Ages." In R. Sternberg (ed.), *Wisdom: Its Nature, Origins and Development.* Cambridge, England: Cambridge University Press, 1990.

Rodgers, R. "Theories Underlying Student Development." In D. Creamer (ed.), *Student Development in Higher Education: Theories, Practices, and Future Directions.* Cincinnati, Ohio: ACPA Media, 1980.

Rudolph, F. R. *The American College and University: A History.* Athens: University of Georgia Press, 1990.

Rundle, B. "History of Logic: Gödel and Church." In P. Edwards (ed.), *The Encyclopedia of Philosophy.* Vol. 4. New York: Macmillan and Free Press, 1972.

Sakalys, J. A. "Effects of a Research Methods Course on Nursing Students' Research Attitudes and Cognitive Development." *Dissertation Abstracts International,* 1984, *43,* 2254.

Sakalys, J. "Effects of an Undergraduate Research Course on Cognitive Development." *Nursing Research,* 1984, *33*(5), 290–295.

Salmon, M. H. *Logic and Critical Thinking.* Orlando, Fla.: Harcourt Brace Jovanovich, 1989.

Sanford, N. *Self and Society: Social Change and Individual Development.* New York: Atherton, 1966.

Schaie, K. W. "Toward a Stage Theory of Adult Cognitive Development. *Aging and Human Development,* 1977–78, *8,* 129–138.

Schmidt, J. A. "The Intellectual Development of Traditional and Nontraditionally Aged Students: A Cross Sectional Study with Longitudinal Follow-Up." *Dissertation Abstracts International,* 1983, *44,* 2681.

Schmidt, J. A. "Older and Wiser? A Longitudinal Study of the Impact of College on Intellectual Development." *Journal of College Student Personnel,* 1985, *26,* 388–394.

Shoff, S. P. "The Significance of Age, Sex, and Type of Education on the Development of Reasoning in Adults." *Dissertation Abstracts International,* 1979, *40,* 3910A.

Sinnott, J. D. "The Relativistic Stage." In M. L. Commons, F. A. Richards, and C. Armon (eds.), *Beyond Formal Operations: Late Adolescent and Adult Development.* New York: Praeger, 1984.

Sinnott, J. D. "Life-Span Relativistic Post-Formal Thought: Methodology and Data from Every Day Problem Solving Studies. In M. L. Commons, J. D. Sinnott, F. A. Richards, and C. Armon (eds.), *Adult Development,* Vol. 1: *Comparisons and Applications of Developmental Models.* New York: Praeger, 1989.

Skinner, S. B. "The Myth of Teaching for Critical Thinking." *The Clearing House,* 1971, *45,* 373–376.

Sternberg, R. J. "Implicit Theories of Intelligence, Creativity and Wisdom." *Journal of Personality and Social Psychology,* 1985, *49,* 607–627.

Sternberg, R. J. "Intellectual Development: Psychometric and Information-Processing Approaches." In M. H. Bornstein and M. E. Lamb (eds.), *Developmental Psychology: An Advanced Textbook.* Hillsdale, N.J.: Erlbaum, 1988.

Sternberg, R. J. (ed.). *Wisdom: Its Nature, Origins and Development.* Cambridge, England: Cambridge University Press, 1990.

Sternberg, R. J., and Powell, J. S. "The Development of Intelligence." In J. H. Flavell and E. M. Markman (eds.), *Handbook of Child Psychology,* Vol. 3: *Cognitive Development.* New York: Wiley, 1983.

Strange, C. C. "Intellectual Development, Motive for Education, and Learning Style During the College Years: A Comparison of Adult and Traditional Age College Students." *Dissertation Abstracts International,* 1978, *39,* 4768A.

Strange, C. C. "Beyond the Classroom: Encouraging Reflective Thinking." *Liberal Education,* 1992, *78*(1), 28–32.

Strange, C. C., and King, P. M. "Intellectual Development and Its Relationship to Maturation During the College Years." *Journal of Applied Developmental Psychology,* 1981, *2,* 281–295.

Study Group on the Conditions of Excellence in American Higher Education. *Involvement in Learning: Realizing the Potential of American Higher Education.* Washington, D.C.: National Institute of Education, 1984.

Taranto, M. A. "Facets of Wisdom: A Theoretical Synthesis." *International Journal of Aging and Human Development,* 1989, *29,* 1–21.

Terman, L. M. *Concept Mastery Test Manual.* New York: Psychological Corporation, 1973.

Thoma, S. J. "Estimating Gender Differences in the Comprehension and Preference of Moral Issues." *Developmental Review,* 1986, *6,* 165–180.

Tinsley, H.E.A., and Weiss, D. J. "Interrater Reliability and Agreement of Subjective Components." *Journal of Counseling Psychology,* 1975, *22,* 358–376.

U.S. Department of Education, National Center for Education

Statistics. *The Condition of Education, 1991,* Vol. 2: *Postsecondary Education.* Washington, D.C.: U.S. Department of Education, 1991.

Van Tine, N. B. "The Development of Reflective Judgment in Adolescents." *Dissertation Abstracts International,* 1990, *51,* 2659.

Voss, J. F., Perkins, D. N., and Segal, J. W. (eds.), *Informal Reasoning and Education.* Hillsdale, N.J.: Erlbaum, 1991.

Walker, L. J. "Sex Differences in the Development of Moral Reasoning: A Critical Review." *Child Development,* 1984, *55,* 677–691.

Watson, G., and Glaser, E. M. *Watson-Glaser Critical Thinking Appraisal Manual.* Orlando, Fla.: Harcourt Brace Jovanovich, 1952.

Watson, G., and Glaser, E. M. *Watson-Glaser Critical Thinking Appraisal Manual.* Orlando, Fla.: Harcourt Brace Jovanovich, 1964.

Webster's New Collegiate Dictionary. Springfield, Mass.: G. and C. Merriam, 1977.

Welfel, E. R. The Development of Reflective Judgment: Its Relationship to Years in College Academic Major, and Satisfaction with Major Among College Students. *Dissertation Abstracts International,* 1979, *40,* 4949.

Welfel, E. R. "The Development of Reflective Judgment: Implications for Career Counseling of College Students." *Personnel and Guidance Journal,* 1982a, *61*(1), 17–21.

Welfel, E. R. "How Students Make Judgments: Do Educational Level and Academic Major Make a Difference?" *Journal of College Student Personnel,* 1982b, *23,* 490–497.

Welfel, E. R., and Davison, M. L. "The Development of Reflective Judgment in the College Years: A Four Year Longitudinal Study." *Journal of College Student Personnel,* 1986, *27,* 209–216.

Whitbourne, S. K. *Adult Development.* New York: Praeger, 1986.

Whiteley, J. M., and Associates. *Character Development in College Students.* Schenectady, N.Y.: Character Research Press, 1982.

Widick, C. "An Attribute-Treatment Interaction Model of Instruction Based on Cognitive Developmental Theory." Unpublished doctoral dissertation, Department of Counseling and Student Personnel Psychology, University of Minnesota, 1975.

Widick, C., Knefelkamp, L. L., and Parker, C. A. "The Counselor as a Developmental Instructor." *Counselor Education and Supervision,* 1975, *14,* 286–296.

Winston, R. B., and Miller, T. K. "Student Developmental Task Inventory (Second Edition) Task Descriptions." Unpublished manuscript, Department of Counseling and Human Development Services, University of Georgia, 1984.

Wood, P. K. "Inquiring Systems and Problem Structure: Implications for Cognitive Development." *Human Development,* 1983, *26,* 249–265.

Wood, P. K. "A Statistical Examination of Necessary but Not Sufficient Antecedents of Problem Solving Behavior." *Dissertation Abstracts International,* 1985, *46,* 2055.

Wood, P. K. "Construct Validity and Theories of Adult Development: Testing for Necessary but Not Sufficient Relationships." In M. L. Commons and others (eds.), *Adult Development,* Vol. 2: *Models and Methods in the Study of Adolescent and Adult Thought.* New York: Praeger, 1990.

Wood, P. K. "Context and Development of Reflective Thinking: A Secondary Analysis of the Structure of Individual Differences." Unpublished paper, 1993a.

Wood, P. K. "Generalized Growth Curve Analysis for Cross-Sectional Skill Theory." Unpublished manuscript, University of Minnesota, 1993b.

Index

315

DATE DUE

MAY 1 1 1994			
MAR 0 2 1995			
JUN 1 2 1998			
FEB 2 8 2000			

Demco, Inc. 38-293